# Praise for *A Guide To Teaching Introductory Psychology*

"No course is more important to our discipline than the introductory psychology class. Sandra Goss Lucas, the coordinator for Introductory Psychology at the University of Illinois, brings together the collective wisdom of her years of experience in teaching and teacher training to deliver a wonderfully useful book. If department heads want to evidence a genuine commitment to teaching, they should give this book to all faculty and graduate students involved in the teaching of this course. It is a treasure house of good ideas from a great teacher."

*Ludy T. Benjamin, Jr., Texas A&M University*

"Sandra Goss Lucas's book, *A Guide to Teaching Introductory Psychology*, will be invaluable for those teaching intro psych for the first time, and even old codgers who have taught intro psych more than 50 times will find new useful and interesting ideas. My copy has 'Good', 'Neat' and other laudatory comments on the margins of many pages."

*W. J. McKeachie, University of Michigan*

"Sandy Goss Lucas offers instructors of Introductory Psychology a fully equipped, functional toolbox, filled with specific, concrete details that can immediately be applied in teaching. This toolbox will be most helpful to instructors teaching the course for the first time, who will undoubtedly breathe a sigh of relief when they realize that, far from being alone and isolated, they are part of large group of people who readily share their approaches, innovations, practices, and challenges. Seasoned instructors will also find much in this book that will be valuable to them, because the advice offered by Goss Lucas, the selection of topics, and her concrete suggestions are all deeply informed by classroom experience—knows what works and what does not.

Even more important than the rich content of this book are the values and dedication that infuse the way Goss Lucas discusses teaching, particularly its more challenging aspects. She models how a caring, thoughtful instructor can apply high standards while making the Introductory Psychology course engaging, challenging, and useful for the students. Goss L⌁⌁⌁ shows how to set the right tone in a classroom—and she doe⌁ ⌁⌁⌁ ⌁⌁⌁ book."

*Robert W⌁⌁⌁* ⌁⌁te University

*Teaching Psychological Science*
Series editors: William Buskist and Douglas A. Bernstein

The *Teaching Psychological Science* series focuses on critical aspects of teaching core courses in psychology. The books share ideas, tips, and strategies for effective teaching and offer all the pedagogical tools an instructor needs to plan the course in one handy and concise volume. Written by outstanding teachers and edited by Bill Buskist and Doug Bernstein, who are themselves well-respected authors and teachers, each book provides a wealth of concrete suggestions not found in other volumes, a clear roadmap for teaching, and practical, concrete, hands-on tips for novice teachers and experienced instructors alike.

Each book includes

- Ideas for beginning the course
- Sample lecture outlines for the entire course
- Examples and applications that link the course content to everyday student experience
- Classroom demonstrations and activities with an emphasis on promoting active learning and critical thinking
- Discussion of sensitive and difficult-to-teach topics and ethical issues likely to be encountered throughout the semester
- Course-specific options for evaluating student performance
- A chapter on available resources for teaching the course

1. *A Guide to Teaching Research Methods in Psychology*
   Bryan K. Saville

2. *A Guide to Teaching Introductory Psychology*
   Sandra Goss Lucas

3. *A Guide to Teaching Developmental Psychology*
   Elizabeth Brestan and Ember Lee

# Contents

# Series Editors' Preface

As the best teachers among us can surely attest, teaching at the college and university level is no easy task. Even psychology, as inherently interesting as it may be, is a difficult subject to teach well. Indeed, being an effective teacher of any discipline requires a steadfast commitment to self-improvement as a scholar, thinker, and communicator over the long haul. No one becomes a master teacher overnight.

Compared to other disciplines, though, psychology has been way ahead of the curve when it comes to taking its teaching seriously. The Society for the Teaching of Psychology (http://teachpsych.org/) was founded in 1946 and continues to be a powerful force in supporting the teaching of psychology in high schools, community colleges, and four-year schools. The annual National Institute on the Teaching of Psychology, or as it is more informally known, NITOP (http://www.nitop.org), has been featuring an impressive venue of pedagogical presentations for the past 30 years. In addition, several annual regional teaching of psychology conferences offer a variety of talks, workshops, and poster sessions on improving one's teaching.

Psychologists have also led the way in writing books on effective teaching. Perhaps the most well-known among these texts is McKeachie's (2006) *Teaching Tips*, now in its 12th edition (the first edition was published in 1951!). Although McKeachie wrote *Teaching Tips* for all teachers, regardless of discipline, other books focused specifically on teaching psychology have appeared in the past several years (e.g., Buskist & Davis, 2006; Davis & Buskist, 2002; Forsyth, 2003; Goss Lucas & Bernstein, 2005). The common theme across these books is that they offer general advice for teaching any psychology course, and in McKeachie's case, for teaching any college course.

Blackwell's *Teaching Psychological Science* series differs from existing books. In one handy and concise source, each book provides all an instructor needs to help her in her course. Each volume in this series targets a specific course: introductory psychology, developmental psychology, research methods, statistics, behavioral neuroscience, memory and cognition, learning, abnormal behavior, and personality and social psychology. Each book is authored by accomplished, well-respected teachers who share their best strategies for teaching these courses effectively.

Each book in the series also features advice on how to teach particularly difficult topics; how to link course content to everyday student experiences; how to develop and use class presentations, lectures, and active learning ideas; and how to increase student interest in course topics. Each volume ends with a chapter that describes resources for teaching the particular course focused on in that book, as well as an appendix on widely available resources for the teaching of psychology in general.

The *Teaching Psychological Science* series is geared to assist all teachers at all levels to master the teaching of particular courses. Each volume focuses on how to teach specific content as opposed to processes involved in teaching more generally. Thus, veteran teachers as well as graduate students and new faculty will likely find these books a useful source of new ideas for teaching their courses.

As editors of this series, we are excited about the prospects these books offer for enhancing the teaching of specific courses within our field. We are delighted that Wiley Blackwell shares our excitement for the series and we wish to thank our Editor Christine Cardone and our Development Project Manager Sarah Coleman for their devoted work behind the scenes to help us bring the series to fruition. We hope that you find this book, and all the books in the series, a helpful and welcome addition to your collection of teaching resources.

Douglas J. Bernstein
William Buskist
April 2007

# References

Buskist, W., & Davis, S. F. (Eds.) (2006). *Handbook of the teaching of psychology.* Boston: Blackwell.

Davis, S. F., & Buskist, W. (Eds.) (2002). *The teaching of psychology: Essays in honor of Wilbert J. McKeachie and Charles L. Brewer.* Mahwah, NJ: Erlbaum.

Forsyth, D. R. (2003). *The professor's guide to teaching: Psychological principles and practices.* Washington, DC: American Psychological Association.

Goss Lucas, S. , & Bernstein, D. A. (2005). *Teaching psychology: A step by step guide.* Mahwah, NJ: Erlbaum.

McKeachie, W. J. (2006). *McKeachie's teaching tips: Strategies, research, and theory for college and university teachers* (12th ed.). Boston: Houghton Mifflin.

Perlman, B., McCann, L. I., & Buskist, W. (Eds.) (2005). *Voices of NITOP: Memorable talks from the National Institute on the Teaching of Psychology.* Washington, DC: American Psychological Society.

Perlman, B., McCann, L. I., & McFadden, S. H. (2004). *Lessons learned: Practical advice for the teaching of psychology* (Volume 2). Washington, DC: American Psychological Society.

# Acknowledgments

This book would not have been possible without the patience and help of many people.

Doug Bernstein, my mentor and my friend, unselfishly edited every chapter I wrote. We have worked together for many years and I am appreciative of the time he takes to help, his excellent editing skills, and his uncanny ability to ask just the right question to trigger a deeper level of thinking.

Thanks to both Doug Bernstein and Bill Buskist, coeditors of the series, who asked me to write this volume and who were extremely patient and understanding, as I balanced writing this book with my other academic responsibilities.

And thanks to Chris Cardone, the Blackwell psychology editor, for her patience and her suggestions and integration of the reviews that helped me refocus and make the book a better one.

Ludy Benjamin shared his wonderful bibliography on teaching introductory psychology which was critical in putting the introductory psychology course in historical perspective. As an undergraduate history major, I enjoyed reading the views on teaching and course construction of the early teachers of the "first course" in psychology. Thanks, Ben.

Houghton Mifflin graciously allowed me to include many of the active learning activities that I have used, some of which I developed, from the Instructor's Resource Manual accompanying Bernstein, Penner, Clarke-Steward, and Roy's *Psychology*, 7th edition.

Thank you to the reviewers of the initial draft for your helpful and insightful comments. Many of your suggestions have been incorporated throughout the book.

And finally, thanks to my husband, Dave, who balanced our family life and made time for me to write. I love you.

# Chapter 1

# An Introduction to Introductory Psychology

A survey of university faculty's views about the chief hindrances in teaching the introductory psychology course elicited the following responses:

> inconveniently large classes . . . lack of assistance . . . lack of equipment or inconvenience in quarters . . . students ill-prepared . . . the mixed and uneven character of the classes . . . lack of a first rate text book.

You might feel the same, and if so, you have company, and you have had company for a long time. The survey was conducted in 1910 as part of the first American Psychological Association (APA) report evaluating the "first course in psychology" (Sanford, 1910, p. 60).

Many of the issues and concerns faced by instructors of the "first course" in psychology remain—and are revisited by every new teacher of the course. So, in an attempt not to have to "reinvent the course," this book addresses the persistent issues and conflicts involved in teaching introductory psychology and provides as many resources, teaching tips, and information as possible. Hopefully both new instructors and veteran instructors looking for a fresh perspective will find value in this book.

Because this is a very personal book, I think it is important that I present my credentials from the very beginning:

- I have taught introductory psychology for over 30 years.
- I earned a teaching certificate—I took all of those "how to teach" courses.
- I went back to graduate school after teaching introductory psychology for 6 years at two different community colleges.
- I earned my Ph.D. in Educational Psychology with an emphasis on "teacher behavior."
- I codeveloped and present every year the University of Illinois, Urbana-Champaign Psychology Department's new teaching assistants' orientation.
- I supervise advanced graduate students teaching the introductory course, and have done so for more than 20 years.
- I love to teach. I like working with first-year college students— helping them adjust to college life and expectations. I like to work with graduate students—both those who immediately resonate to teaching and those who need a bit more guidance and nurturing. I've received teaching awards from an undergraduate organization, a graduate student organization, my college, and my campus.

I want to share with you all of the things I have learned in my 30-year teaching career. This book emphasizes the concepts I think are important, the techniques I've used to help teach the concepts, and the resources I have discovered to aid in my teaching. Obviously, the way I teach the introductory course has evolved, both as I've matured as a teacher and as the content of the course has shifted and expanded. And equally obvious is the fact that you can't teach it all. So I hope you will view this book as a smorgasbord of ideas and information, not a comprehensive "to-do-list."

## What is Introductory Psychology?

In 1908, APA appointed the first committee, the Committee on Methods of Teaching Psychology, to investigate the "first course in psychology" (Goodwin, 1992; Wolfle, 1942). They called it the "first course" because there was debate over whether the first course should be an introductory (i.e., survey) course or an elementary principles course. The report, discussed at the 1909 APA meeting and published in a monograph in 1910, cautioned instructors to focus on psychology as a science, not as philosophy. Although they did not outline a "standard" curriculum, something many instructors of the first course requested, the committee did recommend a "survey" course: "A little from each of all aspects of psychology and much from a few" (Seashore, 1910, p. 83).

Twenty years later, Albert Poffenberger (1929) reported that over 100 people attended a 1928 APA round table to discuss the "first course." However, the results were disappointing as "the contributions were limited mainly to an account of how different individuals teach the first course, with no progress in the direction of a 'one best way,' if such there can ever be" (p. 342).

Today we continue to grapple with many of the same questions about introductory psychology that have been dealt with over the years at APA round tables and conferences—*what* content to cover, *how much* content to cover (the depth vs. breadth issue), *how to teach* the course (e.g., what is the best mixture of lecture and active learning?), *who* should teach the course, and what the *student's role* should be. There are obviously no final answers to these questions, but I hope that this book will provide the background and resources that will help you to answer them in a way that is best for you and your introductory psychology students.

## What Do I Teach?

### The depth versus breadth question

One of the first decisions a teacher makes is *what* to include in their course—the pervasive "depth" vs. "breadth" question. Given that the "knowledge base" in psychology has grown astronomically in the last few decades, how can we cover it all in an introductory psychology survey course? Bob Hendersen and I have been presenting an introductory psychology workshop at the National Institute on the Teaching of Psychology (NITOP) for over 10 years; and every year, no matter what the advertised topic, we have a discussion about whether it is best to teach the entire "standard" course or whether it is better to concentrate on certain areas.

There is no correct answer to this question. You will need to decide for yourself, based on the demands that are placed on the introductory course in your institution as well as your personal philosophy. If instructors of upper-class courses base their course development on the assumption that introductory psychology students likely previewed, and perhaps even learned, the basic ideas they will present in their courses, then you must cover those ideas in some format. If your institution views introductory psychology as primarily a general education course, then you are freer to concentrate on areas that are of interest to you or that you find to be critical for the course.

I come down on the side of "teaching it all." This view reflects, in part, the way the introductory course fits into the curriculum at my university. But it also partly reflects the fact that I truly do not know what to leave out. I've seen too many courses that opt out of teaching biology or sensation and perception, and I think that narrows students' ideas of what psychology is all about. So I cover every chapter in the textbook, and I spend more time on topics that I think will be most difficult for students. For example, I spend considerable time discussing classical conditioning and less time discussing operant conditioning. In my experience, students quickly pick up on the concepts in operant conditioning but have a difficult time understanding the classical conditioning paradigm.

Others disagree with me. They argue that a few core concepts should be taught well. And they might choose to teach concepts that are "most useful" to the students, rather than those that are "most difficult." Whether you prefer to "teach it all" or "teach core concepts," don't worry; this book is organized so that you may focus on chapters of material and topics within those chapters that you deem essential.

## The topics of introductory psychology

In 1946 Claude Buxton wrote an article for *American Psychologist* entitled "Planning the introductory psychology course." His outline of a "typical" introductory psychology course divided 45 class meetings as follows:

- Orientation—Course details (1 meeting); Difficult problems for the psychology student;
- Correction of misbeliefs, psychology vocabulary, scientific method, learning for transfer (3 meetings);
- Individual differences—Psychological measurement, statistics (2 meetings);
- Exam 1 & Review of Exam 1 (1 meeting);
- Abilities—Intellectual (4 meetings);

- Growth and development of behavior—heredity–environment, maturation process, maturation and learning (3 meetings);
- Motivation—Drives, components of motive, incentive & performance, cultural determiners of motivation (4 meetings);
- Exam 2 and Review of Exam 2 (2 meetings);
- Learning and Memory—Including cultural factors and social learning (7 meetings);
- Thinking—Problem-solving (3 meetings);
- Exam 3 & Review of Exam 3 (2 meetings);
- Sensing and perceiving (6 meetings);
- Personality and adjustment (7 meetings);
- Final exam. (Buxton, 1946, pp. 309–310)

Note that his outline includes no discussion of biological psychology, social psychology, consciousness, emotion, stress and coping, health psychology, or other topics typically covered in today's textbooks and courses.

Today, most instructors of introductory psychology take their cue on what topics to teach from the introductory textbook they are using. However, topics covered in introductory texts have changed over the years as well. When Wayne Weiten and Randall Wight (1992) compared texts from the turn of the century to texts from the 1990s, they found that the amount of text devoted to sensation/perception, language/thought, and motivation/emotion had decreased. Coverage of history, methods, introductory material, biological bases, learning, memory, and personality remained about the same, but there was greater coverage of development, psychological testing/intelligence, psychopathology/psychotherapy, and social psychology.

Many veteran instructors argue that current introductory textbooks are essentially clones of each other and lack diversity. A survey conducted among introductory psychology instructors in 1998 found uniformity within the introductory courses, that most courses were indeed centered around the textbook, and that most textbooks included most of the same topics (Miller & Gentile, 1998). A "typical" current textbook covers the topics of history and approaches to psychology; research methods; elementary statistics; development; biological psychology; sensation; perception; consciousness; learning; memory; cognition and language; cognitive abilities (intelligence); motivation and emotion; stress, health, and coping; personality; psychological disorders; treatment of psychological disorders; and social psychology. Not all textbooks cover the material in the same manner or order, but these topics have emerged as the "core" curriculum.

However, we can also argue that textbooks are somewhat diverse. A survey of the glossaries of 44 current introductory psychology textbooks revealed only 14 terms common to every one of the textbooks. Indeed, they found that 93% of the total glossary terms do not appear in even 50% of the textbooks (Griggs, Bujak-Johnson, & Proctor, 2004). Interestingly, the core concepts come almost exclusively from the learning and biology units.

Even back in the 1940s, psychology instructors were commenting that:

> there is one field which students usually consider both uninteresting and unimportant and which deserves special attention—the anatomical and physiological description of the nervous system and sense organs. In these attitudes the students are supported by some of their instructors . . . tradition is not enough to justify us in continuing to teach a diluted, and sometimes obsolete, neural and sensory anatomy. The time devoted to this field in the reviewer's own course is just long enough to refer interested students to the appropriate texts in elementary physiology and neurology. (Wolfle, 1942, pp. 696–697, n. 1)

This view is still prevalent. Many students today do not find biological psychology inherently interesting, and many instructors feel they lack sufficient background and/or interest in this area to teach it well. Accordingly, I have included in this book many suggestions for making biological material more interesting for students to learn and easier for you to teach.

## The organization of content in introductory psychology

Beyond deciding *what* topics should be presented, you will have to decide about the sequence in which they should be taught. This question, too, has been under discussion for many years. Harry Ruja (1948) noted, for example, that

> the problem of order of topics is how to get our students started and, once started, how to keep them going. To accomplish this objective, we need to exploit their readiness for a given topic at a given time . . . from the practical to the theoretical, the familiar to the strange, the concrete to the abstract, the larger context to the detail. (Ruja, 1948, p. 201)

When he polled the authors of introductory psychology textbooks, Ruja found many different preferred topic sequences. He did, however identify two main themes: (a) that the order should promote increasing student understanding (e.g., later chapters should build on early ones); and (b) that the order should "capitalize on the student's current, perhaps superficial, interests in leading him on to broader, more mature ones" (p. 200). But Ruja was also quick to point out that these two themes may be incompatible.

You will need to think about the way that introductory psychology makes sense to you and try to find a way to teach that encourages students to see psychology as a whole, rather than as discrete units. You will need to find an organization that works for you, and re-examine it every few years.

I have not found a textbook that "unfolds" psychology the way I see it, so I assign chapters out of order. Many instructors, especially those who are new to teaching, see the sequence of textbook chapters as "gospel," and thus they teach the course in a sequence that might not actually make the most sense to them.

I begin my own course with the history of psychology, the subfields of psychology, and an overview of the major approaches in psychology. As an undergraduate history major, I truly believe that you "can't know where you are going until you know where you have been." Thus I emphasize that psychology is a relatively new science, and that it has roots in philosophy. I talk about the cultural relevance of psychology and the new impetus for cross-cultural studies.

I often begin by asking students these stimulus questions: "A psychologist gets up in the morning and heads to work. Where does she work? What does she do?" Then I use their answers to illustrate the subfields of psychology. It also allows many students to see that their view of psychology is narrow—many will know about clinical psychology, but few will be aware of quantitative psychology or engineering psychology, for example.

The second day of my course involves an emphasis on research methods and statistics. I find that students are more sophisticated today in terms of statistical background. Consequently, I don't have to spend much time defining and illustrating concepts such as mean, median, and mode. I provide students with a general outline of research methods. I then give examples of research questions and ask them to decide which method would be best for that particular question. I also provide a statistics exercise—giving statistical information about two attractive jobs and having students justify their choice by explaining the statistical concepts. This encourages them to understand the importance of a standard deviation, without having to figure out how to compute one (which I believe is beyond the scope of introductory psychology).

I teach the first couple of days in the same order as the textbook—simply because most textbooks begin with an introductory chapter covering history, subfields, and approaches. Some texts have a separate chapter on research methods, whereas others incorporate that topic into the introductory chapter.

Many textbooks then move into biological psychology. Although I understand the reasoning, to start with a single cell and then progress to social interaction, I have to agree with Buxton (1946) who commented, "A course opening with the nervous system, sensation, and perception could well strike a blow to student morale from which it would never recover" (p. 305). This is exactly what happened when I moved from introductory concepts straight into biological concepts—many of my students' eyes glazed over. So I decided I would teach development before the biological psychology chapter. Why development? Well, a couple of reasons. First, I really like teaching that material—so why not start out teaching in your strong area? Second, the material in development is "catchy" for students and not as unfamiliar as, say, neuroanatomy. As such, students get a relatively easy content chapter "under their belts" before they encounter more difficult material. (I'm speaking in generalities, of course. Some students, especially those majoring in biology, have no difficulty with the biological psychology chapter.)

After development, I move back to a more "traditional" organization —biological psychology, sensation, and perception. After these topics, however, I teach the consciousness chapter. In reality, I think you could teach the consciousness chapter in conjunction with many different units. However, for me, it makes sense to move from the idea of perception—of making meaning from information in the environment—to an internal "perception" or consciousness. Talking about the mind–brain distinction, sleeping, dreaming, hypnosis, and psychoactive drugs fits with my outline. I also take the opportunity to refer repeatedly to concepts in biological psychology when discussing psychoactive drugs.

I then move on to the "cognitive unit" (learning, memory, cognition, and cognitive abilities). It is usually easy for students to see how learning contributes to memory and how memory contributes to thinking, which leads to cognitive abilities. Perhaps more than any other four chapters in your textbook, these units are easy to integrate.

Next I teach motivation and emotion and then the chapter on health, stress, and coping. You can integrate these chapters in many different ways, but I like to use the topics raised in motivation, emotion, stress, and coping to help introduce theories of personality, which is the next unit I cover. Students often find some cohesion in the personality, psychological disorder, and treatment of psychological disorders units because the underlying "approaches" provide a common unifying thread. I end my course with a discussion of social psychology. This is a nice ending point: because we have spent most of the course discussing individual development and differences, it's good to talk in a more "molar" manner about individuals interacting with each other.

My ordering of topics has come from personal trial and error. However, this book will present the topics without presuming any particular content order. The instructor of the course should make the decision about which material to present; and the order of presentation should reflect the personal goals of the instructor and the institution (Fuch, 2000).

## Goals and course objectives in introductory psychology

In 1942, Dael Wolfle, who compiled a history of the "first course in psychology," gave advice to the introductory psychology teacher that is still valid today:

> The first task of the beginning instructor of elementary psychology, and indeed, of any instructor who has not already done it, is to write out specifically the objectives of his course—the changes which he expects to develop in, and the benefits which he expects to be gained by, the students. (Wolfle, 1942, p. 706)

Wolfle integrated several previous versions of goals for the introductory psychology course and came up with five:

- teach facts and principles of psychology;
- develop scientific method or habits of critical thought;
- provide better ability in making personal adjustments;
- prepare students for later courses, or interest them in psychology; and

- teach what psychology is and is not, or eliminate popular superstitions. (Wolfle, 1942, p. 687)

Twenty-five years later, Edward Walker and Wilbert McKeachie (1967) stressed critical thinking as a goal, although they pointed out that there was not general agreement about what actual skills were involved or how to "foster" its development. They paraphrased Roger Heyns, who was then Chancellor at the University of California at Berkeley, as saying:

> the primary goal is to develop learners—individuals who will learn not just in college but throughout life. College instructors, he says, as experts in the learning of their own areas, have two functions: (1) helping students develop skills in learning the discipline, and (2) communicating to students the excitement and satisfaction of learning that discipline so that they may develop long-term motivation to learn. (Walker & McKeachie, 1967, p. 5)

If we modernize Wolfle's (1942) goals, they are an excellent guide for introductory psychology instructors. If we can teach the facts about psychology, encourage students to engage in critical and scientific thinking, help students apply psychological principles to their everyday lives, get students interested in psychology—perhaps motivating them to take more advanced psychology courses—and help students see the common misconceptions surrounding psychology, then I think we are on the right track.

However, it is also important not to lose sight of the fact that our goals are personal ones. As Walker and McKeachie (1967) said:

> What is really important is that the instructor formulate a set of goals or objectives he wishes to meet. Only then can a consideration of the tools and techniques available to him yield the best match between task and tool. (p. 11)

But it is sometimes difficult to sit down and list your personal course goals. That is why I suggest that you complete the Teaching Goals Inventory (TGI), which is available in print (Angelo & Cross, 1993), or online at http://www.uiowa.edu/~centeach/tgi/. The TGI lists 53 skills, abilities, and other student accomplishments, and gives you the opportunity to rate the importance of each of them for your introductory course.

Once you have information from the TGI, you should construct your course to meet your goals. For example, if you think it is important for your students to develop critical thinking skills, you will probably plan a course that gives them the opportunity to critique and debate the validity of research results or use critical thinking in evaluating "psychological claims" in the popular media. If you value collaborative learning skills, you will most likely have students work in teams to summarize research articles, solve course-related problems, or carry out other projects. And if you simply want to ensure that students can define the terms and identify the concepts presented in the course, you will probably create exams and class activities that test these skills.

You must also take into account the role your course plays in your department and on your campus. Most introductory courses are a prerequisite for all other psychology courses. Knowing what your department, or college, expects students to know when they finish your course will help you decide what material to cover (and not cover), and what level of detail is appropriate. Are students expected to leave your course with a detailed knowledge of particular units, with a general appreciation of the major themes in psychology, with improved skills at problem solving, critical thinking, writing, studying, or what?

Keep in mind that it is not enough just to develop course goals or objectives; we also need to "emphasize the course objectives and show the student how the material taught serves to achieve these objectives. In this way students will know from the beginning what they are supposed to learn" (Wolfle, 1942, p. 692).

# How Do I Teach?

## Teaching techniques

The role of the teacher has changed in introductory psychology, as well as in education in general. Although it may sound trite, the idea that the teacher is no longer the "sage on the stage" but is now a "guide on the side" is a good way of summing up the changes. Lecturing is no longer enough. And it probably never was. Nearly a century ago, Carl Seashore (1910) talked about the problems of using only the lecture method.

> There are three common sources of error in a teacher's evaluation of the lecture method: (1) the warmth which the lecturer feels over having made things clear; (2) the pleasure in freedom of expression

and in hearing himself, and (3) the failure to note that he has done the thinking so well that the student gladly accepts his ready made portion without thinking. In the elementary course in psychology the mere information lecture should be tabooed. (Seashore, 1910, p. 86)

Seashore went on to urge instructors to use what we call today active learning. "Keep the student doing things, instead of merely listening, reading, or seeing them done . . . Even if he is to be entertained in the course, let it be most frequently by his own activity" (1910, p. 83). He went on to advocate the use of "the class experiment," specifying that every student should have an active and responsible part and that "each step of the experiment shall be explained and interpreted in print" (p. 87). Over 50 years later, Walker and McKeachie (1967) provided practical guidelines to encourage students to become active participants. These included setting the expectation for student participation during the first meeting of the course, explaining why student involvement is important, continuing efforts to encourage discussion throughout the semester, calling students by name, and rewarding student participation.

Today, there is much emphasis on all types of active learning, techniques that keep learners involved with their own learning and not as passive recipients of information (Bonwell & Eison, 1991; Chickering & Gamson, 1987; see also Bonwell's Active Learning Web Site ⓤ). I agree with this approach. Consequently, this book contains many classroom demonstrations and experiments to help students understand a concept by actually experiencing it in some way.

Seashore also mentioned the discussion method, noting that:

> With the teacher who has the genius to handle it, this is one of the most effective methods of teaching classes of not more than twenty-five; but with the average teacher and the average class, it often becomes a waste of time—an abuse of privilege. An undeserved approbrium [sic] rests upon this method, because instructors who lack resourcefulness usually fall back upon it. Incidental discussion should be strongly encouraged. (Seashore, 1910, p. 88)

(I had to look up opprobrium, too. According to the Oxford English Dictionary it means, "An occasion, object, or cause of reproach, criticism, shame, or disgrace; shameful or disgraceful conduct. Now *rare*.") To help you avoid opprobrium, this book provides a list of stimulus questions, devised to help you start a successful discussion in your class.

In reality, most instructors incorporate an eclectic mix of teaching strategies, including lecture, some discussion, brief writing opportunities, and classroom demonstrations. Integrating these various methods with each topic in the introductory course takes some practice, and one of the goals of this book is to help you choose the appropriate activity for the appropriate topic.

## Teaching outside your major area

Teaching introductory psychology means we are teaching out of our specialty area most of the time. Because of this, the first time that you teach introductory psychology, you may feel a little anxious. However, once you have experience teaching the course, you likely will find that teaching material with which you are less familiar is almost easier than teaching material from your area of expertise. This is because we are often tempted to provide more details and research on topics we know very well—which often minimizes the time we have to teach other topics. Moreover, we have difficulty with the "compromises" in our field, and we want students to understand the complexities of the material.

To alleviate some of your anxiety, I have provided background resources for all of the course topics. Thus, if you are teaching in an unfamiliar area, you should be able to use those resources to gain an understanding of the material and to make a decision about the topics you will want to include in your course.

## A word about teaching technology

What technology to use, and when and how to use it, should be individual teaching decisions. As an old-fashioned teacher who "grew up as a teacher" using the blackboard and overhead, I have not converted to using PowerPoint, although most of the graduate students and new faculty teaching with me do so. For me, the advantages of using Power Point presentations are outweighed by the advantages of using the blackboard. I use the blackboard to slow myself down (I'm a fast talker and the students are taking notes) and to maintain maximum flexibility with regard to content and order of content that I present in class. I've seen excellent teaching with PowerPoint slides, and I've seen awful teaching with PowerPoint slides. There is a tendency for those using PowerPoint to move so incredibly quickly that students have trouble both listening and taking notes. And I've seen far too many teachers use the "as is" PowerPoint presentations that accompany a textbook without modification to reflect their goals and ideas.

Nevertheless, I do believe that technology has greatly aided teaching. I cannot imagine talking about the brain and its structures without showing an overhead (with matching handouts for the students) of the brain and its divisions. When I show my students a video clip of schizophrenic patients being interviewed, they develop a deeper understanding of schizophrenia than they would have by merely reading about the disorder in the textbook. Perceptual processes make more sense when you actually see the illusions. Ultimately, technology has to help you be a better teacher—it cannot be the teacher. Technology should enhance the learning experience, not dictate the learning experience. So choose the technology that makes you a good teacher—and make it a conscious choice, not a default.

## Characteristics of effective teachers

The success of an introductory psychology course depends partly on teaching techniques but also on the personal characteristics and classroom behavior of the teacher. When a group of National Merit Scholars were polled about the characteristics of instructors who contributed most to their desire to learn, they listed the follow characteristics: allowing time for class discussion, modifying course content to meet students' needs and interests, treating students as colleagues, and taking a personal interest in students (Walker & McKeachie, 1967). Research seems to verify that. Harry Murray's (1997) meta-analysis of research on the relation between teaching and student outcomes found three aspects of teacher behavior that were positively correlated with student learning: enthusiasm, clarity, and the ability to have good rapport with students. Perhaps Peter Seldin's summary of the characteristics of effective instructors is most apt.

> Treating students with respect; providing the relevance of information to be learned; using active, hands-on student learning; varying instructional methods; providing frequent feedback to students on their performance; offering real-world, practical examples; drawing inferences from models and using analogies; providing clear expectations for assignments; creating a class environment which is comfortable for students; communicating to the level of their students; presenting

themselves in a class as "real people"; using feedback from students and others to assess and improve their teaching; reflecting on their own classroom performance in order to improve it. (Seldin, 1999, p. 3)

I want to end this section with some words of wisdom for introductory psychology instructors given by two psychologists in 1934.

The student has a tendency to reflect the attitude of the teacher in any course. If the teacher is vibrant with genuine enthusiasm the student bids fair to share this enthusiasm. If the teacher fails to grasp the vital elements in his subject he cannot impart vitality to his students. . . . The introductory course in psychology will become vital to the student in proportion to the vitality which the instructor himself discovers in the course. (Winter, 1934, p. 258)

and

The instructor's understanding of his own behavior is a *sine qua non* of successful teaching in any field. For example no student interest is possible where the instructor indulges in certain forms of sadistic control. No class discussion is likely where the teacher does not encourage freedom of expression. Regularity of preparation can not be expected where the instructor's own presentation is unsystematic or disjointed. . . . And how can notebook work, tests, and attendance be generally satisfactory where the student is not led to perceive the objectives of the course? (Krout, 1934, p. 257)

I truly believe that teaching introductory psychology can be invigorating for us as instructors. As Wilbert McKeachie so eloquently put it:

When you are teaching Introductory, almost everything that you read is relevant. I get a wide variety of journals, and when I'm teaching Introductory, every journal seems to offer me ideas to bring into class. It's a great thing for one's own education. (Halonen, 1992, p. 236)

## Who Are Your Introductory Psychology Students?

Walker and McKeachie (1967) answered this question when they stated, "I think it is fair to say that for most of us, your students are virtually every student in college" (p. 2). In addition, Scheirer and Rogers (1985) stated:

> A better feeling for the size of the introductory course can be obtained by considering that about 27% of all full-time students (18% of all full-time and part-time students) take introductory psychology in any given year. Multiplying this figure across four years, it is clear that a vast majority of the students at any given institution take the introductory course. (p. 13)

According to Miller and Gentile (1998), a "conservative estimate suggests that over one million students take introductory psychology every year in North America" (p. 90).

Although, decades ago, students in psychology mirrored students in higher education in general, being male and upper-class, almost from the very beginning psychology attracted students from many different backgrounds and interests (Morawski, 1992).

Students' motivation for attending college has changed, as well. For many decades, students went to college primarily to gain knowledge. Today most students attend college to gain the qualifications for a particular job (Astin, Parrott, Korn, & Sax, 1997). Wilbert McKeachie lamented this trend in an interview, noting that

> it is disturbing that students are so grade oriented and job oriented, materialistic, which I attribute to the state of the economy. It is realistic that when jobs are scarce, people are more concerned about what is needed in order to get a good job. I'm not, in a sense, critical of them, but it does make it more difficult in teaching where you are trying to get students interested in learning for its own sake and they say, "Is this going to be on the test?" (Halonen, 1992, p. 234)

Nevertheless, I believe that introductory students are still the most fun to teach. At my institution, the Fall semester enrollment is almost 80% first-semester students, and I love teaching these people, many of whom are new to the university and new to our curriculum. Or as McKeachie said, "psychology is fresh and new to them . . . And I like freshmen. They aren't jaded" (Halonen, 1992, p. 236).

Statistically speaking, you would likely find great diversity among students taking the introductory psychology course. Most are not psychology majors, nor will they become psychology majors. In 1946, Buxton estimated that 5–8% of the students enrolled in the course were psychology majors, a percentage that is probably about the same today. Many students will take only one course in psychology and thus that course has to be a coherent experience . . . [and] cannot depend for their meaning on later course work in psychology. For many students there are no future courses to build on the early foundations, and there are no later epiphanies to transform bewildering experiences into visions. (Kulik, 1973, p. 16)

Although many students are taking introductory psychology because it is a required course in their curriculum, it is important not to jump to conclusions. Take the time to learn about the students enrolled in your course. Don't assume that they don't care about the subject or are unmotivated to learn it just because it is required (Zakrajsek, 2004). Remember that your expectations can become self-fulfilling prophesies, so don't let negative assumptions lead you to presume that students lack interest. The enthusiasm of a teacher of introductory psychology who obviously loves and cares about the discipline and about teaching it well can infect even nonmajors.

When teaching the introductory psychology course, you will encounter students who represent a wide range of ethnic backgrounds, abilities and disabilities, interests, motivations, and expectations. Some will be diffident and frightened; others will be overconfident and unrealistically optimistic. Whether they are full-time or part-time students, many will be trying to fulfill academic obligations while dealing with a job, financial pressures, family responsibilities, relationship problems, and other stressors. Preparing to deal with the diversity of today's students is one dimension of the task you will eventually face as a psychology instructor (Goss Lucas & Bernstein, 2005).

## Using This Book

The goals of this book are twofold: to help first-time introductory psychology instructors teach the course well and to provide new resources, information, and ideas for those who have been teaching the course for many years.

I designed the first chapter to introduce you to the special challenges you will encounter as a teacher of introductory psychology. The second chapter will address general teaching issues such as organizing the course, syllabus construction, classroom management issues, evaluation within the course, and the importance of the first day of each class. The final chapter is devoted to helping you reflect on your teaching, end your course well, and provide guidance for any course revisions you may decide to make.

The remaining chapters are devoted to providing you with outlines of course material that is typically taught in introductory psychology and providing you with the resources to prepare and teach well. My hope is that you will be able to pick any topic in general psychology, locate it within this book, and find the resources I provide helpful in preparing to teach it effectively. Thus each chapter has a standard organization.

Chapters 3–13 are organized in the following way: (a) an introduction to the unit, pointing out special concerns or overriding issues; (b) my personal outline for each unit; (c) topics that are typically included in the unit(s) taught; (d) suggestions for ways to organize the concepts; (e) topics that students may find difficult; (f) other important topics to cover; (g) stimulus questions designed to "hook" students on a topic; (h) classroom learning activities that help to illustrate the concepts; (i) possible mini-assignment; and (j) handouts. By using this "outline" organization for each chapter, I hope you will find more information and less verbiage.

## Getting started

### Introduction and important issues in this unit

In this section, I identify some issues that are unique to a particular unit so you can think through these issues. For example, in the biological psychology unit, I note that many students have a difficult time seeing the relevance of the unit, and I provide some suggestions for making the unit more interesting and active.

### My outline for teaching (# days)

These include day-by-day outlines for teaching the material. These outlines are the result of my attempts to maximally organize the material and to structure information so that students can see the connection between topics and concepts. Note, however, that these outlines are constantly evolving and changing to keep pace with changes in content and with changes in student interests. Also note that the times allowed for each topic are approximate and will vary based on your interest in the topic and the number of students in your class. I also discuss where in the course I include a particular unit of information I am describing. Again, this order will vary based on your preferences. In my outlines, I often refer to mini-assignments that will be listed towards the end of the chapter. In some outlines I also include an item I call "summer reading." This refers to books or articles that pertain to the topic we will be discussing that day and that I believe are accessible to the students. I tell my students that I call it "summer reading" because there is so much reading that I *have* to do, I seldom have time to read the things I *want* to read until the summer. And I encourage them to note the resource if it is a topic in which they are interested.

### My transitions

This explains my reasoning for the placement of the content into the structure of the course. In this section, I talk about why I chose to teach the content at this point in the course. I also provide segues from the previous content and to the next content.

### Topics typically included in this unit

This is an encyclopedic listing of topics that *could* be included in this unit. I have tried to be as inclusive as possible—noting that instructors differ in their emphases and orientation. However, this is *not* a list of all topics that you *must* present. There is no realistic way to teach all of these topics. You should review the topics listed and decide which topics to include in your course. The topics that you choose to present will be influenced by the textbook you use, whether you are teaching as part of a multisection course, or the dictates of your institution.

### Some options for organizing the concepts

In this section I discuss different ways to organize the material. Thus one way of teaching a particular unit might be by a timeline (development, for example), whereas another might be by approach to the content.

## Teaching the content

### Topics that many students will find difficult

I've tried to help you identify the topics with which many students will struggle. I've also identified resources to help you teach those topics more effectively. My philosophy is to use class time to teach the concepts that students tend to find the most difficult. Thus I often concentrate on these topics, knowing that the textbook will help students learn other, less challenging, material.

*Other important topics*

There are other important topics that most students will not find difficult. I also identify resources to help you teach this material.

## Classroom tips

*Stimulus questions for discussion*

These questions will help you begin a classroom discussion on a relevant topic. You can use these questions in many different ways. You can just ask them during the class period in which you will cover this material, or you could prime your students for discussion by posing the questions at the class session prior to the discussion. In either case, you can have students write their thoughts about these questions. I have found that students are more likely to participate in a discussion if they have had time to think about the question and have something in writing to which they can refer.

*Some suggested classroom learning activities*

As I stated previously, active learning is important for students to take "ownership" of their own learning. I have suggested classroom demonstrations and experiments to help students understand and apply the important concepts in each unit. Although I have provided an estimate of how long each activity will take, the actual amount of time will vary based on your class size and the way you conduct the activity. (Note that the ⓦ symbol means that a printable version of this activity is available at the web site (www.blackwellpublishing.com/lucas). And the ⓤ symbol means that the URL is available at the web site.)

*Possible mini-assignments (written or groups)*

Writing is another essential means through which students can demonstrate their grasp of the material. I like to use mini-assignments that take only a few minutes to grade or comment on. I provide five mini-assignments that might be useful. Because some of these writing assignments actually work well as a group project, I often provide directions for both individual and group work.

*Handouts*

For some units, I provide handouts that my teaching colleagues or I have developed. We use these handouts to help students understand and organize course material.

Additional suggested resources for instructors

These are additional resources that I have found helpful in my course preparation. You won't necessarily need or want to use all of these resources but, if you feel a "weakness" in a particular area, they should help you to be better prepared.

# In Summary

I think Buxton (1946) may have gotten it right when he said, "also be warned that teaching introductory psychology is a job which calls for compromises of many kinds plus a surprising amount of high-grade clerical work" (p. 303). Aside from the "clerical work," Buxton was correct in stating that teaching introductory psychology involves compromise. We are charged with teaching the basic concepts of the entire field in the introductory course. Unfortunately, it is impossible to include the nuances of every subject. Moreover, because of time constraints, we often have to present prototypes of concepts. And we have to pick and choose the content (as did our predecessors) to present. As a fellow introductory psychology instructor once remarked to me, "Teaching introductory psychology involves a series of white lies." We have to get the basics clear—and we can't dwell on the particulars.

It is my hope that this book will provide the resources and guidelines that will help you develop the type of introductory course that meets your course objectives. By providing a list of potential topics, I hope that you will be able to choose wisely the concepts you teach. By providing many different active learning activities, I hope that you will feel comfortable using such techniques.

I would love to hear from you—both how you were able to use the book and what you wished the book included, but didn't. You can email me at gossluca@uiuc.edu.

References and Further Reading

Angelo, T., & Cross, K. P. (1993). *Classroom assessment techniques: A handbook for college teachers* (2nd ed.). San Francisco: Jossey-Bass.

Arnold, H. (1926). What parts of elementary psychology are most interesting to students? *Pedagogical Seminary, 33,* 729–735.

Astin, A., Parrott, S., Korn, W., & Sax, L. (1997). *The American freshmen: Thirty year trend.* Los Angeles: Higher Education Research Institute,

Graduate School of Education and Information Studies, University of California.

Bonwell, C. & Eison, J. (1991). *Active learning: Creating excitement in the classroom. ASHE-ERIC Higher Education Report No. 1.* Washington, DC: The George Washington University School of Education and Human Development.

Buxton, C. (1946). Planning the introductory psychology course. *American Psychologist, 1,* 303–311.

Chickering, A., & Gamson, Z. (1987). Seven principles for good practice in undergraduate education. *AAHE Bulletin, 39*(7), 3–7.

Dockeray, F. C., & Valentine, W. L. (1935). An analysis of the elementary psychology course at the Ohio State University. *Journal of Applied Psychology, 19,* 503–520.

Fuch, A. (2000). Teaching the introductory course in psychology circa 1900. *American Psychologist, 55,* 492–495.

Gilliland, A. (1932). The introductory course in psychology. *Journal of Applied Psychology, 16,* 614–622.

Gilliland, A. (1934). The introductory course in psychology: Its nature and its aims. *Psychological Exchange, 2,* 254–255.

Goodwin, C. J. (1992). The American Psychological Association and the teaching of psychology, 1892–1945. In A. Puente, J. Matthew, & C. Brewer. (Eds.), *Teaching psychology in America: A history* (pp. 329–343). Washington, DC: American Psychological Association.

Goss Lucas, S. & Bernstein, D. (2005). *Teaching psychology: A step by step guide.* Mahwah, NJ: Lawrence Erlbaum Associates.

Griggs, R., Bujak-Johnson, A., & Proctor, D. (2004). Using common core vocabulary in text selection and teaching the introductory course. *Teaching of Psychology, 31,* 265–269.

Halonen, J. (1992). "I was just lucky": An interview with model teacher Wilbert J. McKeachie. In A. Puente, J. Matthew, & C. Brewer (Eds.), *Teaching psychology in America: A history* (pp. 219–257). Washington, DC: American Psychological Association.

Hartmann, G. W. (1933). The measurement of the relative interest value of representative items taught in elementary psychology. *Journal of Educational Psychology, 24,* 266–282.

Krout, M. (1934). On teaching introductory psychology. *Psychological Exchange, 2,* 254–255.

Kulik, J. (1973). *Undergraduate education in psychology.* Washington DC: American Psychological Association.

Miller, B., & Gentile, B. (1998). Introductory course content and goals. *Teaching of Psychology, 25,* 89–96.

Morawski, J. (1992). There is more to our history of giving: The place of introductory textbooks in American psychology. *American Psychologist, 47,* 161–69.

Murray, H. (1997). Effective teaching behaviors in the college classroom. In R. Perry & J. Smart (Eds.), *Effective teaching in higher education: Research and practice* (pp. 171–204). New York: Agathon.

Nelson, P. & Stricker, G. (1992). Advancing the teaching of psychology: Contributions of the American Psychological Association, 1946–1992. In A. Puente, J. Matthew, & C. Brewer (Eds.), *Teaching psychology in America: A history* (pp. 345–364). Washington, DC: American Psychological Association.

Poffenberger, A. T. (1929). The thirty-seventh annual meeting of the American Psychological Association. *American Journal of Psychology, 41,* 341–343.

Radford, J., & Rose, D. (Eds.) (1980). *The teaching of psychology: Method, content, and context.* Chichester, UK: John Wiley & Sons.

Ruja, H. (1948). The order of topics in general psychology. *American Psychologist, 47,* 161–169.

Sanford, E. (1910). The teaching of elementary psychology in colleges and universities with laboratories. *Psychological Monographs, 12* (Whole No. 4), 54–71.

Scheirer, C. J., & Rogers, A. (1985). *The undergraduate psychology curriculum: 1984.* Washington, DC: American Psychological Association.

Seashore, C. (1910). General report on the teaching of the elementary course in psychology: Recommendations. *Psychological Monographs, 12* (Whole No. 4), 80–91.

Seldin, P. (1999). Current practices—good and bad—nationally. In P. Seldin (Ed.), *Changing practices in evaluating teaching: A practical guide to improved faculty performance and promotion/tenure decisions* (pp. 1–24). Bolton, MA: Anker.

Seward, G. (1931). Students' reactions to a first course in psychology. *Journal of Applied Psychology, 15,* 512–524.

Walker, E., & McKeachie, W. (1967). *Some thoughts about teaching the beginning course in psychology.* Belmont, CA: Brooks/Cole Publishing Company.

Weiten, W., & Wight, R. (1992). Portraits of a discipline: An examination of introductory psychology textbooks in America. In A. Puente, J. Matthew, & Brewer, C. (Eds.), *Teaching psychology in America: A history* (pp. 453–504). Washington, DC: American Psychological Association.

Winter, J. (1934). How to make the first course in psychology more vital to the average student. *Psychological Exchange, 2,* 258.

Wolfle, D. (1942). The first course in psychology. *Psychological Bulletin, 39*(9), 685–713.

Zakrajsek, T. (2004). Teaching a course you feel unprepared to teach. *APS Observer, 17*(11), 33–34, 44.

Zechmeister, J., & Zechmeister, E. (2000). Introductory textbooks and psychology's core concepts. *Teaching of Psychology, 27*(1), 6–11.

# Chapter 2

# Getting Ready to Teach

Now that you are familiar with the major issues involved in teaching introductory psychology, it is time to think about the basics of your course construction. There are many books devoted to teaching and to course development (e.g., Boice, 2000; McKeachie & Svinicki, 2006), some of which focus specifically on teaching psychology (e.g., Forsyth, 2003; Goss Lucas & Bernstein, 2005), so this chapter will provide just a brief look at some of the major teaching decisions you will need to make.

## Beginning to Plan

It is important that you start planning and preparing your course as soon as you can. Being organized and doing as much advance work as possible will pay huge dividends at the end of the course.

### Choosing a textbook

Once you are aware of your teaching goals, you must decide which text best meets your goals and the needs of your students. Kenneth Eble (1994) advised, "the first consideration in choosing texts is whether students are likely to read them, work with them, and learn from them" (p. 126). He also advocated choosing a book that supports students' independent learning. Thus, in addition to holding students' interest, the textbook should be sufficiently clear, current, and free of major errors that you can rely on it to provide further details about—and a broader context for—the information you present in class. This is especially critical for introductory psychology, where it is impossible to cover all course content during class time.

I use my introductory textbook as the "core" of my course and I help my students to learn to use it well. I cue them to read the material that is separate from the "main writing" (e.g., "Thinking Critically" in the textbook that I use) because many students skip these sections. I advise them to pay attention to pedagogical features such as boldface print, italicized or highlighted text, chapter summaries, self-tests, review tables, and the like (Boyd, 2003). Pointing out these pedagogical features helps students as they read and study.

I encourage students to read the assigned material before coming to class and I often start class by asking a couple of multiple-choice questions from that assigned reading. In some units, I assign each study group to become experts on one approach or topic. The "expert" group teaches the information to the rest of the class. Students enjoy being able to demonstrate their knowledge to their peers and they tend to read the section of the text they were assigned to "teach" in greater depth and detail.

Other introductory teachers use the text in different ways. One colleague, Bob Hendersen (2005), has his students use the text as a reference. He wants students to be able to use the text to experience a perspective that might be different from the one he presents in class. And he encourages his students to rewrite and expand their class notes, using the book to fill in incomplete information, to get a better understanding of concepts that might have confused them, and to help them organize class information more coherently.

Talk to colleagues who have taught the course before, both in your institution and in others, for advice on which textbooks have worked for them and why they chose their current text. Contact publishers' representatives and ask for examination copies of textbooks that you think you might be interested in using. Of course, if you do not have enough time to choose your own textbook, or if the textbook choice is made by a committee, be sure to contact the publisher of the text to ask for all of the ancillaries that accompany the book. This most often includes a student study guide, an electronic test bank, an instructor's resource manual (IRM), ready-made

PowerPoint slides, and web-based programs for both you and your students. Make sure that you know of all available resources that accompany your textbook. And be sure to integrate those resources when devising lectures, learning activities, homework, and tests.

# The Course Syllabus

Your course syllabus is one of the most important teaching documents that you will write. It reflects both your personality and the type of course that you plan to teach. It provides students with a "road map" for traversing your course. On most campuses, your syllabus is a legally binding contract between you and your students. It provides the grounds for imposing penalties on students who fail to meet their responsibilities, and outlines your responsibilities to your students (Parkes & Harris, 2002). Accordingly, consider carefully what you want to say in your syllabus, say it clearly, and then stick to it. If you must make changes after the course begins, distribute a written notification to all students.

## Course calendar

The first step in creating your syllabus is to look at a calendar and mark and count the number of class meetings. Mark out standard vacation days, such as Thanksgiving or spring break. Note, too, any class meetings that coincide with religious holidays that may not be official vacation days (e.g., Kwanzaa, Yom Kippur, Eid ul-Fitr). (A comprehensive list of religious holidays is maintained by the Interfaith organization ⑩.) Do not schedule quizzes, exams, or other graded assignments on those days.

Next, decide on the order of the topics you will present and how many class periods you will devote to each. Because I give four exams and do not make my final exam cumulative, I divide the calendar into four segments containing approximately the same number of class days. The last day of each of these segments is the date of the exam covering the information presented during that segment. After noting the dates of the four exams, I then decide when my major paper will be due (usually before a break so I will have time to grade them carefully). And based on when the major paper falls, I decide on when my mini-assignments will be due and when quizzes will take place. Because I require group presentations on particular topics, I also note the optimal placement of those presentations based on their content. Marking the calendar in this way gives me an overview of the course, making it easier for me to see the optimal placement and spacing of all graded assignments.

## Syllabus content

While the exact content of your syllabus is a matter of personal choice, my advice is to include too much rather than too little. Normally your syllabus should begin with the course title and name (e.g., Psychology 100), and the days, time, and location of class meetings (e.g., MWF, 10 a.m., 31 Psychology Building). It should include your name, office address, office phone number, office hours, and email address: in other words, all the information that students need in order to contact you outside of class. You may also provide a home phone number for students to use in case of emergency, but think carefully about whether to do this; if you do reveal your home number, be sure to list the hours during which students may and may not use it.

Your syllabus should be a personal document, in the sense that it should briefly describe your general teaching goals and/or your specific goals for the introductory psychology course. It should clearly state your course policies, pet peeves, and rules of course etiquette (e.g., what students should do if they will be late for class, what they should do if they have to miss a quiz, your feelings about their eating lunch during a noon class). After trying various rules, I've come down to two that I publish in my syllabus:

1. This course is designed for true participation. Please respect your colleagues and be open to perspectives different from your own. You should expect the same respect from all others in the class. Questions, challenges, humor, and feedback are encouraged.
2. Attendance is very important in this class. You miss important information and the class misses your input every time you are not in class. I will take attendance, not to penalize you if you are absent, but to match names and faces. If you must miss class, be sure to talk to a classmate who was in attendance to get the day's notes and assignments.

A list of required learning materials should also be provided— textbooks, study guides, course outlines, and so forth. (And be sure that, if you require something, you actually use it in class, or at least refer to it in a meaningful way. One of students' pet peeves is being asked to buy material that they do not use in the course.) You may also provide a list of optional resources for the benefit of students who might have difficulty in your course or those who might want to pursue particular topics in more depth.

You must include a statement inviting students with special needs to come to see you to explain any accommodations they might be requesting. My statement reads as follows: "Any student requiring special accommodations should notify me as soon as possible. All accommodations will follow the procedures stated in the University Code of Policies Ⓤ."

You must explain clearly in your syllabus the evaluation opportunities that will be available (such as homework, quizzes, exams, papers, online assignments), when they will take place or be due, and how much of each of them contributes toward the student's final grade. In other words, on the first day of class, your students should know what is going to be required of them and when it will be required. Your syllabus also should specify how grades will be calculated. Explain any special policies such as being able to drop one exam score but *not* the final, what research participation points are and how they can be earned, and so forth.

Looking at the syllabi of those who have taught the introductory course previously is a good way to get ideas for your own syllabus. And don't hesitate to talk with colleagues, ask for their input, and have them review your syllabus. Be sure to ask your department chair to review your syllabus to make sure it fits departmental and campus guidelines and curricular needs (Zakrajsek, 2004). Your campus's instructional development center can provide additional general advice and information on writing a syllabus, and the Society for the Teaching of Psychology's Project Syllabus provides, through its Office of Teaching Resources in Psychology (OTRP), a collection of syllabi for introductory psychology courses Ⓤ.

Finally, think of your syllabus as a "work in progress." Be sure to evaluate it periodically throughout the term and make notes on any changes you might like to make in it for the next term.

## Evaluating Student Learning

Deciding how to evaluate my students is one of the most difficult teaching decisions that I make. This will be even more difficult if this is your first time teaching introductory psychology. I am not the only one to feel this way. In his book on teaching, Kenneth Eble (1994) relegates the tasks of testing and grading to a section titled "Grubby Stuff and Dirty Work." Numerous other books include good discussions of student evaluation (e.g., Gronlund & Linn, 1990; Jacobs & Chase, 1992; Ory & Ryan, 1993), and I strongly encourage you to use these resources, especially if you are new to introductory psychology or if you are dissatisfied with your current evaluation plan and instruments. Here I offer just a quick review of some of the most important issues associated with student evaluation.

## General guidelines

First, the process of constructing evaluation instruments should help you think more carefully about your goals for the course, including the goal of providing a learning experience for your students (Ebel, 1965; McKeachie, 2002). "If properly crafted, examinations, papers, and various other graded works can become vehicles for instruction in themselves—real adjuncts to the other material in the course" (Kennedy, 1997, p. 78).

> Tests provide an opportunity for students to show what they have learned and to discover the scope and depth of their knowledge; they also tell students what they do not know and serve as a guide to further study. Students like to find out what they know. (Jacobs & Chase, 1992, p. 7)

Second, remember that students benefit from prompt and constructive feedback (Dinham, 1996). When graded assignments are returned promptly with specific, substantive, and constructive responses, it is easier for students to make decisions about how well their particular approach to studying course material is, or is not, working for them. As Eble (1994) says, "Giving feedback on an examination is as necessary and as worthy of care, intelligence, and imagination as making up the test in the first place" (p. 145).

Ory (2003, p. 35) concurs: "Failing to spend class-time discussing common errors and misunderstanding is missing an opportunity for further learning." Telling students that they should make an appointment or see you during an office hour if they want to go over their test sends the message that the exam was not all that important.

Suskie (2000) used the American Association for Higher Education's "9 Principles of Good Practice for Assessing Student Learning" in devising guidelines for student assessment ⓤ. Six of these guidelines are especially pertinent to this discussion.

1.  Clearly state your learning outcomes and share them with your students. Students should know what goals are most important and what skills they should acquire.
2.  Match your assessment instrument with what you teach and vice versa. In other words, match your goals for the course with your tests and be sure that your tests measure the learning outcomes that you believe are important (Clegg, 1994; Erickson & Strommer, 1991; Jacobs & Chase, 1992; Ory & Ryan, 1993). For example, if one of your goals is to promote critical thinking, assigning "thought papers," analytical essay exams, or comprehension-oriented multiple-choice tests would be better than giving tests focused on defining key terms.
3.  Evaluate students often and by using a variety of instruments. Testing experts agree that the more evaluative components considered in a final grade, the more valid the final grade will be (Ory & Ryan, 1993; Jacobs & Chase, 1992; McKeachie, 2002).
4.  Help students understand the assessment task and goals. If you are assigning a group project, outline what outcomes you expect. Provide students with examples of successful projects. If you are going to use multiple-choice tests, help students learn to take those tests. Provide practice questions in class and describe the process that students should use when deciding how to answer such questions.
5.  Be positive and encouraging—express confidence in students' ability to do well.
6.  Evaluate the outcomes of your assessments. If students do not do well on your assessment instruments, then you need to find out why. Was it a problem with the assessment instrument? Was it a problem with not teaching the concept well or at all? Was it a problem with matching the assessment with your teaching? After every graded component, it is important to look at the assessment instrument and make appropriate adjustments so that the results of future assessments will be as reflective as possible of what you have taught, and what students have learned.

## Quizzes and tests

Do not write tests and quizzes at the last minute. Ideally, you would write one or two questions immediately following each class session, or set aside some time each week to write four or five items (Ebel, 1965; Erickson & Strommer, 1991; Ory & Ryan, 1993). (Remember that classroom tests must be long enough to sample from each objective and content area.) If you can do this, your test items are likely to be content-valid and the process of developing a quiz or test will not seem so stressful.

Linn and Gronlund (2000) classify objective tests into those that require the student to *supply* the answer and those that require the student to *select* the answer. Short answer, completion, and essay are examples of "supply" types, whereas true–false, matching, and multiple-choice are examples of the "select" types. Potential problems with "supply and select" test items include items that are: ambiguously stated, too wordy, contain unnecessarily difficult vocabulary, have unnecessarily complex sentence structure, have unclear instructions, and that may (usually inadvertently) display racial, ethnic, and/or gender bias (p. 162).

Essay and short-answer tests can be constructed relatively quickly, they provide an assessment of students' writing ability, and they can set tasks that require high level analysis of course material (Jacobs & Chase, 1992). However, many testing experts recommend that essay questions be reserved to "measure complex learning outcomes that cannot be measured by other means" (Gronlund & Linn, 1990, p. 212; Jacobs & Chase, 1992; Ory & Ryan, 1993).

For essay and short-answer tests you should develop a grading rubric. Write out an "ideal" answer for each question or create a "template" outlining the important information that should be included in the answer—and then decide how many points each piece of information is worth. Grade these types of questions "blindly" to eliminate potential bias. To create this blind grading situation, ask your students to use an identifying code instead of their names, or to put their names on the back of the paper.

Clegg (1994) summarizes these and other testing ideas in a series of tips for writing good exam questions:

1.  Don't wait until the last minute to start writing tests. Be sure to double check for errors. Don't rely on the test banks that

accompany introductory textbooks. Wolfle's comment on test banks of the 1940s still rings true today . . . "In general they seem not to have had any more careful scrutiny and criticism before publication than the usual course examination has before administration. As a group they place too much stress on memory for isolated factual details" (1942, pp. 703–704).

2. Don't decide on the types of items to include based on what you, personally, prefer. The choice should be made so that items are a good match between the strengths of the item type and the goals of the test. And remember that students will study differently based on the type of exam that they expect. Students who expect open-ended questions, either essay or short answer, consider such tests to be more difficult and thus tend to study more (D'Ydewalle, Swert, & DeCorte, 1983).

3. Look at each item and think about what the student actually has to know and do to answer the questions. Apply Bloom's taxonomy ⓤ here—does the student have to remember, understand, apply, analyze, evaluate, or create? Are these tasks appropriate for the level of your students, the introductory course, and the purpose of your exam?

4. Ask others to read the exam for errors or inconsistencies.

5. Write items that are inclusive of all your students' characteristics, and avoid language that could reasonably be seen as offensive. Your items should include ethnically diverse names and situations. Avoid stereotypes, such as describing all cases of mental disorders as females.

6. Group all similar item types together. All multiple-choice items should be in one part, matching in another part, essay in another part, etc.

7. Write explicit and understandable directions. Indicate the point value of each item and/or the amount of time the student should allocate to the item.

8. Evaluate the amount of time needed for the exam. If in doubt, go with a shorter test so students do not feel time pressure. McKeachie (2002) suggests that you allocate one minute per multiple-choice question, two minutes for a short answer response, 10 to 15 minutes for a restricted response essay (one that is related to only one learning outcome), and 30 minutes for an extended response essay (p. 80).

9. Be careful in formatting the exam. Make it easy to read by using a large enough font, dark enough print, a paper color that

doesn't make the print difficult to distinguish. Be sure to number items sequentially and make sure that an item is not cut off between pages.

10. Proofread and spell-check every exam item.
11. Develop the answer key before administering the exam. In a multiple-choice exam, make sure that you have not overused one response alternative. If your answer key is automatically generated by a computer testing program, be sure to spot-check it to see that it is correct. By developing your scoring criteria for evaluating short answer and essay questions, problems can be detected before the exam is given. For example, if you find it difficult to develop the scoring criteria, you may want to drop that item, or revise it.
12. Count the pages of the collated test to make sure that all pages are included and they are in the proper order. Always make more copies than you think you will need. That way, you will always have enough, even if some copies are damaged or have pages missing.

## Writing assignments

Incorporating writing assignments into your evaluation strategy will help your students to improve their writing and will help you to better evaluate their knowledge of course material. Such assignments might include a long, focused term paper, or multiple "mini-papers" that cover a broader spectrum of course material.

As an alternative to "mini-papers" you could ask students to keep course-related journals, to write letters to friends or relatives in which they explain course material, or to summarize what they find during a course-related search of the Internet (Davis, 1993; Erickson & Strommer, 1991). Some instructors that I work with use "applied concept journals" in which they have the student choose two concepts from each chapter and apply those concepts to their everyday lives.

In other words, think beyond the usual term paper. The results are likely to be more interesting and challenging for your students, and less burdensome for you. But remember, writing assignments deserve as much thought as tests. Students need to know exactly how their assignment is to be evaluated. They need to know how long the paper is to be, how to cite sources, the format of the paper, and the type of resources that are acceptable. Students, and especially introductory students, often do not know the difference between *Psychology Today* and *Psychological Bulletin*. It is important that you educate students about the ranges of resources available, and how they can differ. This is especially critical given the propensity of students to rely on web resources, many of which are not critically evaluated.

Also, keep in mind that material in a typical research journal is inaccessible to most introductory students. Help them learn to read such articles, or allow them to use alternative resources.

Writing assignments can be useful in collaborative learning as well. Allowing peers to critique assignments saves instructor time and allows students to develop skills that will help them be better evaluators of their own work.

## Other assessment instruments

Other strategies of assessment include open-book exams, oral exams, take-home exams, collaborative testing, and portfolios (Jacobs & Chase, 1992). If you are interested in alternative assessment strategies, I recommend that you read "Changing the way we grade student performance" (Anderson & Speck, 1998).

## How I evaluate my students

I incorporate as many diverse evaluation instruments as possible in my evaluation plan. I either give nine quizzes (of which I drop the lowest two) or I ask "quiz questions" every day at the beginning of class (90 opportunities to gain 60 points). I also give three exams and a noncumulative final. The lowest score on the three exams can be dropped. I allow students to drop two quizzes and one exam because I think that this policy alleviates some of the stress surrounding evaluation and allows students to have an "off day."

I also assign 12 "mini-assignments," of which 10 count toward the students' grades. These assignments are devised either to ask students to apply a concept that I think is difficult or to ask them to be creative. For example, in one assignment students set up an experiment to test a hypothesis. In another, they decide which of their five senses they would give up, why they would give up that sense instead of another, and what physiological structures would be impaired. The last "mini-assignment" of the term asks them to violate a social norm, describe their feelings doing so, and how others reacted to them.

I often use small group activities in my teaching and I assign one major group project. Students choose a seminal paper in psychology from a list I provide. They report back to the class explaining the research, the research methods used, the important points of the study, how the study relates to what we are covering in class, and any ethical concerns.

In the major writing assignment of my course, students watch a popular movie that has psychological content or relevance. The students then read about that concept in their textbook and consult at least one additional authoritative source for further information. The guidelines for writing this paper are carefully outlined on the assignment sheet itself, including the number of points awarded for the summary of the movie, summary of the textbook information, summary of the outside source, and an integration of the movie's portrayal of the psychological concept with information from the reputable sources they consult. Students are asked how they would change the movie in order for it to more accurately portray the psychological concept.

By incorporating the guidelines outlined here to develop your course evaluation plan, and making your students aware of the plan, evaluation can become an integral part of your teaching rather than "grubby stuff and dirty work" (Eble, 1994).

## Managing Your Classroom

Beyond developing a plan for how your course is organized and how your students will be evaluated, you must also give some thought to decisions about classroom management issues. Will you accept late assignments, and if so, what penalties, if any, will there be for lateness? Will you offer make-up exams, and how will you determine who deserves one? How will you return exams and quizzes to your students, and when will you discuss their results? Making these and other routine decisions now will make life a lot easier for you as the course proceeds.

You'll also need to think ahead about how to cover sensitive and controversial topics in class, and how you will make your classroom an open and comfortable place for academic inquiry.

## Establishing a good classroom climate

The social and psychological climate you create in the classroom has a strong influence on students' attendance and on their academic progress in your course (Erickson & Strommer, 1991; Leamnson, 1999). All else being equal, students tend to stick with, and learn more from, classes in which they feel comfortable and valued as individuals (Sleigh & Ritzer, 2001; Sleigh, Ritzer, & Casey, 2002). These perceptions are especially important among first-year students, who comprise much of the introductory psychology student population, because they often enter the college classroom with the greatest trepidation and the strongest need for support.

Students are more likely to feel comfortable and valued if you go out of your way to create rapport with them. In the context of teaching, "rapport" refers to the process of "creating emotional connections between teacher and student" (Buskist & Saville, 2001, p. 12). Student surveys suggest that the teacher behaviors that contribute most to the development of rapport are, in order: displaying a sense of humor; being available to students before, after, or outside of class; encouraging class discussion; showing interest in students; knowing students' names; sharing personal insights and experiences with the class; relating course material through everyday terms and examples; and understanding that students sometimes have problems that hinder their progress in the course (Buskist & Saville, 2001). Rapport is also enhanced when teachers make eye contact with students, smile, use an expressive speaking style, stand close to the student they are talking with, use appropriate movements and gestures, appear relaxed, and spend time with students (Andersen, 1986). These behaviors are referred to as *immediacy* because they create the impression that the teacher is psychologically engaged with the students and the class, not an aloof figure going through the motions of teaching. Immediacy can also be expressed by asking students about their work, soliciting students' views on course-related matters, and offering praise for good work. As you might expect, students tend to like teachers who display immediacy. They also tend to like, and to be motivated to work hard in, those teachers' courses (Anderson, 1999; Sanders & Wiseman, 1994).

The most beneficial classroom climate is one in which all students feel comfortable and valued, but it can be a challenge to create this climate. Most teachers would never deliberately make their students feel uncomfortable, but it is easy to do so inadvertently. Some tips for developing an inclusive classroom include:

- *Use diverse references and examples* that let your students know that you don't presume they are all Americans, heterosexuals, Christians, males, females, whites, blacks, or representatives of any other particular group. Don't make sarcastic or joking comments about any condition or any group of people. Don't single out minority students to summarize the views of the group they represent. This not only makes the student uncomfortable, but suggests a stereotype that applies to everyone in that group.
- *Look at everyone* as you lecture or lead discussions. Scan the entire classroom and make eye contact with everyone, not just with your favorite students or the ones who are most responsive and interested. Doing so ensures that you won't miss a raised hand and that you will be able to note when students seem confused or enthused.
- *Create mixed work groups.* Assign students to groups that are diverse in terms of gender, ethnicity, disability, and other demographic characteristics. Assuring diversity in such groups tends to benefit all students, and especially those from majority backgrounds, because it increases involvement in the class and the display of academic and intellectual skills (Marin, 2000).
- *Write inclusive quiz and exam questions.* As noted earlier, be sure to use ethnically diverse names for hypothetical people and make sure that the examples and terms used will be familiar to all your students. For example, an exam item that mentions a reindeer with a red nose will be funny to most students, but might mystify some students who are not from the majority culture. (I learned this the hard way!)

## Dealing with sensitive or controversial topics

It is common in the introductory course to deal with controversial and sensitive issues. I don't profess to have all the answers about how to do this without making the classroom environment uncomfortable, but Anderson (1999) provided some guidelines that I have found to be of value. As he points out, these guidelines are based on establishing an atmosphere of openness and mutual respect early in the term.

- Remind students about sensitive or controversial topics that will be addressed at the next class. This may motivate students to do the reading associated with that topic, and perhaps begin to consider what they think about it and what they want to know about it.

- During your lecture on sensitive material, present that material in a mature and straightforward way, modeling a serious academic approach that students can emulate. If you seem hesitant to use certain words or to address certain topics in your narrative, your students probably will be too, when the time comes to ask questions or engage in a discussion. If you yourself are not entirely comfortable describing or discussing certain topics in class, practice delivering the lecture material in private to help you get used to dealing with it.

- Set the stage by acknowledging that everyone in the room may have strong feelings and differing views on such topics. Point out, too, that although everyone has the right to hold and express those views, discussion in an academic classroom must take place in an atmosphere of mutual respect (Allen, 2000; Marin, 2000). Everyone will be expected to consider the rights and feelings of others and can expect others to do the same.

- If inappropriate or harmful comments are made, they should not be ignored, but they should be handled with care. There is not much point in castigating students who make inappropriate comments because doing so is unlikely to alter—and may even solidify—those students' views. An overly harsh response will probably also lead these students to refrain from further discussions on any topic, and worst of all, will stop the current discussion in its tracks. Take the comment out of the realm of the personal and address it instead from an objective and academic perspective. For example, if a student says, "Everyone knows that women aren't as smart as men" rephrase it into, "Some people do believe that men are smarter than women—where do you think that idea comes from and where can we find some data to examine this question scientifically?"

- Invite students to submit (anonymous) written questions or comments about the topic on the day before it is covered in class (Brooke, 1999). You can use these questions and comments to tailor your lecture and frame discussion so as to characterize and address wide-ranging points of view in a nonprovocative manner.

- You can assign groups of students to study each of several different viewpoints on a sensitive or controversial topic, and then to summarize those viewpoints in classroom presentations. This approach allows the class to consider multiple perspectives on the topic that are based on research and a group consensus, not on the casual comments of one individual. The result may be a more moderate and balanced discussion from which everyone can learn something new (Allen, 2000; Heuberger, Gerber, & Anderson, 1999). This process has been described as disagreeing in an agreeable manner (Desrochers, 2000).
- Recognize your own strongly held views on these topics, and, in accordance with ethical standards, resolve not to let those views turn your teaching into persuasion or proselytizing.

## Developing classroom management routines

The more structure you can apply to common classroom occurrences, the less off-task behavior will occur and the easier your life will be. Establish a routine for handing in papers, taking exams, getting into groups, starting class, and so forth. I teach at 8:30 in the morning and many of my students are barely awake when they get to class. But early in the semester they learn that there will be a handout on the chair when they come in and the directions for using that handout will be on the overhead. This gets them actively engaged from the moment they enter the classroom and leads to a smoother beginning to class.

Another common teaching situation occurs when students miss an exam or the deadline for an assignment. To try to alleviate problems around this situation, when I hand out a writing assignment, I always specify the due date and how late papers will be handled. My strategy is to deduct 2 points for each day the paper is late. I know of instructors who insist that they will never accept a late paper, but I have difficulty with this policy. I think many introductory psychology students are still learning to be college students and thus there should be consequences for their behavior, but not draconian ones. In my experience, the points-off penalty alone acts as a deterrent to late papers.

Of more urgency are students who miss major exams. On my campus, we give a common exam to most students in our large introductory psychology course, and thus our exams are given at night. Because this creates many conflicts for students, I use a "Request for a Conflict Exam" form Ⓦ co-developed with Doug Bernstein. This form outlines the legitimate reasons for missing an exam according to our campus rules (illness, family emergency, another class at the time, etc.) and asks students to document the reason they will miss the class and to obtain a confirming signature. Last minute problems, such as a sudden illness, are handled using the same guidelines—students are encouraged to let me know about the situation as soon as possible and provide documentation that requires them to be seen by a health care professional. Using this form has reduced the number of students seeking a conflict exam from 200 to about 50 per exam—a much easier number to manage.

Because I grade my short answer and essay questions "blindly," I ask my students to write their names on the back of each short answer or essay sheet and to put each question in a separate stack. This saves me untold time in sorting before I grade.

Because students often have questions about how something was graded or have doubts about whether an exam question was fair, Doug Bernstein and I developed a form for students to fill out to request that an exam item's correct answer be reconsidered. I always go over the exam in class and I invite students to ask questions. But rather than getting bogged down in a long discussion of a particular item, I ask students to fill out a form on which they can present their argument in writing. The form is very simple; students indicate the item to be reviewed, what other answer they think could also be correct, and, most importantly, cite supporting evidence from the textbook. These blank forms are put out with the day's handouts, so students do not have to ask me for one. In this way, students have a way to have an item reviewed and there is less confrontation in class. I read each "Request to Review an Exam Item" Ⓦ carefully and I write comments back to the student. If I decide that a complaint is valid, I announce that everyone whose response deserves it will receive credit. If I reject an appeal I explain my reasoning in writing on the review request form before returning it to the student (Goss Lucas & Bernstein, 2005).

## The First Days of Class

Now that you have established goals for teaching your course, selected your textbook, set up your grading system, and created your syllabus, it is time to prepare for the first few days of class. The way you present yourself, and the way you use your time during those first few classes, will tell your students a lot about what they can expect from you and your course, and about what will be expected of them. In other words, the first few days of class tend to set the tone for the rest of the term (Goss Lucas, 2006).

## Getting ready

Be sure to visit each classroom in which you will be teaching and familiarize yourself with its layout and systems. Pay attention to all the details—is the room normally locked, and if so will you have a key? Where are the switches for the lights and projection screens? How is the temperature controlled? Does everything work properly?

If the room is equipped with teaching technology (e.g., a computer-based teaching station) do you know how to use the technology and whom to contact if it malfunctions? If you are connecting your own laptop computer, be sure there is a connection cable available and that you can connect to the campus computer network.

Make sure that there are enough chairs to accommodate every student and that they are not broken or unusable. Will you need special desks to accommodate students who are in wheelchairs? Consider, too, how well the room's seating accommodation fits your instructional style (Chism & Bickford, 2002). If you plan to create a seating circle, be sure that your classroom's chairs can be arranged in this way. Even if you are only planning to have small-group discussions from time to time, figure out how you will set up chairs during these activities—especially if the seats in your class-room are connected or maybe even attached to the floor.

## Introductions

Plan your first day carefully. It has been suggested that students arrive on the first day of class with four questions in mind: "Will this class meet my needs?" "Is the teacher competent?" "Will the teacher be fair," and "Will the teacher care about me?" (Ericksen, 1974; Scholl-Buckwald, 1985). They may have other questions and concerns, too, but it is vital to begin to address these four, through word and deed, during the first class session. Be sure that you not only go over all of the class rules and policies, but that you also give students a taste of the content of introductory psychology. If you distribute your syllabus and let them go early, this sends the message that you don't consider class time to be particularly valuable, that you do not care much about teaching (or them), that they can expect you to do most of the talking, and that they should sit passively and listen.

Other tips for the first day include:

- Be friendly. Be in your classroom as early as possible. Greet students as they come in. I am in my classroom at least 30 minutes early (if possible). This allows me to "set up" early so that as students enter I can chat with them.
- Be human. When you introduce yourself, say a few words about your background, your academic and scholarly activities, and maybe even your hobbies and other outside interests. Be sure to tell students why you are interested in teaching introductory psychology. Remember that enthusiasm for course material, and for teaching in general, is a characteristic typically associated with instructors who are rated as effective by students and peers (Andersen, 1986; Billson & Tiberius, 1998; Davis, 1993; Eble, 1994; Murray, 1997; Scholl-Buckwald, 1985; Timpson & Bendel-Simso, 1996). I tell my students about my academic background, my areas of interest, and my family.
- Invite contact. Let your students know how you would prefer them to address you—as Professor, Dr., Ms., Sandy, or whatever. If you don't have a preference, tell them that, too, and give them some options. Above all, be sure to remove any doubt or ambiguity about this small but important matter. Some students, especially those beginning their first year of college, will avoid contact with us, even if they need help, simply because they are not sure about the proper form of address. I always write my full name and title on the blackboard, but ask students to call me by my first name.
- Express interest in your students. There are many ways to do this, but I begin with an activity described in more detail in Chapter 3. The activity requires students to meet each other and provides me with a segue into a description of course content. Other "opening day" activities can be found in McGlynn's (2003) *Successful Beginnings for College Teaching*.

## Describing the course

Once introductions are accomplished, I distribute my syllabus. I highlight the main points but I know that it contains a lot of information and most students will not be able to absorb all of it at once. So I encourage my students to use the document as a reference when they have questions about the course and its requirements.

I begin by going over the logistics of how to find me outside of class. I make it clear that I am interested in meeting them. I tell them how to find my office, encourage them to stop by to ask questions or simply to introduce themselves, and point out my office hours, emphasizing that I am happy to arrange additional meeting times by appointment.

I then talk about one or two of my course goals. This strategy offers a natural lead-in to how class time will be spent (Davis, 1993). For example, one of my course goals is that students will learn from each other through the study groups that I establish. I emphasize this goal and put students into groups after the first day of class. (It is very important that the instructor creates the groups, rather than just allowing students to form their own, to assure that each group is as diverse as possible in terms of gender, ethnicity, and year of study, and that no one is left out.) And by establishing these groups early in the term, I hope to create the opportunity for students to form a supportive network of classmates from the beginning.

This is also the time when I discuss the number and types of graded assignments and how final grades will be determined.

I am honest with students about the amount of work that will be required in my class. I assure them that it can all be accomplished, but that effort will be necessary to succeed in the course. Most students rise to the challenge (Timpson & Bendel-Simso, 1996), but those who can't handle the workload, or don't wish to, are better off dropping the course before it is too late.

I bring a copy of each of the required readings and other learning materials and display them, while mentioning where they can be purchased and where they can be found in the library. Since a significant percentage of my students are in their first year, I explicitly tell them that I will not have time in class to lecture about all the important information that is covered in the textbook. Therefore they will be responsible for doing a lot of learning on their own. And even though there is a lot of administrative work to do on the first day of class, as mentioned previously, I cover some course content, as well (Scholl-Buckwald, 1985).

Bringing class to an organized conclusion is important for every session, not just the first one. As the end of class approaches, don't just let time run out. Reserve a few minutes to summarize the main points you have covered and to say a few words about the material you will address the next time (Billson & Tiberius, 1998). You might even consider using the final two minutes to have your students jot down and turn in their reactions to the day's lecture. This little exercise not only shows that you care what your students think, it also provides you with immediate feedback on how the class went (McKeachie, 1986). I ask students to answer two questions anonymously before they leave the first day. "In this class I am most excited about . . . ," and "In this class I am most worried about. . . ." This gives me a good idea of concerns that I may not have addressed and an opportunity to correct any misperceptions immediately.

## Summary

This is a quick look at major teaching decisions. As mentioned before, there are entire books on each of the areas I covered and I have written about these topics in much more detail as well (Goss Lucas & Bernstein, 2005). However, I hope that you get the gist of what decisions you will have to make in order to have a successful teaching experience. The following 10 chapters focus on the traditional content in introductory psychology, providing information and resources to help you teach as effectively as possible. The final chapter will talk about the last day of class, obtaining and using frequent student feedback, reflective evaluation of your teaching, and thinking about possible revisions for next time.

### References and Further Reading

Allen, M. (2000). Teaching non-traditional students. *APS Observer, 13*(7), 16–17.

Andersen, J. (1986). Instructor nonverbal communication: Listening to our silent messages. In J. Civikly (Ed.), *Communicating in college classrooms: New directions for teaching and learning, 26* (pp. 41–89). Boston: Jossey-Bass.

Anderson, J. (1999). Faculty responsibility for promoting conflict-free college classrooms. In S. M. Richardson (Ed.), *Promoting civility: New directions for teaching and learning, 77* (pp. 69–76). San Francisco: Jossey-Bass.

Anderson, R., & Speck, B. (Eds.) (1998). *Changing the way we grade student performance: Classroom assessment and the new learning paradigm: New directions for teaching and learning, 74.* San Francisco: Jossey-Bass.

Billson, J., & Tiberius, R. (1998). Effective social arrangements for teaching and learning. In K. Feldman & M. Paulsen (Eds.), *Teaching and learning in the college classroom* (pp. 561–576). Boston: Pearson Custom Publishing.

Boice, R. (2000). *Advice for new faculty members*. Boston: Allyn and Bacon.

Boyd, D. (2003). Using textbooks effectively: Getting students to read them. *American Psychological Society Observer, 16*(6), 25–26, 32–33.

Brooke, C. (1999). Feelings from the back row: Negotiating sensitive issues in large classes. In S. M. Richardson (Ed.), *Promoting civility: New directions in teaching and learning, 77* (pp. 23–33). San Francisco: Jossey-Bass.

Buskist, W., & Saville, B. (2001). Rapport-building: Creating positive emotional contexts for enhancing teaching and learning. *APS Observer, 14*(3), 12–13, 19.

Chism, N., & Bickford, D. (Eds.) (2002). *The importance of physical space in creating supportive learning environments: New directions for teaching and learning, 92*. San Francisco: Jossey-Bass.

Clegg, V. (1994). Tips for tests and test giving. In K. Pritchard & R. McLaran Sawyer (Eds.), *Handbook of college teaching* (pp. 423–37). Westport, CT: Greenwood Press.

Davis, B. G. (1993). *Tools for teaching*. San Francisco: Jossey-Bass.

Desrochers, C. (2000). Establishing expectations for our students. *The National Teaching and Learning Forum, 10*(1), 4–6.

Dinham, S. (1996). What college teachers need to know. In R. Menges & M. Weimer (Eds.), *Teaching on solid ground* (pp. 297–313). San Francisco: Jossey-Bass.

D'Ydewalle, G., Swerts, A., & DeCorte, E. (1983). Study time and test performance as a function of test expectations. *Contemporary Educational Psychology, 8*, 55–67.

Ebel, R. (1965). *Measuring educational achievement*. Englewood Cliffs, NJ: Prentice-Hall.

Eble, K. (1994). *The craft of teaching* (2nd ed.). San Francisco: Jossey-Bass.

Eggleston, T., & Smith, G. (2002). Parting ways: Ending your course. *APS Observer, 15*(3), 15–16, 29–30.

Ericksen, S. (1974). *Motivation for learning*. Ann Arbor, MI: University of Michigan Press.

Erickson, B., & Strommer, D. (1991). *Teaching college freshmen*. San Francisco: Jossey-Bass.

Forsyth, D. (2003). *The professors guide to teaching psychological principles and practices*. Washington, DC: American Psychological Association.

Goss, S. (1995). Dealing with problem students in the classroom. *APS Observer, 8*(6), 26, 27, 29.

Goss Lucas, S. (2002). Returning graded assignments is part of the learning experience. *APS Observer, 9*(15), 19–20, 46–47.

Goss Lucas, S. (2006) The first day of class and the rest of the semester. In W. Buskist & S. F. Davis (Eds.), *The handbook of the teaching of psychology* (pp. 41–46). Malden, MA: Blackwell.

Goss Lucas, S., & Bernstein, D. (2005). *Teaching psychology: A step by step by step guide*. Mahwah, NJ: Erlbaum.

Gronlund, N., & Linn, R. (1990). *Measurement and evaluation in teaching* (6th ed.). New York: Macmillan Publishing Company.

Hendersen, R. (2002). *Introductory psychology forum: Case studies for increasing student engagement.* Presentation to 2nd annual Summer National Institute on the Teaching of Psychology, June 24, 2002, St. Petersburg Beach, FL.

Hendersen, R. (2005). *Introductory psychology forum: Throwing the book at them: Various ways to use the textbook in introductory psychology.* Presentation to 27th annual National Institute on the Teaching of Psychology, January 2, 2005, St. Petersburg Beach, FL.

Heuberger, B., Gerber, D., & Anderson, R. (1999). Strength through cultural diversity: Developing and teaching a diversity course. *College Teaching, 47*(3), 107–113.

Jacobs, L., & Chase, C. (1992). *Developing and using tests effectively*. San Francisco: Jossey-Bass.

Kennedy, D. (1997). *Academic duty*. Cambridge, MA: Harvard University Press.

Leamnson, R. (1999). *Thinking about teaching and learning: Developing habits of learning with first year college and university students*. Sterling, VA: Stylus.

Linn, R., & Gronlund, N. (2000). *Measurement and assessment in teaching* (8th ed.). Upper Saddle River, NJ: Merrill.

Maier, M., & Panitz, T. (1996). End on a high note: Better endings for classes and courses. *College Teaching, 44*, 145–148.

Marin, P. (2000). The educational possibility of multi-racial/multi-ethnic college classrooms. In *Does diversity make a difference? Three research studies on diversity in college classrooms* (pp. 61–83). Washington, DC: American Council on Education and American Association of University Professors.

McGlynn, A. (2003). *Successful beginnings for college teaching: Engaging your students from the first day*. Madison, WI: Atwood Publishing.

McKeachie, W. (1986). Teaching psychology: Research and experience. In V. Makosky (Ed.), *The G. Stanley Hall Lecture Series*, 6 (pp. 165–191). Washington, DC: American Psychological Association.

McKeachie, W. (2002). *Teaching tips: Strategies, research, and theory for college and university teachers* (11th ed.). Boston: Houghton Mifflin.

McKeachie, W., & Svinicki, M. (2006). *Teaching tips: Strategies, research, and theory for college and university teachers* (12th ed.). Boston: Houghton Mifflin.

Murray, H. (1997). Effective teaching behaviors in the college classroom. In R. Perry & J. Smart (Eds.), *Effective teaching in higher education* (pp. 241–367). New York: Agathon Press.

Ory, J. (2003). The final exam. *American Psychological Society Observer*, *16*(10), 23–24, 34–35.

Ory, J., & Ryan, K. (1993). *Tips for improving testing and grading*. Newbury Park, CA: Sage Publications.

Parkes, J., & Harris, M. (2002). The purposes of a syllabus. *College Teaching*, *5*, 55–61.

Sanders, J., & Wiseman, R. (1994). The effects of verbal and nonverbal teacher immediacy on perceived cognitive, affective, and behavioral learning in the multicultural classroom. In K. Feldman & M. Paulsen (Eds.), *Teaching and learning in the college classroom* (pp. 623–636). Boston: Pearson Custom Publishing.

Scholl-Buckwald, S. (1985). The first meeting of the class. In J. Katz (Ed.), *Teaching as though students mattered: New directions for teaching and learning*, *26* (pp. 13–21). San Francisco: Jossey-Bass.

Sleigh, M., & Ritzer, D. (2001). Encouraging student attendance. *APS Observer*, *14*(9), 19–20, 32–33.

Sleigh, M., Ritzer, D., & Casey, M. (2002). Student versus faculty perceptions of missing class. *Teaching of Psychology*, *29*(1), 53–56.

Suskie, L. (2000). Fair assessment practices: Giving students equitable opportunities to demonstrate learning. Retrieved September 25, 2007 from http://faculty.swosu.edu/cindy.carley/share/Blackboard%20Workshops/a_Bbd%206%20Workshops%20Fall%202004/Module%204%20Assessments%20Surveys%20Gradebook/Fair%20Assessment%20Practices.doc

Timpson, W., & Bendel-Simso, P. (1996). *Concepts and choices for teaching: Meeting the challenges in higher education*. Madison, WI: Magna.

Wolfle, D. (1942). The first course in psychology. *Psychological Bulletin*, *39*(9), 685–713.

Zakrajsek, T. (2004). Teaching a course you feel unprepared to teach. *APS Observer*, *17*(11), Retrieved 18 September, 2007 from http://www.psychologicalscience.org/observer/getArticle.cfm?id=1680

# Chapter 3

# Introduction, Research Methods, Culture

## Getting Started

As previously noted, the first few days of class are extremely important in setting the tone for the rest of the semester. Before beginning
a new term, I think about my goals for this particular class and how
I can communicate these goals through content choices and activities
for the first few classes.

My goals for this introductory unit are general and, hopefully,
transferable. I want my students to understand that psychology is
more than Freud and mental disorders. I want them to learn that
there are many subfields in psychology that go beyond what they see
in the popular press. For example, I want them to appreciate the
relevance of biological processes in psychology.

I also explore with students the notion that psychology has changed
in accordance with advances in scientific knowledge. The historical
"schools of psychology" used the research methods available to them
in their time. And that laid the foundation for "modern" psychology. For example, when psychologists used introspection to study
"cognition," the tools used today (PET, MRIs and other protocols)
were not available. But the introspection studies helped lay the
groundwork for cognitive psychology.

Understanding research methodology will help students become
intelligent consumers of information for the rest of their lives. Critical

thinking can be encouraged by having students use a standard set of questions in considering whether claims have validity. This gives them the tools to think critically across a variety of psychological, and nonpsychological, situations.

I also discuss the ethics of conducting research, especially important since my students will be participants in psychological research themselves. I tell them about IRBs (institutional review boards) that rigorously scrutinize research proposals. And I reassure them that another "Milgram-like" experiment is extremely unlikely.

Students also need to appreciate how cultural issues affect research. We are all products of our culture and that culture influences not only what we study, but how we study it. Much psychological research comes from a Western, empirical view and has historically excluded women and people of color. Thus I introduce students to the importance of cross-cultural psychological research.

Finally, I want my students to understand the approaches to psychology which become a common thread throughout the semester, integrating very diverse topics.

## My outline for teaching (3 days—75 minute classes)

*Day 1* (First day of class—students fill out and put on name tags as they enter class.)

I. Administrivia (10 minutes)

Welcome to Psychology 100 (pertinent details)

Show clip from *Ferris Bueller's Day Off* (classroom scene at beginning): "If you promise to not be like those students, I promise to not be like that teacher!"

II. Introductions (20 minutes)

Introduce myself: Include how students can most easily contact me outside of class

Interactive first-day exercise

- Explain Psych 100 relevance to exercise.
- Students introduce themselves

III. Syllabus, class information, grading policies, class rules, administrative details (20 minutes)

Pass out cards asking students for phone numbers, email address, and where they live on campus (for emergency reference and to assign study groups)

IV. Questions and concerns from students (5 minutes)

V. What do psychologists do? (15 minutes)

What is psychology?

History of psychology
Subfields
Approaches to psychology
VI. One minute reaction paper—no names (5 minutes)
In this class, I am most worried about . . .
In this class, I am most excited about . . .
VII. Assignments for next class (listed on board)

*Day 2* (Students fill out and put on name tags as they enter class.)
Directions on board: Pick up a handout and complete the 20 "I am" statements as quickly as possible. (Mini-assignment #2)
Questions from previous class (5 minutes)
Practice questions over material (10 minutes)
I. Administrivia (10 minutes)
Call roll/learn names (tell students to finish "I am" statements as I do this)
Make sure everyone is getting the class email
Pass out study group assignments
Results "Most worried/Most excited"
Questions over readings in the text
Summer reading: Triandis (1994)
II. Finish "what do psychologists do?" (10 minutes)
III. History of psychology in a nutshell (Handout) (15 minutes)
Go over briefly:
• Debt owed to philosophy
• American vs. European Schools
• Evolution of psychology
• Structuralist study of the building blocks of consciousness led to an emphasis on cognitive psychology
IV. Culture (20 minutes)
General introduction to culture
Discussion of "I am" assignment

*Day 3* (Students fill out and put on name tags as they enter class.)
Questions from previous class (5 minutes)
Practice questions over material (10 minutes)
I. Statistics (20 minutes)
Statistics classroom learning activity
Correlation: stimulus questions
II. Research terms (15 minutes)

III. Research methods (25 minutes)
Research ethics
Mini-assignment #1

## My transitions

I spend a lot of class time getting to know my students and letting them get to know me and their classmates. As a result, the students feel freer to participate in class and in their study groups. I begin the course with a discussion of what psychology is, what psychologists do, and the evolution of the discipline of psychology, and then move to research methods. I incorporate statistics, research methods, and ethics. I spend a lot of time on experiments and experimental terminology. Once we have covered the basics, I move on to development, a chapter that most students enjoy and understand.

## Topics typically included in this unit

*What is psychology?* History (schools), subfields, approaches
*Culture and diversity*
*Introduction to critical thinking*
*Research methods*: Naturalistic observation, case study, surveys, correlational studies, experiments, research pitfalls (e.g., choosing subjects, research ethics)
*Statistical analyses*: Descriptive and inferential statistics

## Some options for organizing the concepts

*By timeline*: History, subfields and approaches, research methods and statistical analyses, critical thinking (culture is woven into the content—for example, explaining why psychology developed in Germany, why the approaches developed when they did, the marginalization of women and minorities as psychological researchers, etc.).
*By topic*: Psychology is . . . (history, subfields, approaches), culture, research methods and statistical analyses, critical thinking.
*By research methods*: The entire course could be centered around research methodology—which methodology fits the topic of study, an analysis of the studies conducted on that particular topic. This would be an interesting course theme for an honors section, for example.

# Teaching the Content

Remember that the ⓦ symbol means that a printable version is available on the web site (www.blackwellpublishing.com/lucas) and the ⓤ means that the URL is available on the web site.

## Topics that many students will find difficult

### Controlled experiments
Students often have a difficult time being able to distinguish an experiment from other research methods—understanding the concept of operational definitions and distinguishing the dependent and independent variables in an experiment. Useful resources include:

*Halonen and Gray* (2001). Chapter 1 (pp. 6–19) has several exercises that help students understand operational definitions and how to set up a controlled experiment.
*Research methods in psychology* (2001). This 30-minute video explores research methodology by evaluating the "link" between violence and playing video games. (Insight Media ⓤ)
*A scientific approach* (2003). This 30-minute video presents research methodology, but evaluates attachment research—a good segue into the development chapter. (Insight Media ⓤ)

Flaws in a controlled experiment include sampling errors, experimenter bias, confounding variables—leading to the introduction of the double blind experiment. Useful resources include *How to Conduct an Experiment* (2000). This 20-minute video talks about dependent and independent variables, random variables, and avoiding bias. (Insight Media ⓤ)

### Correlation
In my class, we almost chant, "Correlation does *not* equal causation!" Students often have a difficult time understanding the idea of correlation *and* understanding that the absolute value (+ and − being irrelevant here) determines the strength of the correlation.

### Statistics
The statistical experience introductory students bring to class will vary widely. While some students will have minimal backgrounds, others may have taken an AP Statistics course. Decide what statistical information you think is important for students to be able to

understand and what statistics they should be able to compute. For example, I think students should be able to compute a mean, median, and mode—but be able to understand standard deviation, t-test, and ANOVA. (I put my expectations in Handout #2 ☢.) Useful resources include Huff (1954). This book has stood the test of time and is still available—it has interesting information that you can incorporate into class.

## Other important topics

### Critical thinking

There are many ways to approach this topic and, obviously, it needs to be interwoven throughout the course. I like to use the five questions posed in the Bernstein introductory psychology textbook:

1. What am I being asked to believe or accept?
2. What evidence is available to support the assertion?
3. Are there alternative ways of interpreting the evidence?
4. What additional evidence would help to evaluate the alternatives?
5. What conclusions are most reasonable? (Bernstein, Penner, Clarke-Stewart, and Roy, 2006, pp. 30–31)

Useful resources include Halonen & Gray (2001), Halpern (2003).

### History of psychology

A brief overview of psychology's evolution from philosophy to an empirical science puts psychology's development into a historical context. I start with Wilhelm Wundt's first psychology lab in 1879 and the Structuralist school; then Functionalism (the first American "school"), with a focus on behavior rather than consciousness; then Behaviorism and John B. Watson's influence. I then proceed to Gestalt—a European school with an emphasis back on consciousness/ perception; to Psychodynamic—Freud and the role of the uncon- scious; and finally, I end with more modern views: cognitive psychology—with an emphasis back on consciousness; and humanistic/ phenomenological approaches—views emphasizing the uniqueness and goodness of people. (See Handout #1 ☢.) Useful resources include:

Benjamin (1997). This is a rich resource containing many of the seminal works in psychology.
Benjafield (2005).

## Research methods (other than controlled experiments)

A great way to incorporate research methods and critical thinking is to do a demonstration "showing" that you have psychic ability (obviously there is a trick to this). After doing a "psychic" demonstration, explain that it was only a magic trick and that their assignment for the next session is to try to figure out how the trick could have been performed without psychic power. As students try to explain, you can introduce research terminology—for example, "hypothesis" and "variable." For detailed instructions see Goss and Bernstein (1999).

*Naturalistic observation.* To demonstrate the difficulties of naturalistic observation, pick two students, take them in the hallway and tell them that you want them to record the number of "fidgets" in the classroom for one minute. Don't explain anything, but then ask for their data—it is often very discrepant. This can lead to a discussion of the operational definition of "fidget" and the difficulty in counting such behavior. For full details see Beins (1999).

Examples of how observation can change behaviors include teachers being observed by their supervisors and "real world"/reality shows.

*Surveys.* Advantages include getting a large number of responses quickly. Disadvantages include: phrasing the questions correctly, respondents providing socially desirable (rather than true) responses, the low percentage of returned questionnaires.

*Case studies.* Useful in the study of rare phenomenon—such as Phineas Gage (see The Phineas Gage information page ⓤ) but also problematic, using one in-depth study to make generalizations.

> Case studies therefore illuminate, but can also obscure, the truth. In many cases, they are inherently limited by what their reporter sees, and what their reporter leaves out. This is especially true if the writer is untrained in the scientific method, and thus unaware of the confirmation bias, the importance of considering competing explanations before making a diagnosis, and so forth. To the scientist, therefore, most case studies are useful largely to generate hypotheses to be tested, not as answers to questions. When they are offered as answers, readers should be wary. (Loftus & Guyer, 2002 ⓤ, p. 2)

## Subfields

It is important that students understand the diversity of the field of psychology. Use stimulus questions about what psychologist "do" to broaden student perspectives on this topic.

## Culture

Students have difficulty seeing the influence of culture on their behavior, and in understanding culture as a critical "lens" through which they see the world. I emphasize that culture permeates not only the food we eat, our clothing, how we work, the structure of our families, our government, and religion, but also our science and technology. A useful resource is Chapter 1 of Triandis (1994).

## Approaches to psychology

The various approaches (biological, evolutionary, psychodynamic, behavioral, cognitive, and humanistic) will be a theme through the entire book, so it is crucial that students understand the tenets of each approach (see ⓦ Mini-assignment #5).

# Classroom Tips

## Stimulus questions for discussion

### Subfields

What do psychologists do? They get up in the morning, they interact with their family, they get in their car (or on a train or a bus) and they go to. . . . ? Once they are at work they. . . . ?

### Culture

Respond to this quote:

> Culture imposes a set of lenses for seeing the world . . . We see the world less "as it is" and more "as we are" . . . Depending on the experiences *we* have had, the habits that *we* have acquired, we see events differently. (Triandis, 1994, p. 13)

### Correlation

A survey found that people who often ate Frosted Flakes as children had half the cancer rate of those who never ate the cereal. Conversely, those who often ate oatmeal as children were four times more likely to develop cancer than those who did not. Does eating Frosted Flakes protect you from cancer? (The intervening variable is age—older people are more likely to have cancer, Frosted Flakes weren't around when they were children, so younger people ate Frosted Flakes and older people ate oatmeal.)

A random survey of 2,000 people age 65 and older found that those who did not engage in religious activities had higher average blood pressure readings than those who attended religious services. Does having religious beliefs lower one's blood pressure? (Social support is the intervening variable—the survey found that those who engage in religious services via the radio and/or television had *higher* blood pressure than those who did not.)

## Some suggested classroom learning activities

### First day interactive exercise
(I give students 10 minutes to complete this and then take 5–10 minutes for discussion.) On the first day of class I give each student a paper with 10 statements related to introductory psychology concepts. Their instructions are, "Find someone in this class who meets the following criteria. Only one person per statement." This ensures that each student must talk to at least 10 other students in the class to get all of the statements signed. I then relate the statements to material we will learn in the course.

Here are my 10 statements.

Ⓦ 1.　After eating a turkey dinner, I've felt mellow. (Biological psychology: tryptophan and serotonin—neurotransmitters)
   2.　I slept 8 hours last night. (Consciousness: importance of sleep and effects of sleep deprivation)
   3.　I've seen the movie *Fight Club*. (Mental disorders: dissociate identity disorder)
   4.　I am colorblind or I know someone who is. (Sensation: theories of color)
   5.　A food that I used to like now makes me sick. The food is. . . . (Learning: taste aversion)
   6.　If given a choice in completing an assignment, I prefer to work in groups than by myself. (Introduction: culture and cognition: Problem solving)
   7.　I have read *To Kill a Mockingbird*. (Social psychology: stereotypes and prejudice)
   8.　I have participated in a competitive sport. (Social psychology: social facilitation and social inhibition)
   9.　I have memorized all 50 states. (Memory: mnemonics, encoding)
  10.　I like to bungee jump and/or ride fast roller coasters." (Motivation: arousal theory).

### Introduction to psychology misperceptions quiz
(I give students 7–10 minutes to complete the true–false quiz and then spend 10 minutes going over it.) This is an alternate first-day

exercise which addresses a prevalent belief that "psychology is just common sense." There are many resources for such quizzes (textbook instructor resource manuals, psychology teachers' listserves). I put this quiz together although some questions appear on almost all misperception quizzes I've seen. After students complete the quiz, go over the answers and tell them how the material will relate to your course (as noted in parentheses following each question below).

ⓦ 1. Schizophrenia is split personality. (False)
  2. If you need help, you are more likely to get it if there is only one other person around rather than a crowd. (True: Bystander effect)
  3. Eating turkey will make you more "mellow." (True: Tryptophan and serotonin)
  4. Smile! It will make you happy. (True: Facial feedback hypothesis)
  5. Hearing aids are effective for all types of hearing loss. (False: Not for nerve deafness)
  6. You can learn something without being aware that you learned it. (True: Latent learning)
  7. The facial expression of emotions is the same in all cultures. (False: For basic emotions yes, but not for all)
  8. You only need 5–6 hours of sleep a night to function effectively. (False)
  9. If a teacher believes that particular students will do better in class, they usually do perform better. (True: Rosenthal experiment)
  10. Most people eat because they receive hunger signals from their stomach. (False: Most eating is controlled by signals sent to the brain from the blood)
  11. Children will have a higher need to achieve if their parents punish failure. (False: Parents of children with high need for achievement encourage their children to try new things even if they result in failure)
  12. In normal development, babies will lose reflexes as they mature. (True)
  13. Your attachment to your mother as an infant is predictive of your later romantic relationships. (True)
  14. Some people are "supertasters" and have more "taste buds" on their tongue. (True: Linda Bartochuk's research shows about 25% of the population have many more papillae on their tongues and thus a more acute sense of taste)

15.   When people are color-blind, they can only see shades of brown. (False: Most color-blind people have only one type of cone affected and can see more than one color)

## Critical thinking

(I spend 2 minutes explaining the exercise; give them 2 minutes to get into groups; and 10 minutes to complete. We spend another 10 minutes if groups present to the class.) Choose several print advertisements that make a claim—for example, "makes you look younger," "cats can't resist it," "is the best tasting." Divide the class into groups, give each group a different advertisement, have them analyze the claims that are made and develop an experiment that would validate the claims. Have each group present their analysis to the class. (See ⓦ Mini-assignment #3 for a handout with student guidelines.)

## Culture

(I typically have students complete this as they come into class, so it takes minimal time.) Distribute Mini-assignment #2. Ask students to mark with an S each answer that implies a social response: for example, I am a Catholic (religious group); I am a daughter (family). Triandis (1994) suggests an S response means the student "share[s] a common fate with others who are members of a social unit" (p. 145). Ask students to mark with an I responses that talk about individual attributes (e.g., I am honest, I work hard). Students then add up their S responses and their I responses. In the US, most students will have many fewer S responses than I responses. I use this exercise as a lead-in to a discussion of individualist and collectivist cultures.

*Source for activity: Triandis (1994, pp. 144–5).*

## Statistics

(I spend 2 minutes explaining the exercise; give them 2 minutes to get into groups, and 10 minutes to complete. We spend another 5 minutes discussing their decisions as a class.) Standard deviation is a difficult concept for students to understand, thus in class I give each group the following assignment:

ⓦ You have just graduated from college and have been offered a job with two different small companies. The working conditions and benefits seem to be comparable. However, the president of each company has said only vaguely that your salary "would be comparable to others in the company." In order to give you some basis for comparison, both companies have provided you with the descriptive statistics for salaries throughout the company. Analyze the two salary packages and explain how the numbers could have been derived. Which job would you choose and why?

|        | Company A salaries | Company B salaries |
|--------|--------------------|--------------------|
| N      | 10                 | 10                 |
| Mean   | $33,500            | $28,000            |
| Median | $20,000            | $22,500            |
| Mode   | $20,000            | $20,000            |
| s.d.   | $29,064            | $12,293            |
| Range  | $80,000            | $35,000            |

The statistics I used: Company A salaries: $20,000 (8), $75,000, $100,000. Company B salaries: $15,000 (2), $20,000 (3), $25,000, $35,000, $40,000 (2), $50,000. The "why," demonstrating their understanding of standard deviation is most important. Most choose Company B because there is more chance for salary increases, some choose Company A because of the better starting salary and they think they can be the one earning the $100,000!

## Possible mini-assignments (written or groups)

### ⓦ Mini-assignment #1
You believe that students who are lectured to in class retain more information than students who engage in class discussion. Devise an experiment to test your belief. Be sure to include:

- Your hypothesis
- An operational definition of your variables
- An explanation of how you would set up your experiment. Your explanation should contain the terms (in appropriate context) "experimental group," "control group," "dependent variable," and "independent variable."

Note: this whole assignment can be accomplished in one or two paragraphs.

### ⓦ Mini-assignment #2
(This could be an in-class activity as well.) In the spaces on your paper please complete the 20 sentences. This will *not* be collected so answer the question: "Who am I?" as if giving the answers to yourself,

not to someone else. Write your answers in the order in which they occur to you. Do not worry about importance or logic. Go fairly fast.
I am. . . . (20 times)

ⓦ *Mini-assignment #3*
(Thanks to Sylvia Puente for this assignment on applying critical thinking to advertising claims.)
What are you being asked to believe in the advertisement claims? Design an experiment to test this claim:

- What is your hypothesis?
- What is the independent variable (IV)? How is it operationally defined?
- What is your experimental group?
- What is/are your control group(s)?
- What confounding variables might be problematic in your experiment? What will you do to control for these potential confounding variables?

ⓦ *Mini-assignment #4*
You have decided that you are going to study to become a psychologist. Write a letter to a friend describing what type of psychologist you want to be (e.g., educational, quantitative) and what other fields of psychology you have considered but rejected. Make sure your letter gives your friend an idea of the diversity of psychology.

ⓦ *Mini-assignment #5*
(This would be an ideal group assignment with each group assigned a particular approach.)
Mrs. Jenks, a 4th grade classroom teacher, has asked for an evaluation of Jonathon, a student who acts out in class by hitting other children. As the psychologist in charge of this evaluation, explain the possible causes of Jonathon's aggression and how you would help Jonathon become less aggressive. Take either a biological, evolutionary, psychodynamic, behavioral, cognitive, or humanistic approach.

## Handouts

ⓦ Handout #1 Schools of Psychology
ⓦ Handout #2 A Handy Statistical Reference

# References

Beins, B. (1999). Counting fidgets: Teaching the complexity of naturalistic observation. In L. Benjamin, B. Nodine, R. Ernst, & C. Blair Broeker (Eds.), *Activities handbook for the teaching of psychology, Vol. 4* (pp. 53–55). Washington, DC: American Psychological Association.

Benjafield, J. (2005). *A history of psychology* (2nd ed.). Oxford: Oxford University Press.

Benjamin, L. (1997). *A history of psychology: Original sources and contemporary research* (2nd ed.). New York: McGraw-Hill.

Bernstein, D., Penner, L., Clarke-Stewart, A., & Roy, E. (2006). *Psychology* (7th ed.). Boston: Houghton Mifflin.

Goss, S., & Bernstein, D. (1999). Research methods and critical thinking: Explaining "psychic" phenomena. In L. Benjamin, B. Nodine, R. Ernst, & C. Blair Broeker (Eds.), *Activities handbook for the teaching of psychology, Vol. 4* (pp. 25–27). Washington, DC: American Psychological Association.

Halonen, J., & Gray, C. (2001). *The critical thinking companion for introductory psychology*. New York: Worth.

Halpern, D. (2003). *Thought and knowledge: An introduction to critical thinking* (4th ed.). Mahwah, NJ: Lawrence Erlbaum.

Huff, D. (1954). *How to lie with statistics*. New York: Norton.

Loftus, E., & Guyer, M. (2002). Who abused Jane Doe? The hazards of the single case history: Part I. *Skeptical Inquirer, 26*(3), 24–32.

Triandis, H. (1994). *Culture and social behavior*. New York: McGraw-Hill.

## Additional Suggested Readings for Instructors

Hock, R. (2004). *Forty studies that changed psychology: Explorations into the history of psychological research* (5th ed.). Boston: Prentice Hall.

Pettijohn, T. (2000). *Notable selections in psychology* (3rd ed.). Guilford, CT: Dushkin/McGraw-Hill. (Contains classic papers in psychology.)

Schwartz, S. (1986). *Classic studies in psychology*. Palo Alto, CA: Mayfield/McGraw-Hill. (Contains 15 of the most important studies in psychology.)

Slife, B. (2006). *Taking sides: Clashing views in psychological issues* (14th ed.). Dubuque, IA: Contemporary Learning Series, McGraw-Hill. (A new book is published annually, dealing with current issues in psychology. You can view student and instructor resources related to this book at www.mhcls.com.)

Stanovich, K. (2004). *How to think straight about psychology* (7th ed.). New York: Longman/Allyn & Bacon.

# Chapter 4

# Human Development

## Getting Started

Deciding what content I will exclude from this unit is my biggest issue. If I do not adhere closely to my learning goals, I spend an inordinate amount of time teaching this content, both because this is an area of interest to me, and because many students find this material inherently interesting. My goals for this unit are broad. I attempt to provide an overview of what being human entails, from a cognitive, social, and emotional perspective. I filter the information that I present through the lens of parenthood. Since most of my students will become parents, I present research showing that babies are "a lot smarter than they look." I stress that the fastest rate of development in a human being occurs prenatally. I talk about teratogens, attachment, temperament, and parenting styles. I stress that "mothering" is not instinctive, but learned.

I present Kohlberg's stages of moral development to help them understand the "process" that they use in making such decisions. And I try to touch briefly on adult development, especially recent research showing that impaired cognition due to aging can be mitigated by staying mentally active.

My outline for teaching (2½ days—75 minute classes)

*Day 1*
Questions from previous class (5 minutes)
Practice questions over material (5 minutes)
Administrivia (5 minutes)
  I.   Overview of genetics (10 minutes)
       What is behavioral genetics?
       Phenotype/genotype
  II.  Prenatal lecture (30 minutes)
       Physiological stages
       Critical period/common teratogens
  III. Physical development (20 minutes)
       Childhood
       Adolescence

*Day 2*
Questions from previous class (5 minutes)
Practice questions over material (5 minutes)
Administrivia (5 minutes)
  I.  Cognitive development (30 minutes)
      Piaget—stages of development and his research methods
      Baillargeon–babies' thinking is more advanced than Piaget
        thought
      Vygotsky—impact of culture on children's cognitive development
  II. Emotional and social development (30 minutes)
      Attachment
      Temperament
      Parenting
      Gender roles

*Day 3 (half day development, half day biology)*
Questions from previous class (5 minutes)
Practice questions over material (5 minutes)
Administrivia (5 minutes)
  I.  Beyond adolescence (20 minutes)
      Adult physical development
      Adult cognitive development
      Adult social/emotional development: wisdom
  II. Death and dying (10 minutes)
      Cognitive abilities: terminal drop

*Biology*
I.   Development and biology (10 minutes)
     Reflexes and why they disappear as we develop in infancy and childhood
     Neural connections—few at birth, an overabundance at age 6, a "smart" pruning by adolescence
     Why early exposure to music, language, and math has an impact on children's brain development (See *Newsweek*'s "Your Child's Brain" ⓤ)
II.  Why biological psychology? (5 minutes)
     Important for mental disorders, therapy, development, memory, and so forth.
III. Nature/nurture and the brain (10 minutes)
     The brain is *not* just a product of nature—it is *not* totally prewired. It can be influenced by the environment.
     William Calvin's hypothesis of "The Throwing Madonna" (see stimulus question Chapter 5, p. 82).
     Discussion of Harold Klawans's *Why Michael Couldn't Hit* (see Chapter 5).

## My transitions

I cover Development as the second unit of content, immediately after the introductory, research methods, and culture unit. I tell students that we will talk about the developing person—from zygote to senior citizen. I use developmental material to segue into the next unit, Biological Psychology. I tie developmental and biological principles together through a discussion of reflexes, brain development, and the nature/nurture dilemma.

## Topics typically included in this unit

*Physical development*: Prenatal, the newborn, changes in the brain (tie with biological psychology chapter, e.g., dendritic density at various stages of development, reflexes that drop out as babies mature), puberty, adult aging, death and dying

*Cognitive Development*: Piaget and modifications, information processing

*Social and emotional development*: Temperament, attachment, impact of parenting styles, social skills, gender roles, Erikson's stages, Kohlberg's moral development and critiques

*Heredity and environmental contributions*: Behavioral genetics, geno-type and phenotype, the nature/nurture theme.

## Some options for organizing the concepts

*By theme*: Physical growth, cognitive growth, emotional/moral growth, social growth

*Chronologically*: Prenatal, infancy, childhood, adolescence, early adulthood, middle adulthood, late adulthood

*By heredity and environmental influences*: Physical growth, cognitive growth, emotional growth—the impact of hereditary or genetic influences and the contributions of environmental forces. This could set the stage for discussions in future units—such as personality, intelligence, mental disorders.

# Teaching the Content

Remember that the Ⓦ symbol means that a printable version is available on the web site (www.blackwellpublishing.com/lucas) and the Ⓤ means that the URL is available on the web site.

## Topics that many students will find difficult

### Behavioral genetics

This topic is often very difficult for beginning students. However, having a basic understanding of behavioral genetics, genotype and phenotype, and the nature/nurture discussion is important. Useful resources:

Ⓤ The Human Genome Project Information webpage is a great place to read about basic behavioral genetics.

The official web site of the Ⓤ Nobel Foundation provides information about our genetic code.

Professor John Blamire's web site, Ⓤ Science at a Distance, provides more information about genotype and phenotype.

### Piaget

Many students have a difficult time understanding children's lack of cognitive strategies. It is helpful to show film clips of children at various cognitive stages, as well as asking students to identify the appropriate stage based on examples of cognitive behavior. Useful resources:

The Learning and Teaching web site ⓤ, aimed at providing information for college teachers, has a discussion of Piaget's theory with more references provided.

*Infant and Child Development* (2001) is a film overview of Piaget's theories and other theories of development (Insight Media ⓤ).

Baillargeon (2004) provides an update of Piaget.

A view of cognitive development as influenced by the child's culture, based on the work of Lev Vygotsky, can be found at the Psi Chi ⓤ web site.

## Kohlberg

Lawrence Kohlberg developed his stage theory based on the *reason* for making a moral decision, *not* on the decision itself. Many students will have difficulty with this, so, if possible, present a moral dilemma where the same decision can be classified in all stages (see Miniassignment #4 ⓦ). Useful resources:

Information about Kohlberg's life and theories, as well as a critique of his theories can be found at The Psi Chi ⓤ web site.

*Morality: The process of moral development.* A film on moral development incorporating the theories of Kohlberg and Piaget (Davidson Films ⓤ)

See also Gilligan (1993), which critiques Kohlberg's research from a gender and cultural perspective.

## Other important topics and resources

### Prenatal development

Many of our students will become parents, thus prenatal information is very relevant. I focus on the basic developmental stages—germinal, embryonic, fetal—emphasizing the critical period and teratogens such as smoking, alcohol con-sumption, communicable diseases, nutrition, and illegal drugs. Useful resources:

Images of the developing fetus may be accessed at the National Geographic ⓤ web site.

For a nice graphic of monthly prenatal physical development, see the Dushkin Publishers ⓤ web site.

The March of Dimes Professionals ⓤ web site has updated information about common teratogens. (As I write this, ACE inhibitors used in many blood pressure medications have just been shown to increase the percentage of birth defects.)

## Erikson

Students are fascinated with Erik Erikson's stages of development and usually have no difficulty relating to his crises in social development.

*Everybody Rides the Carousel* is a classic film series describing Erikson's theory of life-span personality development (Pyramid Media ⓤ).

## Temperament

Alexander Thomas and Stella Chess's research distinguishes between difficult, easy, and slow-to-warm-up babies. Their book (Thomas and Chess, 1977) discusses the dimension used to make these distinctions.

## Parenting styles

Diane Baumrind's classic study (Baumrind, 1971) divides parents into four categories (Permissive, Authoritarian, Authoritative, Neglectful) based on the dimensions of warmth and control.

## Attachment

Misperceptions abound about attachment styles and infant bonding. Many students will know something about the classic Harlow study (Harlow, 1959). The take-home message is that "mothering" or "parenting" is a set of learned skills, not genetically determined.

John Bowlby is perhaps the "father" of attachment theory. He advocated the scientific study of children's relationships with their mothers. He used René Spitz's research (Spitz, 1945) on children separated from mothers in penal institutions, and research into mother–child separation during World War II and began a systematic observation of mother–child relationships and interactions. He published a 3-part series titled *Attachment and Loss* (Bowlby, 1982) in which he investigated Attachment (Vol. I), Separation: Anxiety and Anger (Vol. II), Loss, Sadness and Depression (Vol. III).

The Strange Situation assesses attachment styles in the majority culture in the US.

> An infant who has experienced his mother as fairly consistently accessible to him and as responsive to his signals and communication may well expect her to continue to be an accessible and responsive person, despite the fact that she has departed.... On the other hand, an infant whose experience in interaction with his mother has not given him reason to expect her to be accessible to him when out of sight or

responsive to his signals is more likely to experience anxiety even in little everyday separations. . . . such an infant may be identified as anxiously attached to his mother. (Ainsworth, Blehar, Waters, & Wall, 1978, p. 21)

According to Ainsworth and her colleagues:

- Securely attached babies tend to be more cooperative; comply with the mother; are more positive and outgoing to strangers; are more competent, enthusiastic, and less frustrated (Ainsworth et al., 1978, p. 313). They may or may not be upset when the mother leaves, but they are always happy to see her return and actively seek her out (Ainsworth et al., 1978, p. 60).
- Ambivalent attachment comes when the mother is less responsive to the baby's signals and communication. Therefore the infant has more anxiety that the mother will not return. The infant responds to the mother's departure with immediate and intense distress. However, because the mother's "timing" with the infant is not good, the infant may protest when picked up, or protest to be put down when the mother returns, or as Ainsworth puts it "mingle angry resistance with clinging" (Ainsworth et al., 1978, p. 314).
- Avoidant attachment occurs when the baby is comforted by the stranger, and avoids the mother when she returns and displays "detachment behavior." This is the result of the mother being rejecting—such mothers find holding their baby aversive, are angry with their babies, and irritated by them. The infant cries when the mother leaves and shows distress at the separation, but avoids the mother when she returns, even averting their gaze, turning away, and redirecting attention away (Ainsworth et al., 1978, p. 315). Or as Ainsworth explains it:

> Avoidance short circuits direct expression of anger to the attachment figure, which might be dangerous, and it also protects the baby from re-experiencing the rebuff that he has come to expect when he seeks close contact with his mother. It thus somewhat lowers his level of anxiety. (Ainsworth et al., 1978, p. 320)

Other useful resources:

Ainsworth (1973) on mother–child interaction.
*Mary Ainsworth: Attachment and the Growth of Love* (2005) is a 38-minute film detailing her development of the Strange Situation and the attachment styles she found (Davidson Films Ⓓ).

Recent research has emphasized that multiple attachments are good for babies. And attachment styles develop in a cultural setting.

## Adolescence

Issues include physical changes (puberty) and forming a personal identity. Research indicates that most adolescents do *not* experience extreme turbulence during this developmental stage. For current research see *Journal of Research on Adolescence* ⓤ

## Aging

Adult development is often neglected. However, because of stereotypes of older adults and the fact that the percentage of older adults in our population is increasing dramatically, this is an important topic.

    *Aging Successfully: The Psychological Aspects of Growing Old* focuses on aging and the myths surrounding aging (Davidson Films ⓤ)

## Gender roles

It is important to be aware of gender roles and variations based on culture and era. Most students are not consciously aware of how their gender stereotypes influence decisions they make or their interactions with other people. Carol Dweck and her associates have found that gender has an impact on children's learning styles—whether they will be mastery- or performance-oriented. Useful resources:

Hyde (2005) focuses on the many similarities between males and females.
Levy and Dweck (1999) look at children's conception of gender stereo-
    types and whether they see these stereotypes as changeable or not.
*Sex Roles in Motion Pictures* (Questia ⓤ web site).

## Social skills development

This includes self-regulation, empathy, risk, and resilience. Emphasis is on children's development of social skills, the timetable for such development, and the idea that children are resilient. Useful resources:

Luthar and Zigler (1991) review research on resilience in childhood.

Haggerty, Sherrod, Garmezy, and Rutter (1996). This volume focuses
    on the developmental processes that affect coping and resilience.

## Culture and development

It is difficult for students to understand that culture plays a large role in their development of self/identity/autonomy, competence, obedience, verbal communication, learning situations, and child-rearing practices (among others). Useful resources:

Saraswathi (2003). See especially the chapter by Cigdem Kagitcibasi titled "Human development across cultures: A contextual-functional analysis and implications for interventions" (pp. 166–191).
Berry, Poortinga, Segall, and Dasen (2002). See especially the chapter titled "Cultural transmission and individual development" (pp. 19–51).
Triandis (1994). An overview of research on the influence of culture on social behavior.

### Adult Development, Aging, Death and Dying

Students often have negative stereotypes of older people (mentally slow, sexless, bad drivers, nosy, etc.) so it's important to expose them to the research showing that adults are very cognitively active even late in life. I contrast this fact with the idea of terminal drop— that shortly before death, a person's cognitive abilities may decline rapidly. Useful resources:

*Scientific American*'s Ⓤ, "The Truth About Human Aging" (May 13, 2002).
Rowe and Kahn (1987). Looks at how extrinsic factors affect normal human aging.

# Classroom Tips

## Stimulus questions for discussion

### Parenting

Should people have to obtain a license to be parents? Hairdressers, plumbers, doctors, teachers must all obtain a license and in doing so demonstrate their competency. Why not parents?

### Attachment

Children's attachment style with their parents predicts their attachment style in future romantic relationships. Do you agree with this or not? What else might explain this apparent connection? Useful resources are Hazan and Shaver (1987) and Edelstein et al. (2004).

You might also mention that the motherless monkeys of Harlow's studies did not exhibit normal sexual behavior toward males or maternal behavior toward their infants when they matured. They never displayed "normal" behavior towards their offspring—and actually injured or killed their infants (aggression) as well as ignoring them, pushing them away, and not feeding them. See Harlow (1986).

## Behavioral genetics/temperament/nature/nurture

Children are born with a personality and an outlook on life. The environment that they are raised in is irrelevant. Do you believe this statement? Why or why not?

# Some suggested classroom learning activities

## Gender roles

(I spend about 15 minutes on this exercise.) I use pages from a dated children's book that illustrates gender stereotypes. I use *I'm Glad I'm a Boy: I'm Glad I'm a Girl!* (Darrow, 1970); this book is now out of print but there are many other children's books that illustrate the same concepts. The book I use presents the "classic" gender stereotypes—boys are President—girls are First Ladies; boys are pilots—girls are stewardesses and so forth. I show students the children's book and pair it with Mini #1 (that sends students to find gender roles and the impact of culture and history on these roles.) An excellent stimulus for beginning discussion of gender roles.

## Parenting

(15 minutes, although this could also be an out-of-class assignment.) Give students the following two excerpts from two different child care books. Ask them to write their own advice to parents based on what they have learned in the development chapter.

> There is a sensible way of treating children. Treat them as though they were young adults. Dress them, bathe them with care and circum-spection. Let your behavior always be objective and kindly firm. Never hug and kiss them, never let them sit on your lap. If you must, kiss them once on the forehead when they say good night. Shake hands with them in the morning. Give them a pat on the head if they have made an extraordinarily good job of a difficult task. Try it out. In a week's time you will find how easy it is to be perfectly objective with your child and at the same time kindly. You will be utterly ashamed of the mawkish, sentimental way you have been handling it. (Watson, 1928, 81–82)

> Enjoy your baby. He isn't a schemer. He needs loving . . . Your baby is born to be a reasonable, friendly human being. If you treat him nicely, he won't take advantage of you. Don't be afraid to love him or

respond to his needs. Every baby needs to be smiled at, talked to, played with, fondled—gently and lovingly . . . and the baby who doesn't get any loving will grow up cold and unresponsive. When he cries it's for a good reason . . . a little gentle rocking may actually be good for him. (Spock, 1945, 19–20)

*Out of class assignment.* (10–20 minutes for students to share their findings, depending on your purpose.) Ask students to conduct an interview with their own parent(s) or the person who raised them. Some sample interview questions can be found in Bernt (1999).

## Possible mini-assignments (written or groups)

### ⓦ *Mini-assignment #1*
Choose *one* of the activities listed below and write ½–1 page description of what you observe.

1. Go to a toy store and note how the store is organized. Can you tell which aisle has boys' toys and which has girls' toys? If so, how? If not, how is the store organized? Be sure to look at the boxes/wrappings that the toys come in.
2. Go into a card shop and read the cards congratulating parents on the birth of their child (baby cards). Are there different cards for boys and girls? If not, what are the main themes of the cards. If so, how do they differ?
3. Go into the children's section of a public library *or* browse through a small child's book collection *or* if your college has an education library browse through the children's collection there. How are males and females portrayed in general in these books? Note publication dates.
4. Watch a couple of hours of Saturday morning cartoons. Pay special attention to the commercials. Are they gender-specific? How do advertisements differ when only girls, only boys, or both girls and boys are portrayed?

### ⓦ *Mini-assignment #2*
Applying Piaget: List some everyday situations/occurrences (e.g., a teddy bear gets left out in the rain, your dog runs away from home, playing a card game) and ask students to think about that situation as though they were in a particular Piagetian stage of cognitive development (sensorimotor, preoperational, concrete operational, formal operational). Compare the thought process of someone in each stage.

**⦿** *Mini-assignment #3*

Explain how an adult with a childhood attachment style suggested by the Strange Situation (secure, avoidant, ambivalent, and disorganized) would relate to an adult romantic partner. Explain the connection between attachment and romantic relationships.

**⦿** *Mini-assignment #4*

Applying Kohlberg: Larry believes that logging is destroying the environment. He is asked to be part of a human chain that stands between the bulldozers and the trees. Should Larry participate in this activity? According to Kohlberg, which stage of moral development (preconventional, conventional, postconventional) do the following reasons represent?

No, because Larry is likely to be arrested.

Yes, because Larry's friends are also participating.

No, because it is against the law.

No, because chaos would reign if people just ignored the laws they didn't like.

Yes, because Larry wants his colleagues in his environmental group to be proud of him.

Yes, because the most important issue is saving trees and the environment for future generations.

No, because Larry's mother would be upset with him if she knew he participated in a demonstration.

Can you devise a different reason/response for each stage?

**⦿** *Mini-assignment #5*

Aging: Suppose you have started a new job and are introduced to your new supervisor for the first time. Write a paragraph describing what it will be like to work for this person if he or she is:

An 18-year-old female
A 35-year-old male
A 50-year-old female
A 65-year-old-male
A 70-year-old female

Now analyze what you wrote. What qualities did you attribute to each—did gender have an impact? How? Did age have an impact? Why? How might your expectations about your supervisor affect your job performance?

*Source for activity: By permission of Houghton Mifflin.*

# References

Ainsworth, M. (1973). The development of infant–mother attachments. In B. Caldwell & H. Ricciuti (Eds.), *Review of child development research, Vol. 3* (pp. 1–95). Chicago: University of Chicago Press.

Ainsworth, M., Blehar, M., Waters, E., & Wall, S. (1978). *Patterns of attachment: A psychological study of the strange situation.* Hillsdale, NJ: Lawrence Erlbaum Associates.

Baillargeon, R. (2004). Infants' physical world. *Current Directions in Psychological Science, 13,* 89–94.

Baumrind, D. (1971). Current patterns of parental authority. *Developmental Psychology Monographs, 4* (1 part 2).

Bernt, F. (1999). The ends and means of raising children: A parent interview activity. In L. Benjamin, B. Nodine, R. Ernst, & C. Blair Broeker (Eds.) *Activities handbook for the teaching of psychology, Vol. 4* (pp. 244–252). Washington, DC: American Psychological Association.

Berry, J., Poortinga, Y., Segall, M., & Dasen, P. (2002). *Cross-cultural psychology* (2nd ed.). Cambridge, UK: Cambridge University Press.

Bowlby, J. (1982). *Attachment and loss: Vol. I, Attachment* (2nd ed.). London: Hogarth Press.

Darrow, W., Jr. (1970). *I'm glad I'm a boy!: I'm glad I'm a girl!* New York: Windmill Books/Simon and Schuster.

Edelstein, R., Alexander, K., Shaver, P., Schaaf, J., Quas, J., Lovas, G., & Goodman, G. (2004). Adult attachment style and parental responsiveness during a stressful event. *Attachment and Human Development, 6*(1), 31–52.

Gilligan, C. (1993). *In a different voice.* Cambridge, MA: Harvard University Press.

Haggerty, R., Sherrod, L., Garmezy, N., & Rutter, M. (Eds.) (1996). *Stress, risk, and resilience in children and adolescents: Processes, mechanisms, and interventions.* Cambridge, MA: Harvard University Press.

Harlow, H. (1959). Love in infant monkeys. *Scientific American, 200,* 68–74.

Harlow, H. (1986). Maternal behavior of rhesus monkeys deprived of mothering and peer associations in infancy. In C. Harlow (Ed.), *From learning to love: The selected papers of H. F. Harlow* (pp. 281–94). New York: Praeger.

Hazan, C., & Shaver, P. (1987). Romantic love conceptualized as an attachment process. *Journal of Personality and Social Psychology, 52*(3), 511–524.

Hyde, J. (2005). The gender similarities hypothesis. *American Psychologist, 60*(6), 581–592.

Levy, S., & Dweck, C. (1999). The impact of children's static versus dynamic conceptions of people on stereotype formation. *Child Development, 70*(5), 1163–1180.

Luthar, S., & Zigler, E. (1991). Vulnerability and competence: A review of research on resilience in childhood. *American Journal of Orthopsychiatry*, *61*(1), 6–22.

Rowe, J., & Kahn, R. (1987). Human aging: Usual and successful. *Science*, *237*(4811), 143–149.

Saraswathi, T. (Ed.) (2003). *Cross-cultural perspectives in human development*. New Delhi: Sage.

Spitz, R. (1945). Hospitalism—An inquiry into the genesis of psychiatric conditions. *Psychoanalytic Study of the Child*, *1*, 53–74.

Spock, B. (1945). *The common sense book of baby and child care*. New York: Duell, Sloan and Pearce.

Thomas, A., & Chess, S. (1977). *Temperament and development*. New York: Brunner/Mazel.

Triandis, H. (1994). *Culture and social behavior*. New York: McGraw-Hill.

Watson, J. (1928). *Psychological care of the infant and child*. New York: Norton.

## Additional Suggested Readings for Instructors

Bronstein, P., & Quina, K. (Eds.) (2003). *Teaching gender and multicultural awareness: Resources for the psychology classroom*. Washington, DC: American Psychological Association.

Cronin, A., & Mandich, M. (Eds.) (2005). *Human development and performance throughout the lifespan*. Clifton Park, NY: Thomson/Delmar Learning.

Hoyer, W. (2003). *Adult development and aging* (5th ed.). Boston: McGraw-Hill.

Tavris, C. (1992). *The mismeasure of woman*. New York: Simon and Schuster.

# Chapter 5

# Biological Psychology

## Getting Started

One of the challenges of this unit is deciding where to locate it within your course. It must be presented early enough so that students can use this knowledge in future chapters, but not so early that students cannot see the relevance of the information.

It is tempting to just lecture about biological psychology, providing students with, essentially, an anatomy lesson. However, it is vital that you find activities to keep students engaged. Active learning will ensure that they understand the concepts and it will keep them from getting bored or overwhelmed by the material.

I focus on *why* this material is important since many students see it as being irrelevant to psychology. I relate biological functions to future chapters (mental illness, learning, cognition, etc.) and then I make sure that I refer back to the relevant biological concepts in those future units. I talk about how advances in brain imaging have led to a greater understanding of biology's impact on psychological disorders as well as basic human functions such as sleep, eating, and learning. Biological psychology is central to understanding the rest of psychology.

My second focus is to stress the nature/nurture interaction. I want students to understand that the environment has an impact on the brain—the brain is not a static entity, impervious to influence. Nurture does have an impact on nature as well as nature influencing nurture.

I use more visuals in this unit than any other. Visuals help students see the brain structures and graphics of processes (e.g., neurotransmission) often clarify complicated information. And don't forget that students need to have access to these visuals either through a web site or through handouts—they should not have to spend class time trying to draw the brain as you talk.

## My outline for teaching (2½ days—75 minute classes)

*Day 1* (½ day)

I. Development and biology (10 minutes)

Reflexes and why they disappear as we develop in infancy and childhood

Neural connections—few at birth, an overabundance at age 6, a "smart" pruning by adolescence

Why early exposure to music, language, and math has an impact on children's brain development (See *Newsweek*'s "Your Child's Brain" ⓤ)

II. Why biological psychology? (5 minutes)

Important for mental disorders, therapy, development, memory, and so forth

III. Nature/nurture and the brain (10 minutes)

The brain is *not* just a product of nature—it is *not* totally prewired. It can be influenced by the environment

William Calvin's hypothesis of "The Throwing Madonna" (see stimulus question, p. 82)

Discussion of Harold Klawan's *Why Michael Couldn't Hit* (Klawans, 1996)

*Day 2*

Directions on board: Pick a slip of paper out of the bag and pick up the appropriate prop (see Classroom tips: Acting out the structure and function of neurons, pp. 83–5)

Questions from previous class (5 minutes)

Practice questions over material (5 minutes)

Administrivia (5 minutes)

I. Cells of the nervous system (handout packet; 30 minutes—20 minutes for the activity)

Structure of the neuron
Go over action potential handout
Action potential demonstration
II.  Neurotransmitters (15 minutes)
III. Nervous system (15 minutes—the demonstration adds 5–10
        minutes more)
Structure of the nervous system—central/peripheral
Speed of neural transmission demonstration

*Day 3*
Questions from previous class (5 minutes)
Practice questions over material (5 minutes)
Administrivia (5 minutes)
  I.  Brain structures/Brain Game—Check that students have Mini-
        assignment #1 completed as they come into class. (35 minutes)
        Into study groups and play Brain Jeopardy or the Brain Game
 II.  Lateralization/split-brain studies (10 minutes)
III.  Endocrine system (15 minutes)

## My transitions

I teach this unit after development—with brain development and the
nature/nurture dilemma providing nice segues—and before sensation
and perception. I begin this unit by telling my students that the rest
of the course will focus on the individual, from cell structure to
social interaction. I provide a link between the biological psychology
material and materials to come in later chapters. And I tell them that
after learning the basics about biological psychology, we will move
to talking about the sensing and perceiving individual.

## Topics typically included in this unit

*The Nervous System*: Cells of the nervous system—glial cells,
neurons—axons, dendrites, cell body; action potentials—polarization and depolarization, synapses, neurotransmitters, postsynaptic
potentials—EPSP, IPSP; peripheral nervous system—somatic and
autonomic, sympathetic and parasympathetic; central nervous
system—spinal cord, brain
*The Brain*: Imaging techniques; anatomy and function—hindbrain,
midbrain, forebrain, and cerebral cortex; split brain and lateral-
ization; plasticity and repairing brain damage

*Other Systems*: Endocrine—hormones, glands, fight-or-flight syndrome; immune—autoimmune diseases, T-cells

## Some options for organizing the concepts

*In hierarchical format*: Begin by talking about cells in the nervous system, then systems of cells, brain structures, then the systems that control the body (nervous, endocrine, immune).

*Around case studies*: You can teach this chapter using case studies of brain damage (see, e.g., Sacks, 1987). With careful selection of the case studies you can incorporate study of relevant brain structures and biological processes.

*Around biological effects of drugs*: Use student interest in the effects of drugs—over-the-counter, prescription, and illicit—and the impact of each drug on the nervous (brain), endocrine, and immune system. (Cocaine http://www.drugabuse.gov/NIDA_Notes/ NNVol13N5/Cocaine.html is an excellent web site describing the biological effects of using cocaine.)

*Around behavior governed by biology*: Start with higher functions, such as memory and learning, and then explain the biological processes involved in such functions. This method can be interwoven throughout the course—but students need to understand basic neuronal communication before they are introduced to "pieces" of biology throughout the course.

# Teaching the Content

Remember that the ⓦ symbol means that a printable version is available on the web site (www.blackwellpublishing.com/lucas) and the ⓤ means that the URL is available on the web site.

## Topics that many students will find difficult

### Action potentials

Action potentials are the basis of all human thought. Students won't see the "awesomeness" of this, so it's our responsibility to point it out. It is vital that students understand how action potentials occur, or at least appreciate how action potentials operate to allow neurons to communicate with each other. Options for teaching this include:

A good explanation of neurons and action potentials can be accessed
at the Centre for Synaptic Plasticity web site ⓤ sponsored by the
University of Bristol and the Medical Research Council.
The Neuroscience for Kids web site ⓤ also provides an excellent,
and not too basic, description of action potentials.
A classroom demonstration of action potentials, cell communication,
and postsynaptic potentials (see Classroom tips, pp. 83–5).

*Brain structures/anatomy*
Many students are overwhelmed by the need to learn terms and
functions. Using classroom demonstrations, such as the Brain Game
or Neuro-Jeopardy, can take the tedium out of this rote learning (see
Classroom tips, pp. 86–8).

The Wisconsin Online Resource Center ⓤ has a basic lesson in brain
structure and function. (Note that this is a free service but you
will have to sign up to use this site.) As you click on the list of
brain structures, an explanation of that structure and a visual
showing where it is located in the brain appears.
Another excellent resource is the BBC web site ⓤ for information
about brain structure and function.

*Split-brain studies*
Students tend to understand the role of the corpus callosum, but
they have difficulty applying that information to the brain's impact
on behavior—the idea that the right hemisphere has relatively little
language ability and the left has relatively little spatial ability.
An excellent explanation of the split-brain studies may be found at
the Nobel Foundation web site ⓤ. This site also includes a game that
students can play that helps them understand what each hemisphere
is capable of after split-brain surgery (see Mini-assignment #2).

## Other important topics and resources

*Reflexes*
This is a link to the development chapter. Babies are born with
many reflexes which will disappear as they grow. Some basic reflexes
remain and students often have difficulty understanding that these
reflexes can operate entirely within the spinal cord, though they send
feedback to the brain, too.
Sumanas, Inc.—Multimedia Development services web site ⓤ provides a six-slide explanation of the reflex arc.

*Neurotransmitters*
I concentrate on seven major neurotransmitters—dopamine, endorphins, serotonin, GABA, glutamate, acetylcholine, and norepinephrine.

For a directory of web resources about neurotransmitters go to the Cerebral Institute of Discovery web site Ⓤ.
For a basic discussion of the role of these neurotransmitters, see Professor George Boeree's (Shippensburg University) web site Ⓤ.

*The endocrine system*
The basics include: communication between glands and organs of the endocrine system through hormones released in the bloodstream, basic human growth, and sexual development.

For an overview of the endocrine system see the American Medical Association web site Ⓤ and Colorado State's Biomedical Hypertextbooks web site. Ⓤ

*The immune system*
I only emphasize the impact of physical and psychological stressors on immune system functioning. The basic ideas, however, are useful for students and will be expanded upon in the unit on health, stress, and coping.

The Nobel Foundation web site Ⓤ has a good explanation of the immune system, a discussion of the scientists who discovered how it worked, and an Immune System Defender Game that helps reinforce the concepts.

# Classroom Tips

## Stimulus questions for discussion

*Stem cells*
According to the US National Institute of Health:

> *Stem cells* have the remarkable potential to develop into many different cell types in the body. Serving as a sort of repair system for the body, they can theoretically divide without limit to replenish other cells as long as the person or animal is still alive. When a stem cell divides, each new cell has the potential to either remain a stem cell or become another type of cell with a more specialized function, such as a muscle cell, a red blood cell, or a brain cell. (Retrieved June 20, 2006 from http://stemcells.nih.gov/info/basics/)

Scientists are studying how to use adult stem cells in the same manner as embryonic stem cells. If they are successful, what potential do you see for use of adult stem cells?

For more information see the National Institute of Health's web site ⓤ.

### Endocrine system

Recently, baseball players have admitted to taking human growth factor as well as anabolic steroids to enhance their performance. What effect do these substances have on performance? Should these substances be banned?

See *Who will win the drug race?* at NOVA's Science in the News web site ⓤ.

### Aging and the brain

Research has shown that elderly adults who stay cognitively active show less decline in their mental abilities. Thus elderly people are encouraged to do crossword and Sudoku puzzles and to keep their minds active. Some video game developers have even begun to develop video games for older people to keep their brains active. Given what you know about how the brain functions, how do you think doing puzzles and playing video games decreases mental decline?

See a discussion of this trend at CBS News web site ⓤ.

### Brain malleability

In William Calvin's (1991) book *The Throwing Madonna: Essays on the Brain*, he presents a hypothesis that right-handedness led to language being housed primarily in the left hemisphere—rather than the left hemisphere's dominance leading to right-handedness. Working through this hypothesis with your class helps to highlight the idea that the environment can have an impact on the brain. I give a synopsis of Calvin's hypothesis and ask the class, "What do you think of this hypothesis? Why do you think Calvin proposed it?"

You may download Calvin's book for personal reading at his web site ⓤ. He allows teachers to copy one chapter to distribute to students.

### Brain injury/shaken baby syndrome

According to the Brain Injury Association, when a baby is shaken:

> The brain bounces back and forth within the skull cavity, injuring or destroying the brain tissue . . . blood vessels feeding the brain can be

torn, leading to bleeding around the brain [and] retinal (back of eye) bleeding can occur. This can cause blindness . . . [This occurs because] babies' heads are large and heavy, making up about 25% of their total body weight. Their neck muscles are too weak to support such a disproportionately large head. [In addition] babies' brains are immature and more easily injured . . . Immediately after a baby is shaken, the baby may become extremely irritable, experience seizures, have limp arms and legs and a decreased level of consciousness, may vomit, or its heart might stop, leading to death. Long-term consequences of shaking a baby include learning disabilities, physical disabilities, partial or total blindness, hearing impairment, speech disabilities, cognitive disabilities, cerebral palsy, seizures, behavior disorders, and eventual death. (Retrieved March 30, 2007 from http://www.biausa.org/factsheets.htm)

I ask students for information on "shaken baby syndrome" and this leads to a discussion tying development and biological psychology together.

See the above web site for other fact sheets about brain injuries.

### Neuroethics

Advances in imaging and technology have made it possible for us to have a better understanding of how the brain works. But there are ethical questions to consider. For example, what if we had technology that could erase memories (the premise of the movie *Eternal Sunshine of the Spotless Mind*)? Would it be ethical to remove bad memories? How could we be sure the technology would not be used to remove other kinds of memories, or to remove memories without permission? What if a drug were developed to decrease aggression? Would it be ethical to use it on aggressive children as a way of preventing criminal behavior?

For a discussion of these questions and other ethical dilemmas, see the Neuroscience for Kids web site Ⓤ.

## Some suggested classroom learning activities

### Acting out the structure and function of neurons

(10 minute lecture over the basics, then 20 minutes for the activity.) As students enter class they draw a slip of paper from a bag that gives them their role to play in this demonstration. They then pick up their props. I provide a quick introduction of neurons and neurotransmission by reviewing the handout: "A Review of Neurotransmission" (see Handout #1 Ⓦ).

- *Props:* White, red, green, blue, and orange construction paper; a Styrofoam cone; a Styrofoam square; a sheet of Styrofoam with a cut-out that fits the cone; a sheet of Styrofoam with a cut-out that fits the square; several inflated balloons and a safety pin to prick the balloons.
- Roll the construction paper into "hats" and staple—one white hat for the action potential, several green hats for positive electrical charges, several red hats for negative electric charges, several blue hats for a positive postsynaptic potential, several orange hats for a negative postsynaptic potential. (Make as many hats as you need to involve the maximum number of students.)
- Pick one student to wear the white hat and be the action potential, two students to be different neurotransmitters (one should hold the cone, the other should hold the square), two students to be different receptors (one should hold the Styrofoam sheet fitting the cone, the other should hold the Styrofoam sheet fitting the square), one student to be a presynaptic reuptake pump, one student to pop balloons during reuptake. Make the other students positive and negative electrical charges and positive and negative postsynaptic potentials.
- The front of the classroom is the equivalent of the cell body. Students in green hats (positive charges) and students in red hats (negative charges) stand in the front of the classroom. Direct students to move back and forth between different areas to show how the flow of either positive or negative charge affects the relative distribution of charge between two areas. Then tell the person in the white hat (the action potential, or AP) that he or she will "conduct" down the "axon" (an aisle, for example) when pushed in the back by a "threshold" of two hands from positive-charge actors. Green hats physically push and red hats physically pull the AP actor (demonstrating summation). The action potential is "triggered" by a net surplus of two hands pushing the AP actor (showing threshold).
- The AP actor then runs down an aisle (the axon) while maintaining a constant speed, thereby demonstrating the all-or-nothing aspect of neuronal firing (conduction without decay).
- At the aisle's end (axon terminal), the AP actor "tags" one of the two neurotransmitter actors holding a Styrofoam cone or square. The neurotransmitter actor walks across the back of the room (synapse) to the receptor actor holding a compatibly shaped Styrofoam "receptor." Once the neurotransmitter "binds" to the receptor, the membrane pump actor (reuptake) physically walks

the neurotransmitter actor back to the axon terminal. At the same time another student pops a balloon, demonstrating energy to "power" the pump. Depending on which receptor you are using (green or red), students in blue hats (excitatory postsynaptic potential) or orange hats (inhibitory postsynaptic potential) enter the aisle (dendrite) and run toward the front of the room with decreasing speed (passive spread with decay). Be sure that you point out that green=blue and red=orange and that you are differentiating colors to show two distinct cells.

- Once students understand the basics of this demonstration, it is then possible to introduce a second neurotransmitter and a second receptor and demonstrate that neurotransmitters bind only to their own receptors.

*Source for activity: Shenker (1990). By permission of Houghton Mifflin.*

## Mental chronometry and speed of neural transmission

(10–30 minutes, depending on the variations.) This task, first described by Herman von Helmholtz in 1850 and popularized by E. W. Scripture (1895), shows students that (a) even simple mental processing takes measurable time and (b) neural transmission is a physical process that is measurable. See Chapter 9 on Cognition, Language and Cognitive Abilities for an additional variation on this exercise.

- Fifteen to twenty students stand in a line, each student facing the back of the student ahead. Students close their eyes (to avoid picking up visual cues from others) and place their right hand on the right shoulder of the person in front of them. Tell the students to briefly squeeze the shoulder of the next person as soon as they feel their own shoulder squeezed. Stand behind the last person in the line, and start the process by squeezing his or her shoulder, while simultaneously starting a stopwatch. Then go to the front of the line, and stop the watch when the squeeze chain arrives.
- Time elapsed divided by the number of students reasonably estimates the average reaction time to the squeeze stimulus. This estimates the average time needed for a person to perceive a stimulus, select a response, and execute the response. By repeating the procedure, reaction times will fall with practice as students get faster at selecting and executing responses.
- You can estimate the transmission speed of at least some neurons by modifying the basic squeeze chain: Squeeze ankles instead of

shoulders. The impulse must travel from the ankle to the brain, not the shoulder to the brain, and thus should take longer.

• Have the same students, seated in the same order, grasp the right ankle of the person ahead of them with their right hand. Go to one end of the line, have the students close their eyes, and repeat the squeeze experiment. Even after practice, elapsed time for a complete wave of ankle squeezes will be longer than the shoulder trials because the squeeze sensations must travel longer distances to reach the brain. The increase in elapsed time (compared to shoulder squeeze trials) divided by the number of students estimates the increase in individual reaction time due to the extra length of neural transit. The average of that extra distance from ankle to shoulder, (about 3 or 4 feet), divided by the average extra reaction time, estimates the speed of neural transmission in feet per second.

Note: Some students might be reluctant to participate in an exercise requiring touching of other people. While I have never had a student not participate, it might be a good ideas to use only volunteers for this activity.

*Source for activity: Rozin and Jonides (1977); also published in Ware and Johnson (1996, pp. 38–41), and in Scripture (1895).*

### The Brain Game and Jeopardy
(Since I use this activity in lieu of an actual lecture, I spend 30 minutes on it. You could alter this activity to fit your time frame.)

Rather than laboriously lecturing about brain structures and functions I use one of two games to cover this content. For both games, students are instructed to bring their notes from reading the biological psychology unit. I assign Mini-assignment #1 ⓦ to make sure that students read the appropriate sections of the textbook. Students show their notes and are put into groups. (You could put those without notes into a group together. They soon discover the importance of reading the chapter and taking good notes.)

In a true trivia game format, the group that has the answer the quickest gets the point. However, it is difficult to read the question and see which group raised their hand first. So I modify the rules by giving each group a stack of blank paper and a marker. After the question, every group writes their answers on the paper. When the appropriate amount of time has passed, I cue them to hold their paper up at the same time. Every group with the correct answer receives a point.

*The Brain Game.* This game was introduced by Josh Gerow at a National Institute on the Teaching of Psychology conference. Once I have checked that students have completed Mini-assignment #1 and students are in their appropriate groups, I read a series of scenarios involving brain structures and functions. (I'm providing some examples, but these questions are easy to develop.)

- Carol was driving in the rain when a car cut in front of her and as she slammed on the brakes her car began to skid. She got the car under control, but her heart was racing, she was breathing heavily, and her mouth was dry. What part of Carol's nervous system was activated? Answer: sympathetic nervous system.
- Lawrence was brought to the emergency room of the hospital with a gunshot wound to his brain. Although he lost little brain tissue, his brain was no longer able to regulate his breathing or heart rate; therefore, he was pronounced dead. Which part of Lawrence's brain was most likely damaged? Answer: medulla.
- Latifah had surgery on her hindbrain. Unfortunately, some swelling has caused her to lapse into a coma. If one area of the hindbrain is affected, which is most likely the cause of the coma? Answer: reticular formation.
- Lisa reads a newspaper, but moments later she does not recall seeing it. She recalls her name, family members, and her address, but although she meets the same doctor every day for a month, Lisa never recognizes her. Which part of Lisa's brain must have been injured? Answer: hippocampus in the forebrain.

*Brain Jeopardy, also called Neuro-jeopardy.* This game can be found at the Neuroscience for Kids web site ⓤ. Another version of Neuro-jeopardy can be found at the Society for Neuroscience, Atlanta Chapter's web site ⓤ. You can also develop your own categories and questions, using Jeopardy templates available at the James Madison Center of James Madison University's Educational Resources for Teachers web site ⓤ or Graves County Schools' web site ⓤ. Again, students are divided into groups and points are awarded for the correct answer. Christopher Armstrong at the University of Illinois developed the game we use (and other instructors edit his basic game to meet their needs). The categories and a sample question are:

Don't Be Nervous (nervous system)
- Question: Rob Zombie was barbecuing outside when he accidentally touched the hot grill. The pain message was carried to his spinal cord by which nervous system? Answer: somatic.

Lob me a Lobe (lobes of the brain)
- Question: Jose bent over in his garden to pick up a squash but bumped his head on a fence post and passed out. When he came to, he could not let go of the squash in his hand; his hand would not open or close. Jose most likely injured cells in his _____ lobe. Answer: frontal.

Meet Me at the Gap (neurotransmitters)
- Question: Malik always feels sleepy during his afternoon classes. You tell Malik that he should avoid eating high carbohydrate lunches because they increase the effects of which neurotransmitter? Answer: serotonin.

You Know What They Say About a Big Brain (structures of the forebrain)
- Question: Grissom has memorized all of the species of insects that live in the Las Vegas area. The part of his brain that allows him to form new memories is his _____ ? Answer: hippocampus.

Dain Bramage (effects of damage to various parts of the brain)
- Question: Jillian slipped on the ice and hit her head. When she woke up in the hospital she said, "Butter monkeys scanned red Luke". Jillian most likely has damage to which part of her association cortex? Answer: Wernicke's area.

ABCs (Answers start with A, B or C)
- Question: Wayne was injured when a rotary saw blade was accidentally used while playing Frisbee. Wayne had a large cut through the middle of his skull. He seemed OK but when he was asked to place his left hand in his left pocket and verbally describe the contents, he couldn't. Wayne most likely severed his _____? Answer: corpus callosum.

## Other Games

Fayette County Schools Curriculum, Instruction and Assessment web site ⓤ provides templates and instructions for creating games in Jeopardy, Who Wants to be a Millionaire, and Hollywood Squares formats.

## Possible mini-assignments (written or groups)

### ⓦ Mini-assignment #1

(Be sure to space this out so they can write on the sheet. Thanks to Sylvia Puente, University of Illinois.)

*Notes for the Brain Game.* Please take notes on the structures of the following brain structures and neurotransmitters. These will help you score points in the upcoming "Brain Game," which will be played in class.

Neurotransmitters
- Acetylocholine:
- Norepinephrine:
- Serotonin:
- Dopamine:
- GABA:
- Glutamate:
- Peptides: Endorphins:
- Gases: Nitric oxide:

Peripheral nervous system (PNS)
- Somatic nervous system:
- Autonomic nervous system:
  Sympathetic nervous system:
  Parasympathetic nervous system:

Central nervous system (CNS):
- Spinal cord:
  Afferent neurons:
  Efferent neurons:

Brain (write notes below)

Hindbrain
- Medulla:
- Reticular formation:
- Locus coeruleus:
- Cerebellum:

Midbrain
- Substantia nigra:

Forebrain
- Striatum:
- Thalamus:
- Hypothalamus:
- Suprachiasmatic nuclei:
- Amygdala:
- Hippocampus:
- Limbic system:
- Cerebral cortex:
  (1) Anatomical divisions (lobes):
      frontal:

        parietal:
        occipital:
        temporal:
  (2)  Functional divisions (cortex):
        somatosensory:
        motor:
        visual:
        association:
        (a)  Broca's area:
        (b)  Wernicke's area:
Corpus Callosum.

### ⓦ *Mini-assignment #2*

Go to http://nobelprize.org/educational_games/medicine/split-brain/background.html (Nobel Foundation web site) and read the background material on split brains. Then play the split-brain experiments game (at the bottom of the introduction page is a link to the game). What did you learn from playing this game? How would you explain split-brain experiments in your own words?

### ⓦ *Mini-assignment #3*

Your somatic, autonomic, and central nervous systems constantly interact, allowing you to function in the world. Explain how these systems interact in order for you to move away from a fire that is too hot.

### ⓦ *Mini-assignment #4*

(This could be a good group project, with the class divided into neurological diseases and researching the impact on the various nervous systems.) Alzheimer's disease and Parkinson's disease both involve neurotransmitters. Explain the development of each disease, the neurotransmitter involved, and the physiological and behavioral progression of each disease.

### ⓦ *Mini-assignment #5*

The nervous system's three main function are to receive information (input), integrate that information with past experiences (processing), and guide actions (output). Given this model, explain the nervous system's impact on your behavior of waking up to an alarm clock and turning it off.

# Handout

⦿ Handout #1: A Review of Neurotransmission

## References

Calvin, W. (1991). *The throwing madonna*. New York: Bantam.

Klawans, H. (1996). *Why Michael couldn't hit and other tales of the neurology of sports*. New York: W. H. Freeman.

Rozin, P., & Jonides, J. (1977). Mass reaction time: Measurement of the speed of the nerve impulse and the duration of mental processes in class. *Teaching of Psychology, 4*(2), 91–94.

Sacks, O. (1987). *The man who mistook his wife for a hat*. New York: Harper & Row.

Scripture, E. W. (1895). *Thinking, feeling, and doing*. New York: Chautauqua-Century Press.

Shenker, J. I. (May, 1990). *"Acting out" the structure and function of neurons*. Presentation to the Midwestern Psychological Association Annual Meeting, Chicago, IL.

Ware, M., & Johnson, D. (Eds.). (1996). *Handbook of demonstrations and activities in the teaching of psychology*, Vol. III. Mahwah, NJ: Erlbaum.

## Additional Suggested Readings for Instructors

Calvin, W., & Ojemann, G. (1994). *Conversations with Neil's brain: The neural nature of language and thought*. Reading, MA: Addison-Wesley.

Howard, P. (2000). *The owner's manual for the brain: Everyday applications from mind-brain research* (2nd ed.). Austin, TX: Bard Press.

Neuroscience for Kids web site: http://faculty.washington.edu/chudler/neurok.html

# Chapter 6

# Sensation and Perception

## Getting Started

As with the biological psychology unit, there is a large physiological component in the sensation and perception unit. I again reassure my students that this unit has relevance for psychology. And I incorporate as many active learning opportunities as possible.

My goals for this unit are simple but ambitious. I want my students to see the difference between sensation and perception, while understanding that, in reality, they work together. I want them to understand that sensing an object is not the same as perceiving it—that only perception provides meaning. Most importantly I want students to understand that perception is not a passive biological process, but an active *construction* of reality—that our perception is based on our expectations and experiences.

Finally, I want my students to understand that without sensation and perception, we would have no way to interact with our world— sensation and perception essentially define our world.

My Outline for Teaching
(2½ Days—75 Minute Classes)

*Day 1*
Collect ⓦ Mini-assignment #1

Questions from previous class (5 minutes)
Practice questions over material (5 minutes)
Administrivia (5 minutes)
   I.   Definitions of sensation and perception (10 minutes)
        Case studies: Virgil and Michael May (see Stimulus question:
        Sensation without perception, p. 103)
  II.   Sensory basics—what is reality? (5 minutes)
 III.   Discuss Mini-assignment #1 Ⓦ—(10 minutes) What sense would
        you give up? Why? If that sense were impaired, what physi-
        cal structures would be damaged? (Student responses are
        used throughout this unit)
        Sensory modalities handout (See Ⓦ Handout #1)
 IV.   Vision (35 minutes)
        Students who "gave up" vision review the physical structures
        that would be impacted
        Color vision
        •  Theories of color vision: trichromatic vs. opponent process
           Rods and cones: classroom learning activity
           Opponent process demonstration: the flag classroom learn-
              ing activity
        Movement
        •  How do we know when we are moving or the world around
           us is moving?
        Visual dominance
        •  Spiral classroom learning activity
        Lateral inhibition

*Day 2*
Directions on board for olfaction/smell demonstration (see some
   suggested classroom learning activities, pp. 107–9)
Questions from previous class (5 minutes)
Practice questions over material (5 minutes)
Administrivia (5 minutes)
   I.   Olfaction (20 minutes)
        Students review what physical structures would be impacted
           without olfaction
        Olfaction/smell classroom learning activity
  II.   Pain (15 minutes)
 III.   Hearing (15 minutes)
        Students review what physical structures would be impacted
           without hearing

Pinna demonstration (have students hold their pinnas against their head while listening and report the difference in their auditory experience)

IV.  Taste: sweet, sour, bitter, salty (10 minutes)

Note that receptors for each basic taste are spread all over the tongue—not found in particular areas

Students review what physical structures would be impacted without gustation

Importance of texture and heat in taste sensations

Interaction of taste and smell

- Taste classroom learning activity

*Day 3*

Questions from previous class (5 minutes)

Practice questions over material (5 minutes)

Administrivia (5 minutes)

I.  Introduction (10 minutes). I use a snippet of a *Muppet* video in which there is no dialogue, just movement, and I ask my students to tell me what they "sense" from the video and what they "perceive." This leads to a great discussion on the difficulty in discriminating between these processes.

Definitions

II.  Processes of perception (15 minutes)

Bottom-up

Top-down

Subliminal classroom learning activity: bottom-up and top-down processing: making sense of subliminal messages

III.  Organizing the perceptual world (15 minutes)

Figure–ground

Grouping principles

Depth perception

- Monocular cues
- Motion cues
- Binocular cues

Binocular disparity classroom learning activity

IV.  Psychophysics (15 minutes)

Absolute threshold

Signal detection theory

V.  Perceptual illusions/Impossible figures (5 minutes)

Stroboscopic motion/flip books

## My Transitions

I cover sensation and perception after the biology unit because the concepts of these three units build on each other. After perception, many texts go directly to the learning unit, tying perceptual processes into a prerequisite for learning. I teach the consciousness unit next because I see consciousness as the next progression in "building" the individual.

## Topics Typically Included in This Unit

*Sensory systems*: Coding, adaptation, transduction

*Vision*: Anatomy and physiology of the eye and visual pathways; visual processing; physical dimensions of light; color vision

*Hearing*: Anatomy and physiology of the ear and auditory pathways; physical and psychological dimensions of sound; theories of coding

*Chemical senses*: Smell/olfaction—anatomy and physiology of nose and mouth, olfactory pathways, pheromones; taste/gustation—anatomy and physiology of the tongue; flavor

*Somatic senses*: Touch and temperature—physiology; pain

*Proprioception*: Vestibular; kinesthesia

*Synesthesia*

*Sensation/perception*: Differentiation of the two

*Approaches to perception*: Computational, constructivist, ecological

*Psychophysics*: Threshold, subliminal stimuli, signal detection theory, Weber's law

*Organizing perceptions*: Figure–ground; grouping, etc.

*Depth perception*: Monocular, motion, and binocular cues

*Perception of motion*: Visual dominance, stroboscopic motion

*Perceptual constancy*: Shape, brightness, size

*Bottom-up, top-down, network processing*: Parallel distributed processing (PDP), geons

*Culture, development, and perception*

*Attention*: Inattentional blindness, divided attention, Stroop task

## Some options for Organizing the Concepts

*By sensory concepts leading to perceptual concepts*: Start with the physiological basis for sensations then add meaning to the basics to get to perceptual concepts.

*By explaining our interactions with the world as dependent on sensation and perception*: Concepts combined, e.g., "How do I see you? Sensation (structure of eye, etc.) and perceptual processes (depth perception, size, shape constancy, etc.).

## Teaching the Content

Remember that the symbol ⊛ means that a printable version is available on the web site (www.blackwellpublishing.com/lucas) and ⓤ means that the URL is available on the web site.

## Topics that Many Students will Find Difficult

### The basics of sensory systems
Stressing the connection between the physical world and our psychological experience helps in describing coding and transduction.

*The Neural Connection* ⓤ, a 30-minute 1997 video from Insight Media, discusses sensory cells and the transmission of neural impulses.

### Physiology of sensory structure
Rather than lecture on the physical structures important in sensation, I assign students Mini-assignment #1 ⊛, due the first day of the unit. Students then make the case for each sense, explaining the physiological and psychological impact of losing that sense. You could also make this into a group project.

Handout #1 ⊛—Review of sensory modalities—summarizes this information as well.

See Ackerman (1991). The NOVA (PBS) series, *Mystery of the senses* ⓤ (1995, a five-part series, 60 minutes each) is based on this book. The PBS web site ⓤ provides ideas for classroom use of these videos.

A discussion of the anatomy of the ear can be found at the Hyperphysics web site ⓤ.

### Lateral inhibition, ganglion, and bipolar cells in the eye
The idea that we see crisp contrasts because activity is inhibited in some cells and enhanced in those nearby is a difficult one for many students.

The Serendip web site ⓦ supported by Bryn Mawr college has a good description of lateral inhibition and its role in optical illusions. A lateral inhibition simulator helps to explain the concept. Another excellent explanation of this concept can be found at Kevin Douglas's (Northern Kentucky University) web site ⓦ.

## Psychophysics

Threshold is a concept most students will comprehend (although the operational definition often seems arbitrary to them). But signal detection theory and Weber's Law are more difficult.

*Weber's law and the concept of just noticeable difference (JND).* To help students understand this idea, I use a quick classroom demonstration. A student volunteer closes his or her eyes and holds out both hands. On one hand I place a book (not too heavy), on the other hand a sheet of paper. The volunteer is instructed to tell me if he or she notices a difference in weight. When I put a sheet of paper on the book the volunteer usually cannot perceive a difference. However, when I put another sheet of paper on top of the sheet of paper the volunteer usually feels the difference.

For *signal detection theory,* I use a 2 × 2 visual and many examples, such as "hearing" the garage door go up at night when my teenage driver is out. Other standard examples include airport baggage screening and tornado sightings.

|  | *Signal present* | *Signal not present* |
| --- | --- | --- |
| Report signal present | Hit | False alarm |
| Report signal not present | Miss | Correct rejection |

## Proprioception

To show students the importance of proprioception, I present the story of "Christina, the disembodied lady" (Sacks, 1987, Chapter 3). When Christina lost her proprioception, she had no idea where her limbs were in space. She had to watch her feet in order to be able to walk and when she tried to feed herself, her hands would miss or overshoot. Sacks (1987) contains many more case studies that would be nice introductions to many of the sensation/perception topics.

## Parallel and distributed processing

I have difficulty explaining PDP processing. George Hollich's (Temple University) ⓤ "primer" on PDP processing is excellent.

## Other Important Topics and Resources

### Other senses

*Vision.* We primarily rely on visual information (visual dominance), which can lead us to misperceive the world. Several videos discuss the visual system: Insight Media's *Mystery of the Senses—Vision, The Eye: From Light comes Sight* ⓤ and Annenberg Media's Teachers Resources *Discovering Psychology: #7 Sensation and Perception* ⓤ.

- Color vision—Opponent process and trichromatic theories. See "Rods and cones" and the "Opponent processing" classroom learning activities, pp. 106–7.

Color blindness—People with malfunctions in one or more of their three types of cones perceive the world differently. More males than females experience color blindness.

The Web Exhibits web site ⓤ (a web museum) has a description of color blindness and a demonstration of how color-blind people see the world.

See also, "The case of the colorblind painter" (Sacks, 1995, Chapter 1). This book also contains many other case studies that would be useful in the sensation/perception unit.

- Blind spot—The ganglion cells' axons combine into the optic nerve and exit through the eyeball, leaving a "blind spot" in our visual field which our brain fills in. Students can map their blind spot at the Serendip web site ⓤ (Bryn Mawr college).
- Depth cues—Stimulus or monocular cues and cues based on the structure of the visual system.

See the "Floating hot dog" and "A dominant eye" classroom learning activities (pp. 105–6) for two demonstrations of binocular disparity.

Annenberg Media's Teachers Resources *Discovering Psychology: #7 Sensation and Perception* ⓤ shows the Ames room, demonstrating perception of distance.

For a fascinating discussion of a woman who regained her binocular vision as an adult, and how she has to "work" to maintain it, see Sacks (2006).

- Grouping principles—The Gestalt grouping principles—principles that allow us to perceive whole patterns rather than individual objects or object components. See Spokane Falls Community College's web site ⓤ for a presentation of grouping principles.

*Hearing.* Converting physical energy from the environment into neural signals resulting in our sensing sounds.

See the BBC web site ⓤ for basic information about hearing and for an interactive "game" demonstrating characteristics of hearing.
See also Insight Media's *Mystery of the Senses: Hearing* ⓤ.
- Deafness—I differentiate between conduction and nerve deafness to explain why conventional hearing aids help people with conduction deafness but not nerve deafness. There is a lot of current research on using cochlear implants to help those with nerve deafness. The National Institute on Deafness and Other Communication Disorders web site ⓤ has a good explanation of cochlear implants. See also Insight Media's 60-minute, 2002 video, *Sense of Hearing: Cochlear Implants.*

*Gustation.* I explain the tongue map *myth* (sweet is perceived at the tip of the tongue, bitter at the back, sour on the sides, and salty all over). In fact taste receptors for all basic tastes are found all over the tongue.

Basic information about taste can be found at the BBC web site ⓤ and in Insight Media's video, *Mystery of the Senses: Taste* ⓤ.
The Taste Science Laboratory web site ⓤ contains good information about taste research.
Insight Media's CD-ROM, *The Gustatory System* ⓤ explores the anatomy of taste and problems with taste disorders.
Research shows that some people are "super tasters" with more taste buds than normal, while others are "nontasters." The BBC web site ⓤ provides an explanation of this phenomenon.

*Olfaction.* The sense of smell is the only sense that does not send its information through the thalamus.

An excellent resource for olfactory information is Tim Jacob's (Cardiff University, UK) web site ⓤ. Also Insight Media's *Mystery of the Senses: Smell* ⓤ.
Sense of Smell Institute's web site ⓤ provides a description of the importance of olfaction and the impact of its loss on normal life.

See "The Dog Beneath the Skin" (Sacks, 1987, Chapter 18).

See the Vivid World of Odors ⓤ and The Memory of Smells ⓤ at the Howard Hughes Medical Institute's web site.

See Olfaction/smell classroom learning activity (pp. 107–9).

• Pheromones—many students believe that humans communicate through pheromones. I discuss the perfume industry, Martha McClintock's seminal research, and current research.

McClintock (1971). May also be accessed at The Museum of Menstruation and Women's Health web site ⓤ.

For an excellent summary of the research on human pheromones, see Benson (2002). This article can also be accessed at the American Psychological Association's web site ⓤ.

*Touch.* Students often think touch is the sense that they need least. So I stress how essential touch is to navigate the world, and even swallow food.

For basic information about touch see the BBC web site ⓤ. See also, Insight Media's *Mystery of the Senses: Touch* ⓤ.

*How Touch Makes Sense of the World* ⓤ (2004) is a 16-minute Films for the Humanities and Sciences video focusing on how touch influences our communication and experience of the world.

*Pain*—For an excellent resource on pain and the history of pain research see the National Institute of Health: National Institute of Neurological Disorder and Stroke's web site ⓤ. Neuroscience for Kid's web site ⓤ also has excellent information on pain.

• Science Daily web site ⓤ has an article outlining individual differences in the perception of pain.

• The *New Scientist's* online magazine webpage ⓤ discusses gender differences in perception of pain. New research shows that men tend to bear pain better than women and that both sexes feel less pain if the painful stimulus is administered by a female.

• The Neuroscience for Kids webpage ⓤ provides an interesting discussion of why red-haired people feel more pain.

*Vestibular.* Our sense of balance helps us interact with the world. We understand how difficult it is to function when we experience dizziness. The BBC web site ⓤ provides interesting information on balance.

*Sensory adaptation*

I ask my students if they can feel their socks or shoes at exactly the moment I asked. Then we talk about our sensory system being set up to respond to changes and why that is adaptive or not adaptive.

*Bottom-up and top-down processing*

Bottom-up processing, using our basic sensory processes to make sense of the world, and top-down processing, using our expectations and experiences, both impose structure on sensory stimuli. See Classroom learning activities on Top-down processing, Top-down processing and expectancy, and Bottom-up and top-down processing: Making sense of subliminal messages, pp. 109–13.

*Geons*. Irving Biederman believed that our bottom-up processing begins with perception of basic structures he termed geons, used to construct a large number of objects. He proposed a "recognition by components" model.

Kimberly Kirkpatrick's (University of York) webpage ⓤ contains pictures of some geons.
See Biederman (1987), which outlines his theory.

*Subliminal perception*. Many students believe that people are influenced by perceptions occurring below threshold. They believe that tapes they play while sleeping telling them to stop smoking or lose weight will work and that advertisers use subliminal "tricks." To disabuse students of this "knowledge" see a University of Michigan students' project web site ⓤ containing a research-based discussion of subliminal perception.

*Attention*

*Divided attention*. Although students "intellectually" understand that dividing attention is difficult, they divide their attention constantly by walking to class listening to their iPod or talking on their cell phone. Since a student on my campus was killed when she stepped in front of a bus while talking on her cell phone, I stress this topic. I assign Mini-assignment #3 ⓦ and use that as a springboard to discuss attentional resources. (New research indicates that "multitasking," dividing attention, does not work as well as previously thought.)

*Eyewitness testimony.* The controversy about eyewitness testimony revolves partly around the issue of attention. If an eye witness was paying attention to unimportant details, then could he or she really be paying attention to the commission of the crime? See Loftus and Doyle (1997).

*Inattentional blindness—change blindness.* When our attention is focused in one particular direction, stimuli that we are not paying attention to may change without us being aware of them. See Simons and Chabris (1999) for a good explanation of these phenomena.

## Illusion/impossible figures
Students are fascinated by the "failures" of our sensory system that lead us to perceive things that aren't there.

A web site ⓤ sponsored by the Shimojo Laboratory at the California Institute of Technology and IllusionWorks, L.L.C. contains an excellent bibliography of articles on impossible figures.

Wolfram MathWorld's web site ⓤ has a good picture of the impossible fork/blivet/Devil's pitchfork and Hayward's interpretation of it.

Jill Britton's web site ⓤ (Camosun College, Canada) contains an excellent collection of M. C. Escher images of impossible figures. You may also find these illusions in Escher (1992).

Other optical illusions and their explanation can be found in Ernst (1986).

The St. Louis arch is a great example of a visual illusion—it looks taller than it is wide, but it is exactly the same distance across that it is high. See the National Park's Service's Arch History and Architectural Information web site ⓤ.

Michael Bach's (University Augenklinik Freiburg) web site ⓤ presents 64 visual illusions.

Stroboscopic motion is also an illusion—flip books are great ways to demonstrate this concept.

## Influence of culture on perception
Because students are often unaware of how culture permeates their lives, I point out that culture determines what we pay attention to, and thus what information we process, and thus our perception of the world. See Triandis (1994, pp. 120–123) for a discussion of culture's impact on perception.

# Classroom Tips

## Stimulus Questions for Discussion

### Sensation and Perception: our gateway to the world

"What is reality?" Because sensation is very personal, I can't really tell what you are sensing. And past experiences and expectations influence perception. So how do I know that the "chair" that I see is seen the same way by you? When I smell a flower, how do I know that you experience the same smell? Is this important? Is it OK if my smell of "lilac" is different than yours? Why or why not? What impact does this have on "reality"?

### Sensation without perception

Because perception and sensation work together, it is often difficult to disassociate the concepts. "Can there be sensation without perception? What about perception without sensation?" Hallucinations are perceptions without sensory stimuli.

Show students a foreign language newspaper, preferably in a language that uses a different alphabet, and ask them what they are seeing. They will be able to sense the strokes on the paper, but unable to make meaning from it—sensing but not perceiving.

Oliver Sacks's story of "Virgil," a man blind since childhood who regained his "vision" as an adult, puts these ideas into perspective. Virgil could not perceive things—he only had visual sensations which he could not put together into a meaningful whole. This story also highlights the importance of a "critical period" for developing perception. (Sacks, 1993; also in Sacks, 1995, pp. 108–153).

Michael May is another individual who experienced "sight" after being blind since childhood. See Gregory (2003). It may also be accessed at the web site ⓤ of the journal *Nature Neuroscience*. See also Kurson (2007). For Mike May's description of his sensations after having his vision "restored" see the Sendero Group web site ⓤ, developed by Mike May.

### Nerve deafness

Research has shown that nerve deafness is associated with exposure to smoke and to loud noises (e.g., earphones for iPods, etc. that are turned up too loud). How would smoke affect hearing? How would loud noises affect hearing?

## Olfaction

The following quote is from someone who lost his sense of smell.

> Sense of smell? . . . I never gave it a thought. You don't normally give it a thought. But when I lost it—it was like being struck blind. Life lost a good deal of its savour—one doesn't realize how much "savour" *is* smell. You *smell* people, you *smell* books, you *smell* the city, you *smell* the spring—maybe not consciously, but as a rich unconscious background to everything else. My whole world was suddenly radically poorer . . . (Sacks, 1987, p. 159)

## Synesthesia

The doctrine of specific nerve energies does not always apply—some individuals taste shapes, smell visions, and so forth. Physiologically, how do you think that could occur? Psychologically, how do you think it would impact your life? See Cytowic (2002, 2003).

## Pain

How would you experience the world if you had no pain? Would this make your world better? Can there be pain if there is no perception? Pain is "subjective"—how can we understand another's pain?

# Some Suggested Classroom Learning Activities

## Sensory adaptation

(2–3 minutes) Bring an air freshener to class (be sure none of your students have chemical allergies) and after class has started spray the room. Ask students if they "smell" the air freshener and if it is a pleasant or unpleasant smell for them. At the end of class, ask how many students were conscious of "smelling" the scent of the air freshener immediately *before* you asked them. This is an example of sensory adaptation.

## Opponent processing

Many of the sensory systems in the body are set up in an opponentprocess structure. The flag and spiral demonstrations illustrate this principle.

*The flag demonstration.* (2 minutes) This illustrates that ganglion cells work in pairs: blue–yellow, black–white, red–green. Have students stare at an "American flag" that is green, black, and yellow.

The Google Images web site ⓤ has visual stimuli (the American flag and others) used to show an "afterimage." Have students stare at the green, black, and yellow flag for a minute. Tell them not to blink. At the end of the minute, have them shift their gaze to a white screen or piece of paper, and blink a couple of times. They will see the red, white, and blue American flag.

*The spiral demonstration.* (10 minutes) This demonstration illustrates the operation of movement detectors in the cortex, and the mutually inhibitory aspect of cells that detect movement in opposite directions.

- Access an online spiral (see, e.g., the Dogfeathers' web site ⓤ).
- Rotate the spiral in front of the students' eyes (so that the spiral appears to be receding from them) for 60 seconds. Be sure that students view the spiral head-on, not from an angle. Tell the students to fix their gaze on the center of the spiral, not to let their eyes move, and not to blink. This will overstimulate cortical cells that detect outward movement.
- After 60 seconds (try not to abbreviate this so everyone can get the effect), ask the students to shift their gaze to some other object, such as your head. When the outward-movement detectors stop firing, there is a tendency for inward-movement detectors to start firing for a few seconds, creating the dramatic illusion that the object the students now look at is moving toward them; most will experience the object as expanding in size. The same effect occurs when, for example, one looks for a long time at falling water; for a few seconds afterward, other objects will appear to be rising.
- Rotating the spiral in the opposite direction (so that it appears to be expanding) creates the opposite effect on the object to which the students shift their gaze: They will see the object as shrinking, or receding.
- To demonstrate that the effect occurs in cortical, not retinal, cells have the students view the spinning spiral with one eye closed. When they look from the spiral to the object they should change which eye is closed. Since the retina that saw the spiral was not the same as the one that saw the object, the effect must take place in the brain.

*Source for activity: Holland (1965); Wohlgemuth (1911). By permission of Houghton Mifflin.*

## Binocular Vision

*The floating hot dog.* (2 minutes) Instruct students to hold their extended index fingers horizontally before their eyes so that the fingertips barely touch. Then they should focus through the fingers onto a distant target and slowly pull the fingers apart. They should see a floating object/image rather like a hot dog between the two fingers. Encourage students to consider why the illusion occurs. Why do illusions occur more generally? Why is it not possible to avoid seeing the "hot dog" once you realize it is an illusion and false? Is it adaptive for our perceptual systems to permit illusions? Why or why not?

*Source for activity: Gardner (1970). By permission of Houghton Mifflin.*

*A dominant eye.* (2 minutes). Have students roll a piece of paper into a tube. Have them look through the tube with both eyes and focus on a distant stimulus (e.g., a spot on the blackboard, a clock on the wall). Have them close one eye and continue looking through the tube. Have them close the other eye and look through the tube. When they close one of their eyes, the stimulus they are focusing on will appear to "shift." This is the nondominant eye.

## Rods and cones—distribution of rods, cones, and color vision in the retina
(5 minutes to gather materials, 2–3 minutes for the demonstration.)

- Gather objects of various primary colors (pens, etc.), and ask for a student volunteer with normal vision.
- Have the student volunteer stand at the front of the room, facing the class. Tell the volunteer to focus his or her eyes on an object at the back of the room and not to move their eyes or head. Point out that this is difficult, so the volunteer will have to concentrate. (Sometimes it is better to have another student face the volunteer, and instruct them to have a "staring contest.")
- Stand directly to the volunteer's left and hold one of the colored objects about four feet away from his or her left ear, at about eye level. (Do not allow the volunteer to see ahead of time what you will be holding.)
- Tell the volunteer that you are holding something in your hand and ask him or her what it is and what color it is. It is very unlikely that the volunteer will be able to answer either question.

Then move forward, in an arc, about a foot and ask the same questions. Continue to move, one foot at a time, in an arc and ask the questions until the volunteer can correctly identify the color. Eventually your movement will place the object directly in front of the volunteer.

- Most volunteer students have excellent peripheral vision, as reflected in their ability to recognize that the object is present even when it is far off to the side. However, for most of them, it will take another step or two before they can recognize what the object is, and one or two more before they can name its color. Most students will be surprised at how close to the center of the visual field the object must be before its color is clearly apparent.

See Blair Broeker and Bernstein (1999) for a discussion of the distribution of rods, cones, and color vision in the retina.

## Olfaction/smell experiment

(I have students begin this experiment as they enter class. It takes about 5–10 minutes of class time.) Smell (olfaction) is an important, but often overlooked, sensory system. I use this demonstration to lead into a discussion of the sex differences in smell discrimination, the impact of aging on smell, and the large cognitive component involved in identifying different odors. Identifying common odors is a much more difficult task than most students anticipate. Research shows that people can identify only about 50% of common odors (Cain, 1982). In addition, although researchers can find no physical, sensory, differences, women tend to "use" their sense of smell better than men (Cain, 1981). Research shows that the ability to smell diminishes as we age—and indeed our sensory capacity decreases. This is important because one study found that aging impaired elderly people's ability to detect gas odors, thus compromising their safety, not to mention their inability to smell spoiled food (Stevens, Cain, & Weinstein, 1987). However, it may also be the case that because cognition "slows" as we age, being unable to retrieve the "odor word" exacerbates this process (Murphy, Cain, Gilmore, & Skinner, 1991; Cain, 1982). In addition, because cognitive labels are important in identifying smells, culture plays a role. A study found that French subjects most frequently identified garlic, caramel, mushroom, and mustard smells, whereas of these only caramel appears on the list from research in the United States (Sulmont-Rosse, Issanchou, & Koster, 2005).

To lead into this discussion, I modified an experiment by William Cain (1981). He compared people's expectations of what odors they would be able to identify with an experiment testing their expectations. He gave 100 women (and he used only women because of their superior performance on odor recognition tasks) the name of 80 products and asked them how easily they thought they could identify those 80 items by smell. Then he asked different groups to identify those 80 items through smell. His original group's top 10 smells expected to be identified were ammonia, coffee, mothballs, perfume, orange, lemon, bleach, vinegar, nail polish remover, and peanut butter. The top 10 smells actually identified were Johnson's baby powder, chocolate, coconut (extract), Crayola crayons, mothballs, Ivory soap, Vicks VapoRub, Bazooka bubble gum, coffee, and caramel.

- I have 16 cheap plastic salt shakers with masking tape around them so the contents cannot be identified, but you could use any small container thats contents can't be seen. Each bottle has a number on it from 1 to 16. In these bottles I put Johnson's baby powder, chocolate, coconut, Crayola crayons, ivory soap, Vicks VapoRub, Bazooka bubble gum, coffee, caramel, ammonia, orange, lemon, bleach, vinegar, and nail polish remover. (I use cotton balls to hold liquid and to keep contents from rolling around and thus being identified by sound.) However, you can use many other substances. See Cain (1981) and Cain and Potts (1996) for a list of common substances.
- I have a handout ⓦ numbered 1 to 16 with a blank line next to each number. I distribute the "bottles" around the classroom before class begins. As students come into class they pick up a handout and read the directions on the overhead ⓦ.

Follow these directions, please!

1. Pick up one of the sheets on the desk as you come into the room.
2. Put your name on it.
3. Move around the room to the locations where "smell bottles" are located. Each bottle has a unique number on it.
4. Smell the bottles (#1-16) and write down what you think the smell is.

Warning! Do *not* shake the bottle, try to look into it, or do anything else to get cues other than olfactory!

Be cautious! Do *not* take a big whiff right away!

- We discuss what smells they knew and did not know. In addition to the cognitive labeling ("tip of the nose" phenomenon), sex differences, and impact of aging issues, students almost always raise the ideas that: smokers and people with allergies have a less acute sense of smell, and that identifiable smells come from past experience (e.g., more women than men will identify the smell of nail polish remover) although I point out that women can also identify odors that are typically identified as male (Cain, 1982). I also make sure to incorporate the biological psychology section by pointing out that smells and memories are associated via the limbic system (one of my students identified the smell of moth-balls as "this smells like my grandmother and it brought back a memory of . . ."). We also talk about some of the problems with the research design, such as all the subjects being women.

## Top-down processing and expectancy

(It takes some time to prepare the images, but only 5–10 minutes of class time.) This activity demonstrates the effect that prior information or expectancy has on the perception and organization of visual information in an ambiguous figure.

- Enlarge and copy each of the seven images ⦿ from Figure 6.1 so that they can be projected to the class.
- Split your class into two groups and ask the students not to make any comments while you alternately show each group some pictures. Ask Group 2 to close their eyes while you show images to Group 1 (the three drawings of men's faces in Figure 6.1a) one at a time for a few seconds each. Ask Group 1 to close their eyes while you show images to Group 2 (the three drawings of female nudes in Figure 6.1a), one at a time for a few seconds each. Ask everyone to open their eyes and to immediately shout out what they see when you project the last image. Show the entire class the ambiguous "Man and Girl" figure (Figure 6.1b).
- Typically, students in Group 1 (students primed with men's faces) will perceive a man's face when shown the ambiguous figure. And, students in Group 2 (students primed with female nudes) will perceive a female figure in the same drawing. Show the entire class the images that were shown separately to Group 1 and to Group 2. This leads into a discussion of the *priming effect*

(a)

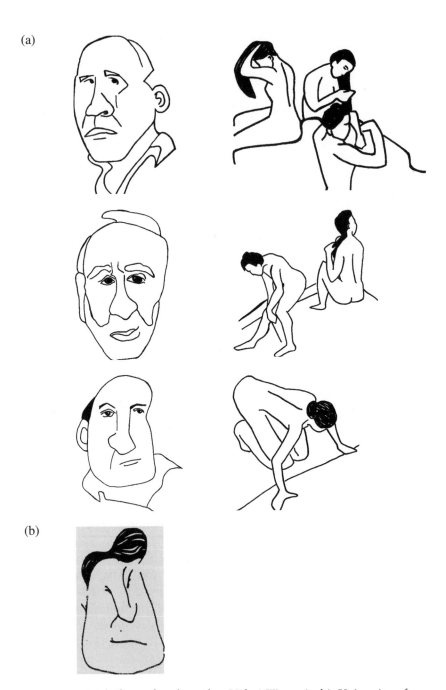

(b)

*Figure 6.1* Male faces, female nudes. Valeri Werpetinski, University of Illinois at Urbana-Champaign; Man and Girl: adapted from Fisher, G. (1967). Preparation of ambiguous stimulus materials. *Perception and psychophysics*, 2, 421–422. Permission Houghton Mifflin.

and *expectancy*. You can also discuss the influence of expectancy and culture on forming differing perceptions of the same stimuli. Connect this demonstration to the *top-down processing* aspect of recognition, and compare this approach to other mechanisms of pattern recognition such as *bottom-up processing* and *parallel distributed processing*.

*Top-down processing.* (5–10 minutes. I would use either the previous demonstration or this one, not both.)

- Divide the class in two and have Group 2 close their eyes while you present the following written instructions (on an overhead or in PowerPoint) to Group 1. "You are going to look briefly at a picture and then answer some questions about it. The picture is a rough sketch of a poster for a trained seal act. Do not dwell on the picture. Look at it only long enough to 'take it all in' once. After this, you will answer *yes* or *no* to a series of questions."
- Group 1 then closes their eyes and Group 2 receives the following written instructions. "You are going to look briefly at a picture and then answer some questions about it. The picture is a rough sketch of a poster for a costume ball. Do not dwell on the picture. Look at it only long enough to 'take it all in' once. After this, you will answer *yes* or *no* to a series of questions."
- The picture shown in Figure 6.2 is presented only for one or two seconds.
- Students are then asked whether or not they saw an automobile (none should), a man (all should), a woman (only the "costume" group), a child (none), an animal (only the "seal" group), a whip ("seal" group), a sword ("costume" group), a man's hat ("costume" group), a ball ("seal" group), a fish ("seal" group). Not all will see the picture they were primed to, but that is because of expectations or experiences that the priming did not influence. A discussion of top-down processing can then follow.

## Bottom-up and top-down processing: Making sense of subliminal messages

(10–15 minutes) In the early 1980s, several fundamentalist Christian ministers insisted that evil and satanic messages were being delivered subliminally in rock music, and that these messages were easily heard when the music was played backward. Two psychologists, Vokey and Read from the University of Lethbridge in Canada, were consulted

*Figure 6.2* Couple in costume or seal act. Permission Houghton Mifflin.

by a local radio announcer who asked them whether such claims were valid or not. The researchers did *not* explore the specific question of whether indeed satanic messages were embedded in rock music. Rather they examined the broader question of whether listeners were influenced by a subliminal message and whether the message was easily heard or was more a product of active construction. They found that, first, there was "no evidence that listeners were influenced consciously or unconsciously by the content of the backward message," and second, "People do hear intelligible phrases in streams of backward speech" (Vokey & Read, 1985, pp. 1236, 1237) but they *cannot* be induced to hear just anything in the backward speech. In other words, there must be sounds that could be constructed into the particular phrases. But most importantly they found that most people do *not* hear the phrases in the backward speech *unless* they have been prepared to hear them.

Vokey and Read (1985) created an interesting classroom demonstration to show the top-down processing that occurs when listening to ambiguous stimuli such as backward speech. Selections and the phrase they are said to contain appear below. First, play the selection forward for the students, asking if anyone heard any messages other than the forward words being spoken. Next, play the same passage backward, asking students if they think they heard anything. About 5 to 10% will report having heard something. This is a good opportunity to discuss bottom-up processing, wherein they are trying to piece together something, but without an expectation for what they should be listening for. Last, give the students the expected phrase and repeat playing the passage backwards. Students find this fascinating, since about 90% or more of them can hear the expected phrase now. Here are examples of the recording and its expected phrase.

*Another One Bites the Dust*   It's fun to smoke marijuana.
*Jabberwocky*   Saw a girl with a weasel in her mouth.
*Revolution*   Turn me on, dead man.
*Stairway to Heaven*   My sweet satan; 666
*Mr. Ed Theme*   He's so nuts; Beelzebub

The findings of Vokey and Read suggest that top-down processing is responsible for people's ability to hear particular messages in backward speech. Some students will believe they have heard something, but this tends to be relatively rare. After you present the expectation, then most students will hear the expected phrase, thus illustrating the power of top-down processing.

You can obtain a CD of forward and backward messages by contacting Blackwell or see the web site.

*Source for activity: By permission of Houghton Mifflin Ⓤ.*

## Divided attention/Stroop task

(5–10 minutes) Pick a volunteer and provide two tasks—one that involves dividing attention and one that does not. The traditional Stroop task divides attention (seeing color words in colors different from the word's meaning, e.g., the word "blue" in green ink). Thus the volunteer is both reading a color word and seeing an ink color and must only give the color, not the word's meaning. This task should take volunteers some time as they process saying the word and ignoring the color. However, if you pick words from a foreign language and have these words printed in colored ink, volunteers should easily be able to tell you the word's color since they are not dividing their attention.

## Possible Mini-assignments (Written or Groups)

🐵 *Mini-assignment #1*
You have been told that you must give up one of your senses.

1. Which one would you choose not to have?
2. Why would you choose this sense and not one of the others?
3. Describe the physiological processes/physical structures that would be affected by your lack of this sense.

🐵 *Mini-assignment #2*
Find a television station such as CNN, Fox News, or CNBC that has information continually moving across the bottom of the screen. Concentrate on watching this "crawl" for two minutes. Then look at a stationary object in the room, or at a page of newsprint. Does that object or the page appear to move? In what direction does it move? Write a paragraph describing what you saw and, based on what you have read in the chapter about opponent processes in vision, explain why this illusion occurs.

*Source for activity: By permission of Houghton Mifflin.*

🐵 *Mini-assignment #3*
Listen to a "talk radio" station for about 5 minutes, and jot down the main points being discussed. Next, call a friend on the phone and have a 5-minute conversation while you also try to keep track of the discussion on the radio. When the call is over, try to write down the main points of what you heard on the radio. Compare these notes with the notes you took earlier. Why do you think it was so difficult to keep track of both conversations at once? Would it have been easier to, say, bounce a ball or make a salad while talking on the phone? If so, why? Write a paragraph or two describing the difficulties in dividing attention.

*Source for activity: By permission of Houghton Mifflin.*

🐵 *Mini-assignment #4*
Go to the BBC webpage Ⓤ at http://www.bbc.co.uk/science/ humanbody/body/interactives/senseschallenge/ and take the "Senses Challenge." What was your score? Which questions did you miss? Explain why you missed the question and what the correct answer is. Do this in your own words.

## ⑩ Mini-assignment #5

Eye witness testimony, when someone actually sees another person committing a crime, is very influential in trials. However, psychologists have found that many eye witnesses provide incorrect information— sometimes even incorrectly identifying the person who committed the crime. Using the information you learned about perception and attention write a paragraph explaining how an "eye witness" could perceive incorrect information.

## Handout

⑩ Handout #1 Review of Sensory Modalities

## References

Ackerman, D. (1991). *A natural history of the senses*. New York: Vintage Books.

Benson, E. (2002). Pheromones in context. *APA Monitor, 33*(9), 46.

Biederman, I. (1987). Recognition-by-components: A theory of human image understanding. *Psychological Review, 94*, 115–147.

Blair Broeker, C., & Bernstein, D. (1999). Distribution of rods, cones, and color vision in the retina. In L. Benjamin, B. Nodine, R. Ernst, & C. Blair Broeker (Eds.), *Activities for the teaching of psychology, Vol. 4* (pp. 125–126). Washington, DC: American Psychological Association.

Cain, W. (1981). Educating your nose. *Psychology Today, 15*(7), 48–56.

Cain, W. (1982). Odor identification by males and females: Predictions vs. performance. *Chemical Senses, 7*(2), 129–142.

Cain, W., & Potts, B. (1996). Switch and bait: Probing the discriminative basis of odor identification via recognition memory. *Chemical Senses, 21*, 35–44.

Cytowic, R. (2002). *Synesthesia: A union of the senses* (2nd ed.). Cambridge, MA: MIT Press.

Cytowic, R. (2003). *The man who tasted shapes* (2nd ed.). Cambridge, MA: MIT Press.

Ernst, B. (1986). *The eye beguiled: Optical illusions*. Cologne, Germany: Benedikt Taschen.

Escher, M. C. (1992). *M. C. Escher: The graphic work*. Cologne, Germany: Benedikt Taschen.

Gardner, M. (1970). Of optical illusions, from figures that are undecidable to hot dogs that float. *Scientific American, 222*, 124–127.

Gregory, R. (2003). Seeing after blindness. *Nature Neuroscience, 6*, 909–910.

Holland, H. (1965). *The spiral after-effect*. Oxford: Pergamon Press.

Kurson, R. (2007). *Crashing through—A true story of risk, adventure, and the man who dared to see*. New York: Random House.

Loftus, E., & Doyle, J. (1997). *Eyewitness testimony: Civil and criminal* (3rd ed.). Charlottesville, VA: Lexis Law Publishing.

McClintock, M. (1971). Menstrual synchrony and suppression. *Nature, 229,* 244–245.

Murphy, C., Cain, W., Gilmore, M., & Skinner, R. (1991). Sensory and semantic factors in recognition memory for odors and graphic stimuli: Elderly versus young persons. *American Journal of Psychology, 104*(2), 161–192.

Sacks, O. (1987). *The man who mistook his wife for a hat.* New York: Harper & Row.

Sacks, O. (1993). A neurologist's notebook: To see and not see. *New Yorker, May 10,* 59–73.

Sacks, O. (1995). *An anthropologist on Mars.* New York: Vintage Books.

Sacks, O. (2006). Stereo Sue. *The New Yorker, 82*(8), 64–73.

Simons, D., & Chabris, C. (1999). Gorillas in our midst: Sustained inattentional blindness for dynamic events. *Perception, 28,* 1059–1074.

Stevens, J., Cain, W., & Weinstein, D. E. (1987). Aging impairs the ability to detect gas odors. *Fire Technology, 23,* 198–204.

Sulmont-Rosse, C., Issanchou, S., & Koster, E. (2005). Odor naming methodology: Correct identification with multiple-choice versus repeatable identification in a free task. *Chemical Senses, 30,* 23–25.

Triandis, H. (1994). *Culture and social behavior.* New York: McGraw-Hill.

Vokey, J., & Read, J. (1985). Subliminal messages: Between the devil and the media. *American Psychologist, 40,* 1231–1239.

Wohlgemuth, A. (1911). On the after-effect of seen movement. *British Journal of Psychology,* Monograph Supplement 1.

## Additional Suggested Readings for Instructors

Association for Psychological Science. List of teaching resources for sensation and perception: http://psych.hanover.edu/APS/teaching.html#sensation

Brandreth, G., DiSpezio, M., Joyce, K., Kay, K., Parquin, C. (2003). *Classic optical illusions.* New York: Main Street/Sterling. This book contains a nice compendium of optical illusions.

British Broadcasting Corporation. Sensation and perception information and student activities. http://www.bbc.co.uk/science/humanbody/

Piatelli-Palmarini, M. (1994). *Inevitable illusions: How mistakes of reason rule our mind.* New York: Wiley. The author goes beyond optical illusions to talk about cognitive illusions.

Wolfe, J., Kluender, K., Levi, D., Bartoshuk, L., Herz, R., Klatzky, R., & Lederman, S. (2005). *Sensation and perception.* Sunderland, CT: Sinauer Associates. This is an excellent sensation and perception textbook that can be used as a reference.

# Chapter 7

# Consciousness, Motivation, and Emotion

## Getting Started

Research on consciousness tends to center on three questions: What is the relationship between the conscious mind and the physical brain? Is consciousness a unified phenomenon or many different ones? What is the relationship between conscious and unconscious mental activities? I present material to encourage my students to consider these issues.

I approach the concept of sleep from a sleep deprivation perspective because almost all of my students are continually sleep deprived. I present research that shows, not just the biological impact of chronic sleep deprivation, but also the cognitive impact. Thus I ask my students to track their sleep cycles and evaluate changes they might want to make in their sleep patterns.

Another goal of mine is to have my students understand that we process information even when we are in a state of unconsciousness. However, I want them to be skeptical about the "subliminal tapes" that promise that listening to them while you sleep will help you lose weight or stop smoking.

Consciousness is an easy unit to teach because my students are inherently interested in sleep, dreams, hypnosis, psychoactive drugs, and so forth. The trick is to contain student discussion!

Because motivation is implicit—difficult to view from outside the person—students often do not see its importance. My student study groups "teach" the theories of motivation to the rest of the class and explain behaviors based on those theories. I also spend time discussing achievement motivation and parental influence on its development. I present emotions as passions that happen to us whether we want them or not. And I am in the process of incorporating more information into my course about happiness—something very relevant to students. Of course, we also discuss the impact of culture on both motivation and emotion.

There are many topics in motivation and emotion and I do not choose to discuss sexual behavior/motivation in class. However, if you do so, be very clear in your terminology. Do not use "cute words" but treat the subject in a professional manner. Be aware that some students will be embarrassed and you need to be sensitive to this.

## My outline for teaching (3 days—75 minute classes)

*Day 1*

Directions on board: Take a handout, complete it, and return it face down. *No names.* (See Achievement motivation classroom learning activity, pp. 136–7.) Collect for use in 2 class days.

Questions from previous class (5 minutes)

Practice questions over material (5 minutes)

Administrivia (5 minutes)

   I.  Definition of consciousness (5 minutes)

  II.  Levels of consciousness (10 minutes)

      Pre/un—sub/non

 III.  States of consciousness (25 minutes)

      Introduction

      Daydreaming

      Sleep

- Stages
- Ⓦ Mini-assignment #1—Mean number of hours slept

      Sleep deprivation

      Scoring the sleep quiz

- Melatonin
- Sleep disorders (Don't list these, let students supply them.)

      Insomnia

      Hypersomnia

      Narcolepsy

Sleep apnea
Nightmares
Night terrors
Sleepwalking
REM behavior disorder
IV.  Dreams (20 minutes)
Doris's Dream (See Classroom learning activity, pp. 134–6)

*Day 2*
Directions on board: Take a piece of paper and write down three
reasons you came to this college (See Theories of motivation class-
room learning activity)
Questions from previous class (5 minutes)
Practice questions over material (5 minutes)
Administrivia (5 minutes)
I.  Psychoactive drugs (10 minutes)
Agonist, antagonist, re-uptake blocker, etc.
II.  Definitions of motivation (5 minutes)
III.  Maslow's hierarchy of needs (10 minutes)
Use their "Reasons for coming to college" (See Theories of
motivation classroom learning activity, p. 136.)
IV.  Motivation—biological aspects (15 minutes)
Eating disorders
V.  Theories of motivation (Classify student reasons for coming to
college by theory or have student groups present important
points of each theory.) (20 minutes)
Instinct/evolutionary
Drive reduction
Arousal
Incentive
Opponent process

*Day 3*
Questions from previous class (5 minutes)
Practice questions over material (5 minutes)
Administrivia (5 minutes)
I.  Achievement motivation (10 minutes)
Definitions
Achievement motivation classroom learning activity
II.  Motivational conflicts (10 minutes)
III.  Emotion: lie detection (15 minutes)
Lie detection demonstration classroom learning activity

IV. Theories of emotion (15 minutes)
   Comparison of James's, Cannon's, and Schachter's Theories
V  Biological aspects of emotion (10 minutes)

## My transitions

I teach these units separately. I follow the sensation and perception unit with consciousness. After consciousness I teach learning and memory, cognition and cognitive abilities, and then motivation and emotion. I find the motivation and emotion chapter to be a good segue into stress and coping. I think that these units are independent enough to be used in almost any order.

## Topics typically included in this unit

*Theories of consciousness*: Materialism, dualism, theater view, parallel distributed processing models

*Levels of consciousness*: Conscious, preconscious, nonconscious, unconscious/subconscious

*Mental processing without awareness*: Priming, blindsight, subliminal

*Neuropsychology of consciousness*: Coma, prosopagnosia, brain damage

*Sleep*: Stages—1–4, REM; sleep disorders—insomnia, narcolepsy, sleep apnea, sudden infant death syndrome (SIDS), nightmares, night terrors, REM behavior disorder; why sleep is necessary— biological restoration, consolidate new learning; circadian rhythms and jet lag; sleep deprivation

*Dreams and dreaming*: Dream attributes—story-like, creative insights; lucid dreaming; theories—wish fulfillment, activation-synthesis

*Hypnosis*: Hypnotic susceptibility; age regression; posthypnotic suggestions; posthypnotic amnesia; theories—state, role, dissociation; applications—pain reduction

*Meditation*: Mantras, stress reduction

*Psychoactive drugs*: Psychopharmacology—blood–brain barrier; effects—substance abuse, psychological dependence, addiction, withdrawal syndrome, tolerance; expectations and drug effects; depressants—alcohol, barbiturates, GHB (Gamma hydroxybutyrate); stimulants—amphetamines, cocaine, caffeine, nicotine, MDMA (Ecstasy); opiates—heroin, morphine; hallucinogens—LSD, ketamine, marijuana

*Motivation*: Intervening variable

*Sources of motivation*: Biological factors; emotional factors; cognitive factors; social factors

*Instinct theory of motivation*: Fixed-action patterns, evolutionary approach

*Drive reduction theory*: Homeostasis, need, drive, primary drives, secondary drives

*Arousal theory*: Optimal level; performance and arousal

*Incentive theory*: Wanting and liking; positive and negative incentives

*Biological signals for hunger and satiety*: Stomach signals, signals from the blood—cholecystokinin (CCK), leptin; brain—lateral and ventromedial nuclei in the hypothalamus, paraventricular nucleus in the hypothalamus, serotonin

*Flavor, cultural learning, and food selection*: Appetite; specific hungers; food culture

*Eating disorders*: Obesity, anorexia nervosa, bulimia nervosa

*Sexual behavior*: Biology of sex—sexual response cycle, sex hormones —estrogen, progestins, androgens; social and cultural factors; sexual orientation—heterosexual, bisexual, homosexual; sexual dysfunction—erectile disorder, premature ejaculation, arousal disorder

*Achievement motivation*: Need for achievement, development, goal setting, success in a work setting, subjective well-being

*Relations and conflicts among motives*: Maslow's hierarchy—biological, safety, belongingness and love, esteem, self-actualization; approach–approach, avoidance–avoidance, approach–avoidance, multiple approach–avoidance conflicts

*Opponent processes in motivation and emotion*

*Characteristics of emotion*: Temporary, positive or negative, cognitive interpretation, alters thought processes, trigger action tendency, passions not decisions

*Biology of emotion*: Brain mechanisms—limbic system, amygdala, pyramidal motor system, extrapyramidal motor system, hemispheres; autonomic nervous system—sympathetic, parasympathetic, fight-or-flight syndrome

*Theories of emotion*: James's peripheral theory—facial feedback hypothesis, lie detection; Cannon's central theory—thalamus; cognitive theories—Schachter-Singer theory—attributions, excitation transfer, cognitive appraisal theories

*Communicating emotion*: Innate expressions—Duchenne smile, disgust, anger; social and cultural influences; learning about emotion —emotion culture, social referencing

## Some options for organizing the concepts

*By topic*: These two units can actually be stand-alone units and taught almost anywhere in the curriculum. I typically teach consciousness after perception and before learning, and I teach motivation and emotion as a lead-in to health, stress, and coping. However, consciousness could be taught immediately before motivation and emotion, or almost anywhere else you find appropriate.

# Teaching the Content

Remember that the ⓦ symbol means that a printable version is available on the web site (www.blackwellpublishing.com/lucas) and ⓤ means that the URL is available on the web site.

## Topics that many students will find difficult

### Theories of consciousness
Consciousness is difficult to define. For a good discussion of what consciousness is and a synopsis of the research, see Crick and Koch (2002). See also the film *The Final Mystery: What is Consciousness?* ⓤ, a discussion of what consciousness actually is and how remarkable it is.

### How psychoactive drugs work
Many students will have difficulty with the concepts of agonists, antagonists, and re-uptake inhibitors. It's helpful to have diagrams of these actions as well as at least one example of each.

A good biological psychology book, such as Kalat (2004), provides more in-depth information about how psychoactive drugs work to alter behavior.

Another reference is Stringer (2005). Chapter 2 explains the basic theory and Part IV provides details about drugs that act on the central nervous system.

A nice demonstration of psychoactive drugs' influence on the brain can be seen in a 25-minute video from Films for the Humanities and Sciences titled *Animated Neuroscience and the Action of Nicotine, Cocaine, and Marijuana in the Brain* ⓤ.

### Opponent process theory of motivation
While the other theories of motivation seem to "make sense," opponent process theory is less intuitively clear to some students. I

talk about this theory last and use it to bridge my discussion of motivation and emotion. Richard Solomon's basic ideas are that any reaction to a stimulus is followed by an opposite reaction and that after repeated exposure to the same stimulus, the initial reaction wanes and the opponent process becomes stronger. Thus, when a person first parachutes, they experience intense fear, but then relief when they land safely. After repeated parachuting, the fear weakens, and the relief becomes stronger. Another classic example is drug abuse. When a person first takes a psychoactive drug they experience a "high" which wears off and is followed by a "low." As the person continues to use the drug, the "high" becomes shorter and the "low" occurs more quickly. Soon the person is taking the drug, not only to achieve the "high" but also to avoid the "low." See Solomon (1974).

## Biological motives

Understanding the biological basis for hunger provides students with an understanding of obesity and eating disorders. However, remembering the brain structures that have an impact on eating behavior can be difficult for some students.

The hypothalamus is central for biological motives. The lateral nucleus is often thought of as the "start eating center" (thus if it is destroyed the animal will not eat, and if it is stimulated the animal will overeat). The ventromedial nucleus is often thought of as the "stop eating center" (thus if it is destroyed the animal will overeat, and if it is stimulated the animal will not eat). The paraventricular nucleus (PVN) is important in regulating "specific hungers".

## Sexual behavior

Typical topics include: sex hormones—androgens, estrogens, and progestins; the sexual response cycle and how it differs for males and females; social and cultural factors in sexuality including attitudes, mores, etc.; and sexual orientation and its origin. The idea that sexual orientation may be prewired and that homosexuality is *not* considered a psychological disorder is something that students need to hear. See the University of Chicago survey on sexual behavior within the United States (Laumann, Gagnon, Michael, & Michaels, 1994). See also Laumann and Michael (2000).

## Theories of emotion

Distinguishing among the three major theories of emotion (James–Lange, Cannon–Bard, and cognitive) is difficult for many students. I highlight the similarities and differences to help students differentiate the theories.

1.  James–Lange or peripheral theory is counterintuitive to most students. The idea that you have a perception (I see a bear) that causes a peripheral response (change in facial expression, increased heart rate) which is then perceived and the emotion is felt (I am afraid) is not obvious. It is often expressed as "I am afraid because I run from the bear." This theory postulates that every emotion has a slightly different physiological "identity." Changing Minds web site ⓤ presents a nice summary of this theory. One of the variations of the James–Lange theory is the facial feedback hypothesis—involuntary facial movement provides enough peripheral information to create an emotional experience.
2.  Cannon–Bard or central theory—Walter Cannon and Philip Bard believed that the experience of emotion starts in the thalamus which then activates the autonomic nervous system and the cerebral cortex at the same time. Research has shown that there really is no one "emotion center" in the brain, but that there are widespread connections throughout the brain. See Insight Media's *Emotion* ⓤ (2001), a 30-minute video that discusses the nature of emotion and compares the James–Lange and Cannon–Bard theories of emotion, or *Emotion* ⓤ (2006) for a more integrated discussion of what is an emotion.
3.  Cognitive theories—Stanley Schachter believed that emotions have a cognitive component. Unlike William James, he believed that generalized arousal could be cognitively interpreted as several different emotions. He stressed cognitive interpretation of the arousal. Cognitive appraisal theory stresses that cognitive interpretation of the event itself (not the arousal) is most important in shaping emotional experiences.

## Communication of emotion

Some emotional expressions seem to be innate while others are learned and have cultural implications. Research suggests that the smile is related to positive emotion, the "long" face associated with sadness, and disgust seems to lead to the same type of facial contortion across cultures. The facial expression of anger also tends to be innate.

*   Emotion culture—rules that govern what emotions are appropriate in what circumstances and what emotional expressions are

allowed vary from culture to culture and even differ according to gender and age within a culture.

- Social referencing is the idea of letting another's emotional state guide our own, especially when we are in an ambiguous situation. Babies and children often "social reference" their mother when in a new situation. See the visual-cliff studies where infants were urged to cross an area that appeared to be a cliff—and they looked at their mother's expressions for guidance as to whether or not they should crawl over the area. See Gibson and Walk (1960). See also the MSN Encarta web site ⓤ for a picture of an infant in the visual-cliff experiment.

*Biology of emotion*

For many students, these concepts are difficult to remember. I emphasize only the major aspects:

- The limbic system, especially the amygdala, is central to emotion.
- Controlling emotional and nonemotional facial expressions is controlled by the pyramidal (voluntary movements) motor system and *extra*pyramidal (*in*voluntary movements) motor system. (A helpful mnemonic is matching the prefixes, "extra is in.")
- The right cerebral hemisphere seems to be more important in experiencing and expressing emotion. However, the left cerebral hemisphere might be more important in experiencing positive emotion.
- The sympathetic nervous system and parasympathetic nervous system, part of the autonomic nervous system, also play a role. The sympathetic nervous system prepares the body for "flight or fight."
- *In the Heat of the Moment: The Biochemistry of Feeling* ⓤ (2000) (Films for the Humanities and Sciences) discusses the importance of brain structures and neurotransmitters in experiencing emotion.

## Other important topics in consciousness

*Sleep*

An excellent general resource on sleep—functions, stages, and so forth—can be found at the Neuroscience for Kids web site ⓤ. Other general sleep web resources include the National Sleep Foundation web site ⓤ, the American Academy of Sleep Medicine web site ⓤ, the Sleep Research Society web site ⓤ, and Sleep Medicine Home Page ⓤ.

- Sleep stages—the stages of sleep and a "typical night's sleep." See ThinkQuest (Oracle's Education Foundation web site ⓤ) and, of course, the standard graphic of a "typical night's sleep" found in Cartwright (1978). There is a wonderful internet resource from the National Sleep Foundation titled *Sleeping and Waking with the Doze Family* ⓤ that demonstrates the effect of age, shift work, caffeine, alcohol, and stress on sleep.
- *The Biology of Sleep* ⓤ (Insight Media) is a 30-minute video that looks at sleep patterns and how they change across the life-span.
- See *Consciousness* ⓤ (Insight Media), a 30-minute video that discusses stages of sleep, sleep disorders, and circadian rhythms.
- Sleep is important in the consolidation of new learning of spoken language. See Fenn, Nusbaum, and Margoliash (2006). This article may also be accessed at the web site of the journal, *Nature* ⓤ.
- Sleep helps improve memory. See Science Daily web site ⓤ.

*Melatonin.* Melatonin has been touted as helping with the rhythms of sleep and in decreasing jet lag. However, there has not been research on the long-term effects of the drug and it is not regulated by the FDA, so that adds additional concerns. See the Family Doctor (sponsored by the American Academy of Family Physicians) web site ⓤ and the National Sleep Foundation web site ⓤ for a discussion of what melatonin is and how it impacts sleep.

*Sleep disorders.* Students are fascinated with sleep disorders so I spend time discussing them, especially sleep deprivation.

Sleep deprivation—Have your students keep a sleep journal for a week (see ⓦ Mini-assignment #1). Many students are chronically sleep deprived and I think it is important that they understand the consequences. Coren (1996) is an accessible book about the problems of sleep deprivation. See also *The Sleep Famine* ⓤ (2000) (Films for the Humanities and Sciences) and *Sleep Disorders* ⓤ (Insight Media), a 28-minute video explaining the major sleep disorders. For a discussion of the impact of sleep deprivation on physical health see VanDongen, Maislin, Mullington, and Dinges (2003), which is also available at the APA web site ⓤ. Sleep deprivation also impacts your ability to perform physical tasks— such as swinging a golf club. See the APA web site ⓤ.

Insomnia—inability to go to sleep or to stay asleep. For some tips on combating insomnia see the U.S. Department of Health and Human Services' Women's Health web site ⓤ.

Nightmares—these occur in REM sleep, involve a dream that causes extreme fear and/or anxiety, and usually occur in the early morning hours (when you are spending more time in REM sleep). See Medline Plus ⓤ, a National Institute of Health web site.

Night terrors—distinct from nightmares, night terrors are not dream-like and occur in Stage 4 sleep, not REM. Typically more males than females experience night terrors. See Medline Plus ⓤ, a National Institute of Health web site.

SIDS—the leading cause of death in babies over a month old. The "Back to Sleep" campaign, putting sleeping babies on their backs, has decreased the incidence of SIDS. See the National Institute of Child Health and Human Development (National Institute of Health) web site ⓤ.

REM behavior disorder—the sleeper's muscles do not become paralyzed, as is normal, during REM sleep, making it possible to act out dreams—most common among older males and tends to be caused by diseases that affect myelin. See the National Sleep Foundation web site ⓤ.

Apnea—the sleeper wakes up hundreds of times throughout the night, but is not consciously aware of this. Research shows that sleep apnea can lead to severe health problems—including an enlarged heart. For a discussion of sleep apnea, its effects, and treatments see the Mayo Clinic ⓤ and the NIH ⓤ web sites. In addition, there is new evidence that children experiencing sleep apnea may have decreased mental development. See the NIH web site ⓤ.

Narcolepsy—victims suddenly enter REM sleep, thus paralyzing the body. See the National Institute of Neurological Disorders and Stroke (NIH) web site ⓤ for a discussion of narcolepsy and its current treatments. This web site also provides links to current research literature.

*Human circadian rhythms.* Understanding basic information about circadian rhythms can help students understand the impact of shift work and jet lag. For general information see Round-the-Clock Systems ⓤ and the National Sleep Foundation ⓤ web sites.

Shift work—for general discussion of the impact of shift work on sleep patterns see the National Sleep Foundation web site ⓤ.

A study of how hormonal changes affect shift workers can be found at the Association for Psychological Science web site ⓤ.

Zeitgebers are external time cues that have an impact on our sleep/wake cycle. See Sharma and Chandrashekaran (2005) for an interesting discussion.

Jet lag, or the effect on your body from crossing multiple time zones, can be debilitating. For information on jet lag see the National Sleep Foundation web site ⓤ. In addition, jet lag has a negative impact on cognitive functioning. See Cho, Ennaceur, Cole, and Suh (2000). This is also on the *Journal of Neuroscience* web site ⓤ.

*Dreams.* Many students will be convinced that they can interpret their dreams. A discussion of the latent (actual dream) and manifest (meaning) content and of Freud's emphasis on dream interpretation is always of interest. However, it is important to make a balanced presentation, so I also explain the activation-synthesis theory of dreaming. See Freud (1915/1980). See also *Dreams: Theater of the Night* ⓤ (Films for the Humanities and Sciences), a 28-minute video that discusses what dreams are, what they mean, and Freud's theory.

## Hypnosis

Theories typically presented in introductory textbooks—state, role, and dissociation—are discussed in Gruzelier (2000) and Kirsch and Lynn (1995).

## Psychoactive drugs

Students have been exposed to antidrug messages since grade school and yet many of them know little about addiction or abuse. This is important information for them.

A 25-minute video *Under the Influence: The Science of Drug Abuse* ⓤ and *Addiction and the Human Brain* ⓤ (Insight Media) are two videos showing the physical attributes of addiction and discussing why adolescents are at the highest risk for drug addiction.

The National Institute on Drug Abuse ⓤ has an excellent web site detailing the effects of cocaine on the brain.

Alcohol and the adolescent brain—recent research has indicated that adolescent alcohol abuse has special significance—it "wreaks havoc" in the hippocampus and impairs memory formation. Since

many of our adolescent students do drink this is important information. See APS Staff (2001).

## Other important topics in motivation

### Maslow's hierarchy of needs/motives

Although modern psychologists consider Maslow's hierarchy to be
simplistic, it is a great way to organize motives and give students a
framework for thinking about motives—physiological → safety →
belongingness → esteem → self-actualization. It gives students a
different perspective on social issues—when thinking that lower
motives, like hunger and shelter, must be met before higher motives
become important.

### Theories of motivation

I talk about drive-reduction theory, evolutionary theory (with a
reference to instinct theory, its antecedent), arousal, incentive, and
opponent-process theories.

For a general overview of theories of motivation, see *Motivation* Ⓤ
(Insight Media), a 30-minute video.

Drive reduction—homeostasis (all physiological systems in balance
or at equilibrium) becomes imbalanced, creating a need (physiological) which leads to a drive (psychological—creating an arousal),
leading to behavior to satisfy the need and achieve homeostasis.

Primary drives are physiological, while secondary drives are learned—
associated with reducing a primary drive. Money and grades are
good examples of secondary drives.

Evolutionary theory—the idea that we are motivated by inborn factors,
especially a desire to maximize our genetic contributions, is a
different approach to motivation. See David Buss's homepage Ⓤ.
See especially his interview on teaching evolutionary psychology
(Barker, 2006). See also Bernard, Mills, Swenson, & Walsh (2005).

Arousal theory—everyone has an optimal level of arousal and
those with high internal arousal need less external stimulation,
while those with low internal arousal need more external stimulation. An example is Ritalin—a stimulant being given to people
with ADHD. The *very* simplistic explanation is that with higher
internal stimulation (caused by the Ritalin), those with ADHD
aren't forced to seek external stimulation. This example resonates
with students.

Incentive theory—this theory makes the most sense to students. While other theories are considered "internal" this theory is external—going along with the behaviorist idea of rewards and punishments. Students believe that they are more likely to be motivated if there is an external reward for it, such as paying students for grades in an attempt to increase their motivation to study. However, some research shows that extrinsic rewards can decrease intrinsically motivating behaviors. See Deci (1971).

### Achievement motivation

Students are fascinated with the idea of achievement motivation and the role of culture in encouraging the development of such motivation. I talk about Henry Murray's needs model (including need for achievement, or nach) and David McClelland's research on achievement motivation; how women vary (Dweck's research); and parental influence on the development of need for achievement. See the Tripod.com web site ⓤ for a short description of Murray's needs model and the Thematic Apperception Test he developed. See also Shneidman (1980) and McClelland (1961). For a discussion of women and achievement motivation see Dweck (2000).

### Job motivation

Understanding that one's job can have both positive (satisfiers) and negative (dissatisfiers) aspects is not intuitive to most students. I assign ⓦ Mini-assignment #5, asking students to analyze a job they have held as a lead-in to a discussion of this topic. Although this is not a standard introductory psychology topic, I think it has important application to students' future lives. See Spector (1997).

### Motives in conflict

Students typically understand the idea of conflicting motives. I have them provide examples of approach–approach (they are invited to two great parties occurring at the same time in separate cities); avoidance–avoidance (they have a bad tooth and have to bear that pain or the pain of going to the dentist to get it treated); approach–avoidance (they can go to a concert that has been sold out for months, but it is with someone they really don't like); and multiple approach–avoidance (they are offered a great job in a terrible city or a mediocre job in a great city). They often confuse approach–avoidance—one event has both attractive and unattractive features—with multiple approach-avoidance, in which a choice has to be made between two or more alternatives, each of which has both positive and negative features.

### Eating disorders

Because many of our students are vulnerable to developing eating disorders, or possibly already have an eating disorder, I talk about anorexia nervosa, bulimia, binge eating disorder, and obesity. I also talk about how "culture" defines beauty—for example, that "Miss Americas" from the 1950s weighed considerably more than those current—and were considered beautiful.

The National Institute of Health has a webpage ⓤ that provides the latest research on eating disorders.

See also *Dying to Be Thin* ⓤ, a 60-minute video which looks at the psychological aspects of eating disorders, the damage they cause to the body, and therapies. *Eating Disorders* ⓤ (Insight Media) is a 28-minute video that defines eating disorders and treatments and has students who have suffered from eating disorders discuss their experiences.

Obesity has become more of a problem in recent years. For general information see the Center for Disease Control web site ⓤ and The American Obesity Association web site ⓤ.

## Other important topics in emotion

### What is an emotion?

Emotions are temporary, positive or negative, triggered partly by your thoughts, alter thought processes, trigger an action tendency, and are passions that happen to you. See *Emotion* ⓤ (Insight Media, 2006), a 30-minute video exploring what constitutes an emotion.

Disgust—Paul Rozin has done extensive studies of disgust and the cultural influence on disgust. For a comprehensive discussion of disgust see Rozin, Haidt, & McCauley (2000). For pictures that tend to promote disgust you can go to Dr. Val Curtis's (London School of Hygiene and Tropical Medicine) web site ⓤ. For a discussion of "disgust" as an emotion go to the University of Pennsylvania's Arts and Sciences' webpage ⓤ.

Positive emotions—Martin Seligman and Edward Diener have presented research on positive psychology and happiness. See Seligman and Csikszentmihalyi (2000), Diener and Diener (1995), Diener and Seligman (2004).

Emotion and gender—recent research suggests that there might be a gender bias in perceiving emotion. Observers more quickly see anger on male faces and happiness on female faces. See Becker, Kenrick, Neuberg, Blackwell, and Smith (2007).

### Lie detection

Students are fascinated with the idea of lie detection. Sophisticated polygraphs have been developed, using more basic biological information. See the How Stuff Works web site ⓤ for an in-depth discussion of how lie detectors work. See also *Why we lie* ⓤ (2002, Insight Media), a 50-minute DVD that discusses why people lie and demonstrates polygraphs, facial analysis, and ways of detecting lies. For further reading see Etcoff, Ekman, Magee, and Frank (2000), Farwell and Donchin (1991), and Grubin and Madsen (2005).

# Classroom Tips

## Stimulus questions for discussion

### Daydreaming

I refer to James Thurber's *Secret Life of Walter Mitty*, a story of a man who does little with his life because he lives it through daydreams (see the geocities web site ⓤ). I also read excerpts from a 1927 journal article on the dangers of daydreaming to college students (without first telling them the year of publication) to promote a discussion of the pros and cons of daydreaming. See Brown (1927).

### Hypnosis

I often start out asking if anyone has been hypnotized and if so, what the experience was like. If no one has experienced it directly, I ask if they have observed others being hypnotized and what they thought was happening. I then do the Barber Suggestibility Scale classroom learning activity (see p. 136).

### Motivation

I put Maslow's hierarchy of needs on the overhead or on a PowerPoint slide and ask students to provide examples of when the hierarchy works (e.g., hungry children can't be motivated to learn—thus the free lunch program) and when it doesn't work (e.g., suicide bombers who kill themselves and others for a political principle).

### Emotion

Smile! It will make you happy! True? Asking this question can lead to a discussion and a demonstration of the facial feedback hypothesis (see classroom learning activity, pp. 138–9).

"What is happiness?" This question has been researched extensively in the last few years. Students are often surprised at the predictors of happiness. For example, happiness is only slightly related to age, race, gender, educational level, parenthood, or wealth. However, happy people tend to have high self-esteem, be optimistic, sleep well, exercise, and have close friendships or a good marriage. See Diener and Lucas (2000) and Ryan and Deci (2001). See also Gilbert (2006), an excellent, readable book about what happiness is (and is not).

## Some suggested classroom learning activities

### Sleep diary

(Students complete this outside of class, 10–15 minutes of class time) I assign ⦾ Mini-assignment #1 10 days before I cover this topic in class. You may collect the diaries the class period before or ask students to share their information the same day you discuss it. I graph the average number of hours that students sleep—divided into week nights and weekend nights. I compare the students' weekend sleeping compared to their weekday sleeping patterns. Then I talk about their "sleep debt" and use that to segue into sleep deprivation and its impact.

### Sleep questionnaire

(Students complete this outside of class and bring it to the discussion.) *How large is your sleep debt?* is a questionnaire on sleep deprivation found in Coren (1996, pp. 264–265). It also provides the scoring and interpretation of scores. This is an excellent lead-in to a discussion of the functions of sleep and the impact of sleep deprivation.

### Circadian rhythms in body temperature

(An out-of-class activity that can be collected and compiled before you discuss it in class. This is a nice segue into circadian rhythms.) This exercise was developed by Michael Renner (1999). He had students track their temperature for 72 hours and record their state of alertness. He asked students to get an oral thermometer. He then had them record their temperature every 2 hours for 72 hours (he allowed ± 20 minutes). Then he had them rate their state of alertness on a scale of 1 (asleep—the alarm clock woke me up) to 10 (I'm hyper-aroused). He also told them not to eat or drink anything for 15 minutes before they took their temperature, and to be sitting still. He then had them write responses to questions—Did they find evidence of a circadian rhythm? When was their temperature low and when was it high and how did that correlate with alertness?

## Doris's Dream

(15–20 minutes) Divide your class into groups of four or five students. Give each group a copy of one version of Doris's dream. For example, Group 1 may get the version that includes no information about Doris, Group 2 might get the 18-year-old version of Doris, Group 3 the 28-year-old version of Doris, and Group 4 the 65-year-old version of Doris. Continue the same process for other groups, so if you have eight groups, two groups have each version.

Print the dream on the handouts as well as showing it on the overhead or via Power Point.

Ⓦ Doris's Dream

> I am at my friend Betty's house. I call Ann up to make an appointment to get my hair highlighted. I speak to the receptionist at the beauty parlor. I speak in a Russian accent. She asks when I can come. I say in a couple of days. I think that might be Wednesday. She asks "Are you sure because we are changing things around here," implying that it won't be good if I change my mind and cancel the appointment. After speaking to her, I realize that I don't need to have my hair highlighted yet, because my hair hasn't grown out yet. But George and I go on the "A" train to the beauty parlor. It goes through a neighborhood that I have never seen before. The train travels outside. George gets out at a stop as if he nonchalantly is doing something. The train leaves without him. I wave to him and feel bad that he is not on the train. (Ullman, 1986, p. 539)

Jot down notes about your interpretation of the dream in the space below:

#1.  Ⓦ No description of Doris—just the dream

#2.  ⓦ 18-year-old Doris: At the time of the following dream, Doris S. was an 18-year-old woman living in a rural area. She was getting ready to graduate from high school and begin the long road towards a medical degree (she would have been the first child in her family to become a doctor) when she found out that she was pregnant. Her parents were not yet aware of the situation and she and her boyfriend were in the midst of deciding whether to try to arrange an abortion or to get married, though the latter option meant the end of her medical school aspirations. Beyond these rather unfortunate problems, Doris lived a very normal life and had never experienced serious psychological problems.

#3.  ⓦ 28-year-old Doris: At the time of the following dream, Doris S. was a happy and healthy 28-year-old woman living in a comfortable Chicago condominium with her husband of 5 years. Both she and her husband had high-paying jobs in advertising (they had met at work) and were generally enjoying life as "yuppies." They got along well together and, beyond the usual conflicts over small things, the only problems they had were her overbearing mother (who tried to run their lives) and a very stressful decision about whether to move to Los Angeles, where her husband, but not she, had the opportunity for an exciting new job at even higher pay. Beyond these rather routine problems, Doris lived a very normal life and had never experienced serious psychological problems.

#4.  ⓦ 65-year-old Doris: At the time of the following dream, Doris S. was a 65-year-old woman living in a Chicago suburb. She had four grown children, two boys and two girls. Her husband of 40 years died two years before she had the dream. Though in excellent health for decades, she had just been diagnosed as having breast cancer. Her prognosis was good, but she worried about her health. She also worried about one of her grandchildren, a boy, who was born autistic and retarded. Other than these rather unfortunate problems, Doris had lived a very normal life and never experienced serious psychological problems.

I give the groups about 5–7 minutes to read the dream and come up with an interpretation of it. I ask each group to report their interpretation. I start with the group with no directions because they often have little to say and whatever they say can't be contradicted by other groups' directions.

Once groups with a description of Doris start reporting, other groups get "agitated" about where the group came up with their information. I "confess" the different information about Doris and put up the three versions (4th has no information) on the overhead.

We talk about the difficulty of interpreting dreams and the lack of reliability. We talk a bit about Freud and his symbols but also about the fact that even when a therapist would use dream analysis, it would relate to a series of dreams, not just one individual dream.

*Source for activity: By permission of Houghton Mifflin.*

## Dream analysis by mail
(10 minutes) In 1927 Freud corresponded with an American woman and interpreted her dreams. Ludy Benjamin and David Dixon wrote an article about this correspondence (Benjamin & Dixon, 1996), including the letters. Give students one of the dreams and ask them to interpret it. You could also read a dream in class, ask for student interpretation, and provide Freud's.

## Barber suggestibility scale
(15 minutes) Since it is unethical to hypnotize students, the Barber suggestibility scale works very well as a substitute. It provides a similar experience to hypnosis and demonstrates suggestibility. Barber and Calverley (1963) provides all of the directions you need for this activity.

## Theories of motivation
(5 minutes) Later in class, I give them the following ⓦ handout: "Write down 3 reasons why you chose to attend this campus this year."

Then I ask them to share their reasons. I write the reasons on the board and I classify them into groups that match Maslow's hierarchy *and/or* the theories of motivation.

## Evolutionary theory of motivation
(10 minutes) To help students understand this theory I pose a series of questions. "You and your spouse have just had your first child. Both sets of grandparents are ecstatic about the baby. Who will be kinder to the child—the mother's parents or the father's parents?" (Mother's—because they know that it is their genetic grandchild.) "You are on a boat that has just capsized and you can save only

one of your grown children. You have a 20-year-old child and a 40-year-old, both of the same sex. Which child would you save?" (20-year-old because of more "fertile" years to reproduce and perpetuate your genes). This leads to a great discussion of evolutionary theory.

### Achievement motivation—the classic demonstration

(10 minutes) Ask students to wad up pieces of paper. Ask for volunteers to "shoot baskets," or in a small class, have everyone shoot at the waste basket. Allow students to stand anywhere in the room. Students who stand at a challenging, but "makeable," distance are the ones displaying the highest need for achievement.

*Source for activity: McClelland (1958, 1985).*

### Achievement motivation and gender

(10 minutes to prepare the material, 30 minutes to analyze the material, 10 minutes of class time.) This exercise must be done at least the class session before you will discuss the material. I have two sets of papers, both with the same directions:

ⓦ Do not put your name on this paper!
Sex (circle one): Female      Male
Write a short story about the sentence below. (A paragraph or two is fine.)

But with different sentences:

John is sitting in a chair with a smile on his face.
Anne is sitting in a chair with a smile on her face.
I alternate the papers, so that half the class has John and half has Anne. Students begin writing when they enter class and I give them a few minutes of class time to finish. I collect their stories and then analyze them according to their achievement themes. This is based on Matina Horner's "Fear of Success" classic study on women's "fear of success"—women's conflicting motives to achieve and still fit their gender stereotype.

*Source for activity: Horner (1972).*

### Lie detection

I put the following directions on the overhead as students come into class:

Ⓦ Come to the front of the room.

Take a card from the bag. Don't show it to anyone.

Write a paragraph about *one* of the topics listed below. If your card says TRUTH, write something that is true. If your card says LIE, write something that is untrue.

Your paragraph should be written so that you would not be embarrassed to read it to the class.

Topics:

Something interesting that happened to you.

Your earliest memory.

Your favorite vacation.

Where you would most like to live.

A surprising talent that you have.

Your favorite meal.

An interesting aspect of your family.

The most interesting person you have ever met.

An elementary, middle school, or high school teacher who had the most impact on you.

I have a brown "lunch" bag with 3 × 5 cards, half that say TRUTH and half that say LIE. (Varying this—maybe with all saying TRUTH or all saying LIE could provide an interesting twist.) Students take a card out of the bag as they enter class and I give them a few minutes to finish them at the beginning of class. When we begin to discuss emotion, I ask for volunteers to read their story to the class. The other students record whether they think the volunteer is telling the truth or a lie. After five or six volunteers, we decide as a class whether the student was lying. We are often wrong! This leads to a great discussion of the cues we were looking for and cues that actually are important in detecting lies.

For a list of cues about "lying behavior" see Vrij (2000). There is a list on p. 33 of nonverbal behaviors during deception, including speech hesitations, pitch of voice, speech rate, gaze, blinking, and so forth.

### James-Lange theory of emotion/facial feedback hypothesis

This is a good demonstration of the facial feedback hypothesis. Pick a cartoon that you think is very funny. Put it on a transparency or in your PowerPoint. Pass out a plastic drinking straw to everyone and ask them to take out a pencil and paper. Divide the class in half and have Group 2 shut their eyes. Display the following written instructions to Group 1.

❺ "Please place your straw in your mouth as the instructor demonstrates. Rate the following cartoon on a scale of 1 to 5 with 1 = Not at all funny and 5 = Very funny."

For Group 1, you should put the straw horizontally between your teeth in a way that will cause your face to approximate a smile and then display the cartoon. Once students have rated the cartoon, ask Group 1 to close their eyes and Group 2 to open their eyes. Show the same directions, but this time place the end of the straw in your mouth (so that your face approximates a frown) and show the cartoon. If the facial feedback hypothesis works, those students approximating a smile should rate the cartoon as funnier than those students approximating a frown.

*Source for activity: original idea from Strack, Martin, and Steper (1988), the outline for using this as a classroom activity comes from Schallhorn and Lunde (1999).*

## Possible mini-assignments (written or groups)

### ❺ *Mini-assignment #1*

Keep a sleep and dream diary for the next week. Record the time you went to sleep, the time you awoke, and any dreams that you can remember.

Average the number of hours of sleep that you get on weekdays and the number of hours of sleep that you get on weekends. Feel free to make any comments about your sleep patterns.

### ❺ *Mini-assignment #2*
(Could be an in-class activity as well)

1. Read the story below and answer the questions.
   Rodney Denman was an outstanding volleyball player his first three years of high school, but he did not perform as well in the classroom. At the end of his junior year, he discovered that he would not be eligible for any college volleyball scholarships unless he raised his grades. During his senior year, Denman's grades rose from a D average to a B+ average while his outstanding performance on the volleyball court continued.
   - Pick a theory of human motivation (instinct, drive reduction, arousal, or incentive).
   - Using this theory, explain Rodney Denman's change in behavior.

2. Using *another* theory of motivation, explain some behavior that *you* engage in. Describe the behavior, then explain how the theory explains it.

### ⓦ *Mini-assignment #3*
(Could be an in-class activity as well) Design a program to help *one* of the people below using *one* of the major theories of motivation.

1. Alice needs to lose 50 pounds.
2. Jacob is performing poorly in school.
3. Louise is trying to organize a group of people to vote for her.
4. Henry is trying to improve the performance of the people who work for him.

### ⓦ *Mini-assignment #4*
(Instructor—see Changing Minds web site ⓤ for a list of Murray's needs that you can distribute to your class for this assignment.)

Read a short children's story. Write a summary of the story. Analyze the story using Henry Murray's list of needs, especially the need for achievement and need for affiliation.

### ⓦ *Mini-assignment #5*
Think about a job that you have held, even if it was part-time or a summer job. Make a list of the aspects of the job that you liked (satisfiers) and a list of the aspects of the job you did not like (dissatisfiers). Write a paragraph summarizing the positive aspects of the job and the negative aspects of the job.

## References

APS Staff. (2001). Adolescents and alcohol abuse: New knowledge, new challenges. *APS Observer, 14*(10), 33–36.

Barber, T., & Calverley, D. (1963). "Hypnotic-like" suggestibility in children and adults. *Journal of Abnormal and Social Psychology, 66*(6), 589–597.

Barker, L. (2006). Teaching evolutionary psychology: An interview with David M. Buss. *Teaching of Psychology, 33*, 69–76.

Becker, D., Kenrick, D., Neuberg, S., Blackwell, K., & Smith, D. (2007). The confounded nature of angry men and happy women. *Journal of Personality and Social Psychology, 92*(2), 179–190.

Benjamin, L., & Dixon, D. (1996). Dream analysis by mail: An American woman seeks Freud's advice. *American Psychologist, 51*, 461–468.

Bernard, L., Mills, M., Swenson, L., & Walsh P. (2005). An evolutionary theory of human motivation. *Genetic, Social, and General Psychology Monograph*, *131*(2), 129–184.

Brown, G. (1927). Daydreams: A cause of mind wandering and inferior scholarship. *Journal of Educational Research*, *16*(4), 276–279.

Cartwright, R. (1978). *A primer on sleep and dreaming*. Reading, MA: Addison-Wesley.

Cho, K., Ennaceur, A., Cole, J., and Suh, C. (2000). Chronic jet lag produces cognitive deficits. *The Journal of Neuroscience*, *20*, 1–5.

Coren, S. (1996). *Sleep thieves*. New York: Free Press.

Crick, F., & Koch, C. (2002). The problem of consciousness. *The Hidden Mind* (Special edition of *Scientific American*), 10–17.

Deci, E. (1971). Effects of externally mediated rewards on intrinsic motivation. *Journal of Personality and Social Psychology*, *18*(1), 105–115.

Diener, E., & Diener, C. (1995). Most people are happy. *Psychological Science*, *7*, 181–185.

Diener, E., & Lucas, R. (2000). Subjective emotional well-being. In M. Lewis & J. Haviland (Eds.), *Handbook of emotions* (2nd ed., pp. 325–337). New York: Guilford.

Diener, E., & Seligman, M. (2004). Beyond money: Towards an economy of well-being. *Psychological Sciences in the Public Interest*, *5*, 1–31.

Dweck, C. (2000). *Self-theories: Their role in motivation, personality, and development*. Philadelphia, PA: Psychology Press.

Etcoff, N., Ekman, P., Magee, J., & Frank, M. (2000). Lie detection and language comprehension. *Nature*, *405*, 139.

Farwell, L., & Donchin, E. (1991). The truth will out: Interrogative polygraphy ("lie detection") with event-related brain potentials. *Psychophysiology*, *28*(5), 531–547.

Fenn, K., Nusbaum, H., & Margoliash, D. (2006). Consolidation during sleep of perceptual learning of spoken language. *Nature*, *425*(6958), 614–616.

Freud, S. (1915/1980). *Interpretation of dreams*. New York: Avon.

Gibson, J., & Walk, R. (1960). The visual cliff. *Scientific American*, *202*, 64–71.

Gilbert, D. (2006). *Stumbling on happiness*. New York: Knopf.

Grubin, D., & Madsen, L. (2005). Lie detection and the polygraph: A historical review. *Journal of Forensic Psychiatry and Psychology*, *16*(2), 357–369.

Gruzelier, J. (2000). Redefining hypnosis: Theory, methods and integration. *Contemporary Hypnosis*, *17*(2), 51–70.

Horner, M. (1972). Toward an understanding of achievement-related conflicts in women. *Journal of Social Issues*, *28*(2), 157–176.

Kalat, J. (2004). *Biological psychology*. Belmont, CA: Thomson Wadsworth.

Kirsch, I., & Lynn, S. (1995). The altered state of hypnosis: Changes in the theoretical landscape. *American Psychologist 50*(10), 846–858.

Laumann, E., Gagnon, J., Michael, R., & Michaels, S. (1994). *The social organization of sexuality: Sexual practices in the United States.* Chicago: University of Chicago Press.

Laumann, E., & Michael, R. (Eds.). (2000). *Sex, love, and health in America: Private choices and public policies.* Chicago: University of Chicago Press.

McClelland, D. (1958). Risk-taking in children with high and low need for achievement. In J. W. Atkinson (Ed.), *Motives in fantasy, action, and society* (pp. 306–321). Princeton, NJ: Van Nostrand.

McClelland, D. (1961). *The achieving society.* Princeton, NJ: VanNostrand.

McClelland, D. (1985). *Human motivation.* Glenview, IL: Scott, Foresman.

Murray, H. (1938). *Explorations in personality.* New York: Oxford University Press.

Renner, M. (1999). Circadian rhythms in body temperature. In L. Benjamin, B. Nodine, R. Ernst, & C. Blair Broeker (Eds.), *Activities handbook for the teaching of psychology, vol. 4.* (pp. 109–11). Washington, DC: American Psychological Association.

Rozin, P., Haidt, J., & McCauley, C. R. (2000). Disgust. In M. Lewis & J. Haviland (Eds.) *Handbook of emotions* (2nd ed., pp. 637–653). New York: Guilford Press.

Ryan, R., & Deci, E. (2001). On happiness and human potentials: A review of the research on hedonic and eudaimonic well-being. *Annual Review of Psychology, 52,* 141–166.

Schallhorn, C., & Lunde, J. (1999). The facial feedback hypothesis: Are emotions really related to the faces we make? In L. Benjamin, B. Nodine, R. Ernst, & C. Blair Broeker (Eds.), *Activities handbook for the teaching of psychology, vol. 4* (pp. 228–231). Washington, DC: American Psychological Association.

Seligman, M., & Csikszentmihalyi, M. (2000). Positive psychology: An introduction. *American Psychologist, 55,* 5–14.

Sharma, V., & Chandrashekaran, M. (2005). Zeitgebers (time cues) for biological clocks. *Current Science, 89*(7), 1136–1146.

Shneidman, E. (1980). *Endeavors in psychology: Selections from the personology of Henry A. Murray.* New York: Harper & Row.

Solomon, R. (1974). An opponent-process theory of motivation. I. Temporal dynamics of affect. *Psychological Review, 81*(2), 119–145.

Spector, P. (1997). *Job satisfaction: Application, assessment, cause, and consequences.* Thousand Oaks, CA: Sage Publications.

Strack, F., Martin, L., & Steper, S. (1988). Inhibiting and facilitating conditions of the human smile: A nonobtrusive test of the facial feedback hypothesis. *Journal of Personality and Social Psychology, 54,* 768–777.

Stringer, J. (2005). *The basics of pharmacology: A student's survival guide* (2nd ed.). New York: McGraw-Hill.

Ullman, M. (1986). Access to dreams. In B. B. Wolman & M. Ullman (Eds.), *Handbook of states of consciousness* (pp. 524–532). New York: Van Nostrand Reinhold.

VanDongen, H., Maislin, G., Mullington, J., & Dinges, D. (2003). The cumulative cost of additional wakefulness. *Sleep*, 26(2), 117–126.

Vrij, A. (2000). *Detecting lies and deceit: The psychology of lying and the implications for professional practice.* New York: John Wiley & Sons.

## Additional Suggested Readings for Instructors

Braddon-Mitchell, D., & Jackson, F. (2006). *Philosophy of mind and cognition.*

Brewer, M., & Hewstone, M. (Eds.). (2003). *Emotion and motivation.* Oxford: Blackwell.

Buss, D. (Ed.) (2005). *The handbook of evolutionary psychology.* Hoboken, NJ: John Wiley & Sons.

Ekman, P. (1992) *Telling lies: Clues to deceit in the marketplace, politics, and marriage.* New York: Norton. See also Paul Ekman's web site Ⓤ for more resources.

Landau, T. (1989). *About faces: The evolution of the human face.* New York: Doubleday.

Markus, H., & Kitayama, S. (1991). Culture and the self: Implications for cognition, emotion, and motivation. *Psychological Review*, 98(2), 224–253.

Maslow, A. (1970). *Motivation and personality.* New York: Harper & Row.

Oatley, K., Keltner, D., & Jenkins, J. (2005). *Understanding emotions* (2nd ed.) Oxford: Blackwell.

Ryan, R., & Deci, E. (2000). Self-determination, theory and the facilitation of intrinsic motivation, social development, and well-being. *American Psychologist*, 55(1), 68–78.

Tavris, C. (1989). *Anger: The misunderstood emotion.* New York: Simon and Schuster.

# Chapter 8

# Learning and Memory

## Getting Started

I think that the learning and memory unit is one of the most important of the entire term. One of my goals is to have my students understand their own learning process—and to be able to use that information to adjust the way they study, write, take exams, and approach learning situations throughout their lifetime. I also want my students to broaden their definition of learning. Learning is *not* just what occurs in a school context, but is a lifelong process that occurs without effort in many contexts. And, while learning is more than an automatic response to a stimulus, classical and operant conditioning do contribute to learning in our everyday lives.

Students often do not understand that learning and memory have a biological component, and new research is focusing on these processes. This discussion often runs the gamut from information about Alzheimer's disease to the idea of a "memory" pill.

I want my students to understand that memory is *not* a photograph of what occurred but a *construction* of reality. There is no one place that memory is stored, but when we remember something many different areas of the brain "put together" that memory—every time we retrieve it. But most importantly, I want my students to envision what they would be like without memory—that memory provides each of us with our individual identity.

My outline for teaching (3 days—75 minute classes)

*Day 1*
Questions from previous class (5 minutes)
Practice questions over material (5 minutes)
Administrivia (5 minutes)
  I.   Introduction to learning (10 minutes)
       Definitions of learning
  II.  Classical conditioning (50 minutes)
       Basic concepts
       See Classical conditioning classroom learning activities (I pick
         one based on time available—pp. 156–7)
       Pavlov video (Discovering Psychology #8 Learning Ⓤ)
       Paradigm—lots of examples!
       Watson and Little Albert videoclips (Discovering Psychology
         #8 Learning Ⓤ)
       *Seabiscuit* Ⓤ (2003) movie—group assignment (See Ⓦ Mini-
         assignment #2)
       Classical conditioning concepts: acquisition, spontaneous
         recovery, stimulus generalization, stimulus discrimination,
         extinction, reconditioning, higher order conditioning

*Day 2*
Questions from previous class (5 minutes)
Practice questions over material (5 minutes)
Administrivia (5 minutes)
  I.   Operant conditioning (30 minutes)
       Introduction/B. F. Skinner
       Basic concepts
       Acquisition
       Other concepts: law of effect, stimulus generalization, stimulus
         discrimination, avoidance and escape learning
       Schedules of reinforcement
  II.  Learning from a cognitive viewpoint (5 minutes)
  III. Introduction to memory—definitions (10 minutes)
  IV.  Types of memory and models—information-processing view (Ⓦ
         Handout #1) (10 minutes)
  V.   All-purpose memory classroom learning activity, p. 159
         (5 minutes)

*Day 3*
Questions from previous class (5 minutes)
Practice questions over material (5 minutes)

Administrivia (5 minutes)
  I.   Remembering (15 minutes)
       Recognition vs. recall classroom learning activity (pp. 159–60)
       What is remembered?
       Eyewitness testimony
 II.   Forgetting (20 minutes)
       Encoding strategies classroom learning activity (p. 162)
       Elaborative vs. maintenance rehearsal levels of processing class-
          room learning activity (pp. 160–2)
III.   Biological bases of memory (15 minutes)
       Anterograde amnesia—loss of memory for events after the injury
       Retrograde amnesia—loss of memory for events before the injury
       ⓦ Handout #2
IV.   Improve your memory tidbits (10 minutes)
       Loftus—learn to pay attention
       Mnemonics
       Metamemory—knowledge of how your memory works
       Distributed practice/rehearsal rather than massed

## My transitions

I teach the learning and memory unit after consciousness—often
using the concept of attention to segue between the two. I think
learning and memory are a package, so it would be difficult to teach
them as separate units. After memory, I move to cognition and cognitive abilities (intelligence), two other units I find to be integrally
connected. I tell my students that we have talked about how an
individual learns and remembers; now we will talk about how those
cognitions are formed and put together into a hypothetical construct,
"intelligence."

## Topics typically included in this unit

*Classical conditioning*: Pavlov, classical conditioning paradigm, acqui-
    sition, extinction, spontaneous recovery, stimulus generalization
    and discrimination, second order conditioning, biopreparedness,
    phobias
*Operant/instrumental conditioning*: Operants; law of effect; reinforcers
    —negative, positive, primary, and secondary; escape and avoidance
    conditioning; discriminative stimuli and stimulus control; stimulus
    generalization and discrimination; shaping; schedules of reinforce-
    ment; partial reinforcement; extinction effect; punishment

*Cognitive processes in learning*: Learned helplessness, latent learning, cognitive maps, insight and learning, observational learning and vicarious conditioning

*Neural networks and the biology of learning*: Connectionist models, synaptic connections, associations

*Other learning concepts*: Habituation, opponent process theory, Thorndike's law of effect, culture's impact on learning, active learning, skill learning

*Basic memory processes*: Encoding, storage, and retrieval; types of memory—semantic, episodic, procedural; explicit and implicit memory

*Models of memory*: Levels of processing, transfer-appropriate processing, parallel distributed processing, information processing

*Storing memories*: Sensory, short-term and working memory, chunking, long-term memory, primacy and recency effects

*Retrieving memories*: Encoding specificity, context and state dependence, semantic networks, tip-of-the-tongue phenomenon, feeling of knowing

*Constructing memories*: Constructive memories, PDP models, schemas, eye-witness testimony

*Forgetting*: Ebbinghaus and method of savings, decay, interference—retroactive and proactive, recovery of repressed memories

*Biological bases of memory*: Neurotransmitters, hippocampus, thalamus, retrograde and anterograde amnesia

*Improving your memory*: Mnemonics, studying, PQ4R

## Some options for organizing the concepts

*By approach*: Learning and memory can be taught from the viewpoint of the different approaches—behaviorist, cognitive, biological, evolutionary.

*By topic*: Learning most often is taught immediately before memory—with learning concepts leading into memory concepts. Learning and memory are often taught following the perception or consciousness unit. Memory is a good unit to cover before the first major exam in the course—it allows students to use what they learn about memory research to improve their studying.

# Teaching the Content

Remember that the ◍ symbol means that a printable version is available on the web site (www.blackwellpublishing.com/lucas) and ⓤ means that the URL is available on the web site.

## Topics that many students will find difficult

### Classical conditioning paradigm

Many students will have difficulty understanding classical conditioning, especially that the UCS → UCR link is *unlearned*. I explain the paradigm first and then provide numerous examples and have students fill in the paradigm for each example.

UCS → UCR
CS + UCS → UCR
CS → CR

Note: Some textbooks present the CS (conditioned stimulus) as the NS (neutral stimulus) in the second step. I prefer the paradigm I presented, but you should be consistent with the textbook you use.

For information about Ivan Pavlov and his discovery of classical conditioning see the Nobel Foundation web site Ⓤ.

Footage of Pavlov and a more detailed description of his experiments can be found in the *Discovering Psychology: #8 Learning* Ⓤ video.

Students may also learn about classical conditioning by teaching an "on-line dog" at the Nobel Foundation web site Ⓤ.

The McGraw-Hill Higher Education web site Ⓤ provides an interactive classical conditioning paradigm allowing students to classically condition, extinguish, and see spontaneous recovery of a response.

### Vicarious conditioning

Differentiating vicarious conditioning from the larger concept of observational learning is tricky. I emphasize the key difference—the observation of *consequences*; either rewards or punishments. Albert Bandura's Bobo doll experiments are good illustrations of this concept. Another example: If on the first day of class a student asks me a question and I respond negatively and "punished" the student for asking, then the rest of the class would learn vicariously not to ask me questions. They wouldn't have to ask me a question to personally experience the negativity—they would learn from watching the consequences of their classmate's behavior.

See Christopher Green's Classics in the History of Psychology web site Ⓤ for Bandura's classic paper on vicarious conditioning.

See Davidson Films web site ⓤ for an outline and learner's guide of a video highlighting Bandura's work—this also ties in nicely with the personality unit and Bandura's social cognitive theory.

## Discriminative stimuli

Understanding that a discriminative stimulus signals the availability of reward is difficult for students. Use as many examples as possible— for example, that Grandpa (who always gives his grandchildren a dollar) is a discriminative stimulus for money and that many people trying to lose weight find that the TV set is a discriminative stimulus for eating (and thus they try to gain *stimulus control* by limiting their eating to their kitchen table).

## Negative reinforcement

Negative reinforcement, in which the removal of a negative stimulus increases the probability of the response that preceded the removal, is often confused with *punishment*—or the application of a negative stimulus following some behavior to decrease the likelihood of that behavior. Many textbooks do not do a good job explaining this difference, so it's important to emphasize that reinforcers increase the likelihood of a response while punishment decreases the likelihood of a response.

A 2 × 2 grid works well in helping students understand the concept.

|  | *Stimulus presented* | *Stimulus withdrawn* |
|---|---|---|
| Positive stimulus | Positive reinforcement | Punishment 2/penalty |
| Negative stimulus | Punishment 1 | Negative reinforcement |

See the Maricopa Center for Learning and Instruction web site ⓤ for a good discussion and examples of negative reinforcement.
See the Shippensburg University faculty web site ⓤ for a compilation of examples of negative reinforcement from various textbooks.

## Neural networks and learning

For the purposes of an introductory course, I believe that I just need to provide a basic understanding of this process. I usually provide a handout of this information (see ⓦ Handout #2).

See the Intelligen, Inc. web site ⓤ for a basic discussion of network processing.

The Serendip web site ⓤ (Bryn Mawr college) provides information about basic biological neural networks and how research is progressing on AI versions of this.

### Synaptic plasticity and long-term potentiation
The Medical Research Council Centre for Synaptic Plasticity (University of Bristol) web site ⓤ discusses these concepts in an excellent, easy to understand manner.

### Implicit memory
The idea that some memories influence our behavior without being brought to consciousness is a difficult concept for students. I provide as many examples as possible.

### Constructive memory
Because many students have a conception of memory as a snapshot of "real life," it is difficult for them to grasp that we construct our memories all the time—and that most of the time this construction works well for us. However, errors can occur.

See Stanford University's Encyclopedia of Philosophy web site ⓤ for a short discussion of memory as a constructive process.

For a nice discussion of the history of memory research see Alexander Riegler's Constructive Memory web site ⓤ.

Elizabeth Loftus is a leading researcher in constructive memories. See Loftus and Pickrell (1995) for a discussion about implanting false memories. See also Loftus (2003).

The Eureka Alert web site ⓤ has a discussion of how false memories are formed.

The Eureka Alert web site ⓤ also describes a study finding that false memories can be detected by imaging activity in the prefrontal cortex.

See Schacter, Norman, and Koutstaal (1998), which can be found at Annual Reviews in Psychology web site ⓤ, for a discussion of the neuroscience underpinnings of constructive memory.

### Repressed/recovered memories
Because many students have a "snapshot" conception of memory, they believe that memories can be repressed for many years, despite the lack of scientific evidence for this belief.

See the Skeptic's Dictionary web site ⓤ for a discussion of "repressed memory," therapists' claims, and the scientific evidence refuting it. See Loftus and Ketcham (1994) for a comprehensive discussion of evidence on the issue.

## Other important topics

### Watson's "Little Albert" experiments

Watson's famous experiments with a baby named "Little Albert" demonstrate classical conditioning principles. Watson (1928) contains a picture of the conditioning experiments. *Discovering Psychology: #8 Learning* ⓤ contains video of the Little Albert experiments with both Watson and Rosalie Raynor, his assistant (and future wife). For more information on Watson's fascinating life and his work and theories see the Psi Chi Café web site ⓤ.

These experiments often lead to a discussion of the ethics of psychological research. See the American Psychological Association's code of ethics at APA's webpage ⓤ.

### Taste aversion and the Garcia effect

Students are fascinated by this research and often can trace their dislike of a food to a specific time when they ate the food and then were ill. See Anthony Riley and Kevin Freeman's (American University) webpage ⓤ for an annotated bibliography of taste aversion literature and research.

### Operant conditioning

Examples of operant conditioning are easy to generate and most students will be able to do this. I use an anecdote (I'm not sure of the original source) from World War II—the British operantly conditioned seagulls to spot German submarines off the coast of Britain. The British first arranged for their submerged subs to release their garbage when they were close to the English coastline. As the garbage came to the surface, it attracted seagulls. The gulls soon learned to follow submerged submarines because these vessels were associated with food. Watching the location and flight pattern of large flocks of gulls allowed the British to improve their detection of German submarines.

[Interestingly, sea lions are now being operantly trained to help protect British and American ships in the Persian Gulf. They have been trained in mine recovery and to alert humans when they

detect an intruding diver. They even have been trained to attach a restraining device to a diver. For more information, see V. Murphy (2003) "Let slip the sea lions of war" at the BBC web site ⓤ.
For examples differentiating classical and operant conditioning see Marilla Svinicki's (University of Texas) webpage ⓤ.

*B. F. Skinner.* The father of operant conditioning, Skinner spent his life applying his ideas to practical problems in the world. See the B. F. Skinner Foundation web site ⓤ for a concise biography discussing both Project Pigeon and the baby tender.

Project Pigeon: During World War II Skinner proposed using trained pigeons to guide missiles. See Greg Goebel's In the Public Domain web site ⓤ for a discussion of this and Ari Schindler's web site ⓤ for a picture. See also Capshew (1993).
Baby tender: Skinner developed a safer crib he called the "baby tender" for his daughter Deborah. However, his article in the *Ladies Home Journal* (Skinner, 1945) carried the title "Baby in a box." For Deborah Skinner's version of growing up, see the B. F. Skinner, works and life web site ⓤ.
Programmed learning—Because Skinner's daughter's schools were overcrowded, Skinner developed programmed learning to help students learn on their own—this concept has been used extensively, especially in computer programs. See Skinner (1986).

## Thorndike and the law of effect
Thorndike's "law of effect"—that behavior followed by positive consequences tends to be repeated and that behavior followed by negative consequences tends not to be repeated—will make sense to students and can be used as a context for explaining some of their own behaviors.

See Thorndike (1927), available at JSTOR (Archives of Scholarly documents) web site ⓤ.
Footage of Thorndike and a discussion of his law of effect can be found in the *Discovering Psychology: #8 Learning* ⓤ video.

## Punishment
While punishment decreases the likelihood of a response, it also has some undesirable consequences, for example: fear of the punisher, only suppressing the undesired behavior, behavior reoccurring when the punisher is not present, modeling of aggression that may affect the behavior of the punished child. Students will be interested in the

"spanking" controversy as well (see Classroom tips: punishment stimulus question, pp. 155–6).

## Schedules of partial reinforcement

The idea that our behavior is made more resistant to extinction by partial reinforcement than by continuous reinforcement is not intuitive. I explain it as involving expectations—that is, with continuous reinforcement you expect that every time you behave in a certain way, you will get a reward. So, when the reward doesn't appear, you immediately know that something has changed and that further rewards are unlikely. With partial reinforcement, you don't expect a reward for every behavior so when you aren't rewarded one time you still expect to be rewarded later. Examples of fixed ratio, variable ratio, fixed interval, and variable interval can be found at a web site compiled by faculty at Shippensburg University Ⓤ.

## Latent learning

The idea that we learn things without conscious knowledge of the information until we need it is intriguing for most students. I use an example from my life that many students can identify with. When I received a parking ticket, I knew exactly where to go to find the "box" to deposit my fine. I was not consciously aware that I knew where the parking ticket deposit boxes were—but when I needed one, I knew where to go.

## Learned helplessness

Students can relate to the idea that continuously engaging in a behavior that has no effect on the environment can result in a tendency to stop trying. This concept is a good beginning point for discussion of children who experience helplessness in schools and adults who experience helplessness in relationships. See Seligman and Maier (1967) for the original article articulating the concept of learned helplessness.

## Memory—A basic overview

Stanford University's Encyclopedia of Philosophy web site Ⓤ provides a good general overview of memory processes. The BBC web site Ⓤ provides some tests of memory (see Ⓦ Mini-assignment #4).

## Ebbinghaus and the method of savings

Ebbinghaus's rather unsophisticated research methods, experimenting on himself with made-up nonsense syllables, provides a nice tie to research methods. Ebbinghaus's discovery of the method of savings was important to show that forgetting is not complete. His research also demonstrated the forgetting curve and how long-lasting savings in long-term memory can be. You can access Ebbinghaus's book (translated into English) at Christopher Green's Classics in the History of Psychology web site ⓤ.

## The capacity of short-term memory

George Miller's research on the capacity of working memory (7 ± 2 pieces of information) still holds today, even when more sophisticated research methods are used.

## Models of memory

Much of the way we discuss memory is based on the information-processing model. Sensory, short-term, and long-term memory are all aspects of this model. I provide a summary of this model (see ⓦ Handout #1). I also give students a one-page story about the stages of memory (see ⓦ Handout #3).

## Forgetting

We all are fascinated by why we forget things and strive to improve our memories. The primary theories of forgetting include decay and interference. I provide many examples of proactive and retroactive interference, as students often confuse these concepts. I use a mnemonic that the first vowel in proactive is an o—old interferes with new; the first vowel in retroactive is an e—new interferes with old. It also helps if students understand that *pro* refers to forward and *retro* refers to backward.

## Retrieving memories

Understanding that it is easier to retrieve memories in the same manner that they were encoded highlights the relevance of context and state-dependent memory. One practical implication of this research is to advise students to study in the rooms where they will be taking their exams. (But don't overemphasize this, because students will get the wrong idea and think they are at a disadvantage if they can't do this.) See Encoding and retrieval classroom learning activity, p. 162.

*Flashbulb memories.* Memories for surprising and emotional events are *not* perfect memories. Often what we remember is affected by other people's recounting the event. After the terrorist attacks of 9/11 several psychologists studied people's flashbulb memories and their memories years later. Their research found that the memory was dependent on each person's personal connection with the attack and that the memories a year later did not always match the immediate memory.

All articles in a special 2003 issue of *Applied Cognitive Psychology* contain research on memories of 9/11; see especially Neisser (2003). See also Luminet et al. (2004).

## Memory and smell
As we discussed in the sensation/perception unit—biological structures tie memory and our sense of smell.

# Classroom Tips

## Stimulus questions for discussion

### Learning and memory begin in the womb
There is evidence that babies remember what they heard while in the womb and that they prefer that stimulus even 12 months later. What implications does this have for parents? How would this knowledge change the way you would behave while pregnant or while a significant other was pregnant? See Educational CyberSpace Playground web site Ⓤ for information about this research.

### Watson's behaviorist view of parenting

> *No one today knows enough to raise a child.* The world would be considerably better off if we were to stop having children for twenty years (except those reared for experimental purposes) and were then to start again with enough facts to do the job with some degree of skill and accuracy. Parenthood, instead of being an instinctive art, is a science, the details of which must be worked out by patient laboratory methods . . . The behaviorists believe that there is nothing from within to develop. If you start with a healthy body, the right number of fingers and toes, eyes, and the few elementary movements that are present at birth, you do not need anything else in the way of raw material to make a man, be that man a genius, a cultured gentleman, a rowdy, or a thug. (Watson, 1928, p. 13)

Read this quote to your class. Ask them if they believe that any child could be taught to take up any occupation. How would they use learning principles to accomplish this?

### Punishment
The basic principles of punishment are outlined at Mark Plonsky, University of Wisconsin, Steven's Point, Dr. P's web site Ⓤ which is

a site for dog trainers. Print out the list—show it to the class and ask them if they agree with the principles applied to childrearing. Then reveal that these principles are for training dogs and ask the class if their opinion has changed.

Spanking has been hotly debated as a discipline technique. Ask the class to discuss the pros and cons of spanking in terms of shaping or changing a child's behavior. Be aware that this is a controversial topic for many students and you need to be sensitive to this. See APA's web site ⓤ for a discussion of spanking that incorporates the latest research.

### Memory tips

I summarize memory information into four practical tips for students. I put this on an overhead (in large font) and ask for student responses.

1. Learn to pay attention (Loftus).
2. Use mnemonics.
3. Understand your metamemory—how your memory works.
4. Use distributed practice/rehearsal rather than massed.

## Some suggested classroom learning activities

### Classical conditioning: An all-purpose demonstration using a toy water gun

(2 minutes to set up, 5 minutes for the demonstration, 5–10 minute for discussion) You will need a volunteer who does not wear contact lens and does not mind getting wet, a rain poncho (or plastic garbage bag with a hole for the head), a towel, and a squirt bottle or toy water gun.

- Ask students in class to keep track of the learning principles that you will be demonstrating. Ask them *not* to laugh or provide any cues to the volunteer.
- Have the volunteer sit in a chair at the front of the room, facing the class. Tell the volunteer that you are going to read a list of words and all the volunteer has to do is listen. Have the volunteer close their eyes and you crouch down in front of him or her (so the class can see the volunteer's face.) Read the following list of words and when the word is capitalized read the word and then spray the student in the face with the squirt gun. Be sure that you say the word BEFORE you spray the volunteer.

Cup, can, lime, CAN, dish, girl, chalk, can, dish, CAN, key, screen, ran, CAN, desk, CAN, knob, bag, tape, CAN, dish, clip, CAN, air, ban, cheese, CAN, door, can, box, dish, hair, CAN, ring, nail, CAN, boat, cap, dish, CAN, crane, wheel, fire, CAN, dish, king, cape, apple, CAN, dog, blue, can, dish, CAN, take, call, brick, pair, CAN, spin, chair, CAN, camp, CAN, bridge, scale, can, fan, board, CAN, cool, three, horn, dusk, can, cast, test, pen, dime, can, dish, van, can, card, stand, meat, pad, can, dish, eye, juice, can, food, can, van, disk, tree. (This is an abbreviated list that I use from the much longer one provided by Shenker.)

- Students will report that the volunteer originally had no reaction to "can" but after pairing the word "can" with water in the face, they often showed a grimace or flinch when the word was uttered. You can demonstrate the classical conditioning paradigm, acquisition, stimulus generalization, stimulus discrimination, and extinction with this activity.

*Source for activity: Shenker (1999).*

## Classical conditioning: Demonstration using balloons

(5–10 minutes) A quick demonstration of classical conditioning involves a very large needle (hat pin or darning needle) and enough balloons for every student. As students enter the classroom, they pick up a balloon, blow it up, and keep it at their desk. I start class and as I lecture on classical conditioning, I walk around the classroom with my large needle popping students' balloons. Soon, every time my pin approaches a balloon, most of the class is flinching—even before the balloon bursts. I then have the students fill in the classical conditioning paradigm so they understand the process by which they were classically conditioned.

*Source for activity: Vernoy (1987), also in Ware and Johnson (2000, pp. 143–144).*

## Shaping behavior through operant conditioning

(5 minutes to shape a simple behavior to 15 minutes to shape a complex behavior) Explain to the class that they are going to shape behavior by clapping when a student volunteer engages in behavior that approximates the desired target behavior and by being silent when the behavior is not close to the target behavior (this is a version of the old game, "hot and cold.") Pick a volunteer and have that person leave the room. Have the class pick a behavior to be

shaped. Explain to the class the idea of *successive approximations*—the first behavior rewarded with clapping only has to vaguely approximate the desired behavior, or at least be in the right direction. But then it must get closer and closer to the desired behavior for reinforcement to continue.

Two things to keep in mind. First, the volunteer must "operate" on the environment—he or she must move around and try different things; just standing in one place will be pointless. Second, the behavior has to be something the volunteer would be comfortable with—erasing the board, writing on the board, moving a chair—something along those lines. Reject your class's suggestions to have the volunteer disrobe, for example.

For a more elaborate version of this demonstration see Fernald and Fernald (1999).

### Learned helplessness

(5 minutes—be aware that one group will not finish) While many students are empathetic to the concept of learned helplessness, actually "artificially" experiencing it is more powerful. In this exercise students complete a series of six anagrams, provided on the following two handouts:

1. Instructions: Unscramble each anagram below. Work as fast as you can, proceeding in order from the first anagram to the last. LAIN SRUH EDHA UDMR OBKO DOLS
2. Instructions: Unscramble each anagram below. Work as fast as you can, proceeding in order from the first anagram to the last. YAKE ITNC HOLO FELM CORL DOLS

- Make copies of the two handout versions and interweave them, so that half of the students get the first list of solvable anagrams (NAIL, RUSH, HEAD, DRUM, BOOK, SOLD) and half of the students get the second list (unsolvable except the last one, SOLD). Do *not* tell the students that they are working from two different lists.
- Tell students to say "I'm done" when they have completed all six anagrams. Students who have the unsolvable anagrams should experience some learned helplessness, especially as other students complete the task effortlessly, and should be less able to solve, or even try to solve, the sixth anagram.
- Show the entire class the two different lists that were distributed and use this demonstration as a lead-in to discuss the concept of learned helplessness.

*Sources for activity: By permission of Houghton Mifflin.*

## All-purpose memory demonstration

(5 minutes) Based on a paper by Henry Roediger and Kathleen McDermott, this activity can be used as an introduction to memory concepts or a summary of material covered.

- Ask the class to listen as you read, at about one word per second, the following list: BED, QUILT, DARK, SILENCE, FATIGUE, CLOCK, SNORING, NIGHT, TOSS, TIRED, NIGHT, ARTI-CHOKE, TURN, NIGHT, REST, DREAM.
- After a brief pause, give the class 30 seconds to write down as many of the words as they can recall. Then repeat the word list in order and ask for a show of hands by those who correctly recalled each word. Plot the frequency of correct recall for each of the words on the chalkboard. At the end ask if they recalled the word *sleep* from the list. Many students will indicate that they recalled the word *sleep*, demonstrating constructive memory.

A serial-position curve should show that words at the beginning of the list (primacy) and end of the list (recency) are remembered best. *Artichoke* should be recalled because of semantic distinctiveness, *night* because it was presented three times, and *toss* and *turn* are often chunked and recalled together.

Roediger and McDermott (1995) contains an appendix supplying different word lists that should lead to a constructive memory.

*Source for activity: Roediger and McDermott (1995). By permission of Houghton Mifflin.*

## Memory and the seven dwarfs: Recognition vs. recall

(5 minutes) Students have experience taking multiple-choice and essay exams, so they know the difference between being able to recognize information and being able to recall it. This is a very simple demonstration of the same distinction, and of the fact that recognition tends to be easier than recall. Divide the class into two groups and have Group 1 close their eyes while you display the following written instructions to Group 2: "Write down the names of the seven dwarfs." Turn off the display and let Group 1 open their eyes while Group 2 is allowed one minute to complete their task. Then have Group 2 close their eyes and show Group 1 the following written instructions: "Find the names of the seven dwarfs." Allow Group 2 to open their eyes and then put up the following display^ (in large font) and give Group 1 one minute to complete the task (be sure that Group 2 does not use this display to amend the list they made earlier).

| | | | |
|---|---|---|---|
| GROUCHY | DUMPY | DROOPY | HAPPY |
| GABBY | SNEEZY | DOPEY | DOC |
| FEARFUL | LAZY | SNIFFY | DANNY |
| SLEEPY | POP | WISHFUL | TEACH |
| WHEEZY | JESSIE | GRUMPY | PUFFY |
| SMILEY | BASHFUL | STUBBY | JUMPY |
| CHEERFUL | HOPEFUL | SHORTY | SHY |
| AWESOME | NIFTY | POKEY | MOPEY |
| SLEEZY | GEORGE | SNOOZY | DOZER |

- Students who had to recall the information will be less likely to have all seven names than students who only had to recognize the names.
- This leads to a nice discussion about differences in studying for recognition vs. recall exams; mnemonics—some people use a mnemonic; tip-of-the-tongue phenomenon—many students will feel as though the information is right on the tip of their tongue; and cultural impact—students who have not seen Disney's *Snow White and the Seven Dwarfs* will have no idea.
- The seven dwarfs are Sleepy, Dopey, Grumpy, Sneezy, Happy, Doc, and Bashful.

*Source for activity: Miserandino (1996).*

## Levels of processing
(10 minutes) This activity demonstrates the levels-of-processing model of memory and helps students appreciate the relationship between the depth to which information is processed and the likelihood that it will be encoded or retrieved from long-term memory.

- ⓦ Divide the class into two groups and ask Group 1 to close their eyes while you display the following written instructions to Group 2: "For each of the words that I am going to read, mentally count or estimate the number of vowels in the word." Next, ask Group 2 to close their eyes while Group 1 opens their eyes to read a display showing the following written instructions: "For each of the words that I am going to read, mentally rate the usefulness of the item, on a 1–5 scale, if you were stranded on a desert island."
- Ask students to follow their instructions as they listen carefully, without writing anything, to the following words as you read them aloud:

ⓦ UMBRELLA, ORCHESTRA, YACHT, DIAMOND, UNIVERSITY, MACARONI, EYEGLASSES, GARDEN, UNDERWEAR, NEWSPAPER, ALCOHOL, BOUQUET, MICROSCOPE, CAMOUFLAGE, POLLUTION, RESTAURANT, INSECT, ELEPHANT, SULPHUR, LEMONADE, MOSQUITO, BOTTLE.

- To displace from short-term memory the words in the latter part of the list, ask the students to spend about 30 seconds performing tasks such as writing their name, address, phone number, major, and social security number (such a distraction is analogous to the one used in the Brown–Peterson procedure).

- After the distracting task, give the students one minute to write down as many words from the list as they can recall. Then display the words shown above so that students can check the number of words that they correctly recalled.

- There are 22 words on the list. Ask students to raise their hands if they got one item correct (almost all will). Tell them to keep their hands up until you reach the number of items that they correctly remembered, e.g., if they had 7 correct, they lower their hand when you say 8. Retention scores from those who processed the words superficially (by estimating the number of vowels) should be much lower than those from students who processed the information more deeply (by thinking about, and probably visualizing, the usefulness of each item in a particular situation). Another twist to this is to make joking comments about the "less intelligent" side of the room. Then, either now or when you discuss mental abilities in a later chapter, you can link this exercise with a discussion of how factors other than mental ability (in this case encoding strategy) can affect mental ability test performance.

- Ask students who remembered more words on the list to explain how they were able to recall the words.

- Show the entire class the set of instructions that each group received. Due to the instructions that students were given, they will differ in terms of the depth with which they elaborate upon and think about the material. Link this demonstration to the levels-of-processing model of memory.

- Link levels of processing to study advice—students should avoid study methods that process material superficially (e.g., by simply reading or underlining) in favor of deeper processing by outlining chapters, writing examples of the relationship between new and already learned material, or writing test questions about the material. This would be a good time to distribute ⓦ Handout #4 and discuss study strategies.

*Source for activity: By permission of Houghton Mifflin.*

## Encoding and retrieval

(5 minutes) This is a quick and easy demonstration of our tendency to recall information the way we encoded it. Ask students to write down the names of all of the 50 U.S. states. Give them a minute or two to do this. Then ask students to read their list in order. Some students will start alphabetically, some geographically, some learned a mnemonic in grade school and their list will be a result of that mnemonic. And some students will seem to have no "reason" behind the order of their list but when asked to explain will often report that they started with states they had lived in or had visited or had family in.

## Rumor chain—constructive memory

(5–20 minutes, depending on the number of students involved). The rumor chain, similar to the childhood game of "telephone," provides an illustration of how information in long-term memory can be distorted during encoding or retrieval by prior knowledge.

Ask for volunteers who think they have a "good memory." Send two to five of the volunteers out of the classroom, keeping one in class. Tell the class that you want them to keep track of the story that is being told and caution them not to laugh or provide cues for the volunteers. Read aloud a story to the class and the volunteer in class, whose task it is to repeat the story to one who has been out of the room. This next volunteer's task is to repeat the story to the next student who is readmitted and so on until the last student who hears the story repeats it to the class. Here is a sample story (developed by Mindy Bergman, Texas A & M University):

> On December 15, Joanne Hinckle, an executive for Exxon Oil, was brought into St. Luke's Episcopal Hospital in Houston. Ms. Hinckle had collapsed at an office party and complained of chest pains, shortness of breath, and shooting pains down her left arm. A cardiologist, Michelle Jackson, examined Ms. Hinckle and concluded that surgery was in order. The surgery was long and difficult, requiring a triple bypass, 6 pints of blood, and over 4 hours of surgery. Michael Smith, head cardiac nurse, was on duty that night and watched for any postsurgery complications. Fortunately, Ms. Hinckle seemed to come out of the surgery well and was expected to be released from the hospital in 6 days.

The errors made in each successive telling of the story are usually quite predictable and follow some basic principles of constructive memory. First, the story will get progressively shorter as nondistinctive details are left out. This is sometimes referred to as *leveling*. Particularly distinctive details are often retained, a process called *sharpening*. Because many elements of the story are encoded semantically, they are likely to be altered in line with the teller's schemas. For example, because many students, even today, think of doctors as men and nurses as women, Michelle Jackson may be remembered as the nurse and Michael Smith as the doctor.

*Source for activity: By permission of Houghton Mifflin.*

### Eye-witness testimony—a staged event

(1–2 minutes for the staged event, 5 minutes for students to write down what occurred) This activity is a good link between perception (top-down processing), memory (PDP memory model), research methods (naturalistic obser-vation and observer bias), cognition (scripts), and social cognition (attributions).

- Arrange a "script" with an accomplice, so that you know exactly what to say and do. Have the accomplice interrupt your class, claiming to be bringing quiz scores from the department. The accomplice comes to the front and briefly talks with you before leaving. After the accomplice leaves, continue class for a few minutes and then feign panic, realizing that your watch (which had been on your desk) is missing. Tell students to write a description of the departmental messenger so that you can file a complaint. Or, if you do not want to deceive your students, just have a messenger deliver the quizzes and a few minutes later ask the class to describe the messenger.
- Have students compare their descriptions—they won't be the same. Discuss why they have different descriptions and then relate this to eyewitness testimony. Have your accomplice return and share your "script" so students can see the errors in their memory of the event.

*Source for activity: Kite (1991). By permission of Houghton Mifflin.*

## Possible mini-assignments (written or groups)

### ⍵ Mini-assignment #1

You have just inherited a circus from a long-lost relative. All of the circus acts are "stale" and out of date. At an employee meeting, you explain the principles of classical and operant conditioning and provide examples of how the circus acts could be improved by using classical and operant conditioning. Below write one example demonstrating how classical conditioning could be used in one circus act. Write another example demonstrating how operant conditioning could be used in another circus act. Be sure to label all of the concepts.

Classical conditioning example:

Operant conditioning example:

### ⓦ *Mini-assignment #2*
(This is an in-class activity which works well in a group).

You are going to watch a clip from the movie, *Seabiscuit*. In this clip Seabiscuit is being classically conditioned as part of his training. Please fill out the following information.

Unconditioned stimulus =
Unconditioned response =
Conditioned stimulus =
Conditioned response =
Classical conditioning paradigm

(Note to instructors—this clip is when Seabiscuit is conditioned to run at the sound of a bell.)

### ⓦ *Mini-assignment #3*
(This works well as a group activity)

Read the following story and then retell it using the appropriate learning terminology. (Thanks to Amanda Allman for this activity.)

*Going to the store: A story about parenting and operant conditioning.*

A father often took his three-year-old son grocery shopping with him. They had a system worked out that if the son would be the father's "helper" by helping to put the groceries in the cart and not crying or whining, then he would get a Milky Way bar (his favorite) to eat on the way home. This worked very well for quite a while.

One day the father and son went to the store and the son kept crying and whining and wouldn't help his father at all. He begged and begged for the Milky Way bar, and finally his father bought the Milky Way bar to stop his crying and whining (which it did). The next several times they went to the store, the son whined and wouldn't help, and the father still bought him a Milky Way bar to stop his fussing. The father noticed, though, that his son only whined at the grocery store. He behaved very well when they went to a clothing store or other type of store without Milky Way bars.

Finally, the father decided he was not giving in to his son anymore. He never again gave his son Milky Way bars when he cried and whined at the grocery store, and eventually the son stopped being so difficult when they went grocery shopping.

Now the son is eight, and he still goes grocery shopping with his father. The father decided that now that his son is older he doesn't want to give him candy bars for being good any more. He always tells his son, though, that he is proud of him when he behaves when they go shopping, and overall the son behaves pretty well.

Retell this story using the following terms: operant, positive reinforcer, negative reinforcer, primary reinforcer, secondary reinforcer, discriminative stimuli, stimulus discrimination, stimulus control, extinction.

### ⓦ Mini-assignment #4
Go to http://www.bbc.co.uk/science/humanbody/mind/interactives/intelligenceandmemory/memorytest/ (a BBC web site) and take a memory test. How did you score? Explain your score and develop a plan to improve your score (and thus your memory) using terminology from the memory unit.

### ⓦ Mini-assignment #5
Recall an incident that happened to you when you were a child that also involved another person with whom you are still in contact (e.g., a parent, sibling, close friend). Write down all that you remember about the incident. Then ask the other person to write down what they remember, without sharing your version. How are the two descriptions alike? How do they differ? Explain the two versions using the ideas of constructive memory, encoding, and retrieval processes.

## Handouts

ⓦ Handout #1 Informational processing model of memory
ⓦ Handout #2 Biological bases of memory
ⓦ Handout #3 Stages of memory
ⓦ Handout #4 Study dos and don'ts

# References

Bernstein, D., Penner, L., Clarke-Stewart, A., and Roy, E. (2006). *Psychology* (7th ed.). Boston: Houghton Mifflin.

Capshew, J. (1993). Engineering behavior: Project Pigeon, World War II, and the conditioning of B. F. Skinner. *Technology and Culture, 34*(4), 835–857.

Fernald, P., & Fernald, L. (1999). Shaping behavior through operant conditioning. In L. Benjamin, B. Nodine, R. Ernst, & C. Blair Broeker (Eds.), *Activities handbook for the teaching of psychology, vol. 4* (pp. 176–80). Washington, DC: American Psychological Association.

Kite, M. E. (1991). Observer biases in the classroom. *Teaching of Psychology, 18*, 161–164.

Loftus, E. (2003). Make-believe memories. *American Psychologist, 58*(11), 867–873.

Loftus, E., & Ketcham, K. (1994). *The myth of repressed memories: False memories and allegations of sexual abuse.* New York: St. Martin's Press.

Loftus, E. F., & Pickrell, J. E. (1995). The formation of false memories. *Psychiatric Annals, 25*, 720–725.

Luminet, O., Curci, A., Marsh, E., Wessel, I., Constantin, T., Gencoz, F., & Yogo, M. (2004). The cognitive, emotional, and social impacts of the September 11 attacks: Group differences in memory for the reception context and the determinants of flashbulb memory. *The Journal of General Psychology, 2004, 131*(3), 197–224.

Miller, G. A. (1956). The magical number seven, plus or minus two: Some limits on our capacity for processing information. *Psychological Review, 63*, 81–97.

Miserandino, M. (1996). Memory and the seven dwarfs. In M. Ware & D. Johnson (Eds.), *Handbook of demonstrations and activities in the teaching of psychology, vol. II* (pp. 178–180). Mahwah, NJ: Lawrence Erlbaum.

Neisser, U. (2003). New directions for flashbulb memories: Comments on the ACP Special Issue. *Applied Cognitive Psychology, 17*(9), 1149.

Roediger, H., & McDermott, K. (1995). Creating false memories: Remembering words not presented in lists. *Journal of Experimental Psychology: Learning, Memory, & Cognition, 21*(4): 803–814.

Schacter, D., Norman, K., & Koutstaal, W. (1998). The cognitive neuroscience of memory. *Annual Review of Psychology, 49*, 289–318.

Seligman, M., & Maier, S. (1967). Failure to escape traumatic shock. *Journal of Experimental Psychology, 74*, 1–9.

Shenker, J. (1999). Classical conditioning: An all-purpose demonstration using a toy watergun. In L. Benjamin, B. Nodine, R. Ernst, & C. Blair Broeker (Eds.), *Activities for the teaching of psychology, vol. 4* (pp. 163–165). Washington, DC: American Psychological Association.

Skinner, B. F. (1945). Baby in a box. *Ladies' Home Journal*, 30–31, 135–36, 138.

Skinner, B. F. (1986). Programmed instruction revisited. *Phi Delta Kappan*, *68*(2), 103–110.

Thorndike, E. (1927). The law of effect. *American Journal of Psychology*, *39*(1/4), 212–222.

Vernoy, M. (1987). Demonstrating classical conditioning in introductory psychology: Needles do not always make balloons pop! *Teaching of Psychology*, *14*(3), 176–177.

Ware, M., & Johnson, D. (Eds.) (2000) *Handbook of demonstrations and activities in the teaching of psychology, vol. II.* Mahwah, NJ: Lawrence Erlbaum.

Watson, J. (1928). *Psychological care of infant and child.* New York: Norton.

## Additional Suggested Readings for Instructors

Baddeley, A. D. (1999). *Essential of human memory.* Hove, UK: Psychology Press.

Bartlett, F. (1932). *Remembering: A study in experimental and social psychology.* Cambridge, UK: Cambridge University Press.

Kotre, J. (1996). *White gloves: How we create ourselves through memory.* New York: Norton.

Skinner, B. F. (1948). *Walden two.* New York: Knopf.

Skinner, B. F. (1971). *Beyond freedom and dignity.* New York: Knopf.

Skinner, B. F. (1974). *About behaviorism.* New York: Knopf.

# Chapter 9

# Cognition, Language, and Cognitive Abilities

## Getting Started

When I first started teaching these two units were the most boring in the course. But I rethought my learning objective and I worked to find, or create, memorable examples and classroom demonstrations that allowed the students to experience the material. Now this is one of my favorite units to present.

I start with the basic truth—thought has a neural basis. All our thoughts, plans, and decisions can be traced to the depolarization of neurons. I want students to understand that the most complicated thinking we do all starts with the depolarization of neurons. This also reinforces the importance of the biological psychology unit.

I talk about ways of thinking and patterns of thinking becoming more sophisticated with age and experience—that children do not think the same way that most adults do. This idea is important when students become parents or when they interact with children in a professional capacity (e.g., as social worker, lawyer, or teacher). And this ties back to the developmental unit.

Other learning objectives include recognition of the shortcuts we all use in our thinking—heuristics, mental sets, schemas, and so forth. And understanding that most of the time, these shortcuts work well for us but, sometimes, they cause us to make errors.

Language is an exciting topic because we all rely on language to communicate with others. I stress that almost all babies are born able to make every sound necessary for any language. But as sounds aren't used, the ability to imitate them is lost.

I want my students to understand that intelligence is a culturally determined concept. I want them to grapple with the *idea* of intelligence. I also want them to see that psychological research has had an impact on government policy, for example, Cyril Burt and the educational structure in the United Kingdom, and IQ testing and immigration laws in the U.S. Thus I spend time talking about the history of intelligence testing.

I also want them to understand that "success" in a culture is often predicted by doing well on "culturally biased" IQ tests. And that there is less variability in IQ scores between ethnic groups than there is within ethnic groups.

And finally, because there is so much misinformation about mental retardation, I want them to understand that mentally retarded individuals' ways of thinking do not differ that much from everyone else's—mentally retarded individuals just know fewer facts about the world and do not have metacognitive skills/abilities.

## My outline for teaching (3 days—75 minute classes)

*Day 1*
Directions on board: Take a handout, read it, put it away (Schemas/
   Playing hooky classroom learning activity)
Collect ⊛ Mini-assignment #4
Questions from previous class (5 minutes)
Practice questions over material (5 minutes)
Administrivia (5 minutes)
  I.   Cognition: Schemas/scripts (10 minutes)
       Absence of information
  II.  Biological aspects (10 minutes)
       Reaction times
       Evoked brain potentials
  III. Thinking and concepts (students to do on their own)
  IV.  Algorithms/heuristics (15 minutes)
       Definitions
       Experiment
       Types
  V.   Problem solving (15 minutes)

VI. Schemas/Playing hooky classroom learning activity (10 minutes)

*Day 2*
Questions from previous class (5 minutes)
Practice questions over material (5 minutes)
Administrivia (5 minutes)
  I. Language (15 minutes)
     How language is learned
       Stages
       Theories
       Genie
     Language basics/organization
       Phonemes
       Morphemes
       Words
       Syntax
       Semantics
       Surface/deep structure
     Gender and language
     Learning a language changes the brain
     Dyslexia
  II. Definitions of cognitive abilities (15 minutes)
     Definitions from ⍵ Mini-assignment #4
  III. History of heredity vs. environment arguments (20 minutes)
  IV. Culture free/culture fair (10 minutes)
     Use their items from ⍵ Mini-assignment #4

*Day 3*
Questions from previous class (5 minutes)
Practice questions over material (5 minutes)
Administrivia (5 minutes)
  I. Teacher expectancies—Rosenthal and Jacobson research (10 minutes)
  II. Distribution of IQ scores (5 minutes)
  III. Intelligence and age/fluid vs. crystallized (5 minutes)
     Speed slows, difficulty holding information in STM to solve problems
  IV. Modern approaches to cognitive abilities (20 minutes)
     Gardner
     Sternberg
  V. Test construction (20 minutes)

## My transitions

I cover the cognitive unit immediately after memory. I often segue into cognition by doing the Rumor chain classroom learning activity (see Learning and memory unit, pp. 162–3). Discussing what is "left" at the end of the rumor chain leads into a nice discussion of schemas. I move to cognitive abilities after cognition, trying to get students to see the "units of cognition" as possible indications of "intelligence." I typically segue into motivation and emotion after cognitive abilities. I stress that once we know the basics of *how* we think or our cognitive building blocks, then we need to know the *why*. Motivation and emotion explore the *whys*.

## Topics typically included in this unit

*Thought*: The circle of thought—describe, elaborate, decide, plan, act; mental representations; concepts—formal, natural, prototypes; propositions; schemas and scripts; mental models; images and cognitive maps; thinking strategies—formal reasoning, informal reasoning, heuristics: anchoring, representativeness, availability

*Measuring information processing*: Mental chronometry; evoked brain potentials; neuroimagining

*Problem solving*: Strategies—means–end analysis, working backwards, using analogies; obstacles—multiple hypotheses, mental sets, ignoring negative evidence, confirmation bias; problem solving by experts—analogies, chunking, similarities, mental sets, confirmation bias; by computer—symbolic reasoning and computer logic, neural network models

*Decision making*: Process—evaluating options, comparing attributes, estimating probabilities; flaws and biases—gains, losses, probabilities, gambler's fallacy; naturalistic decision making—situation awareness; group processes in decision making—group polarization, groupthink, social loafing, brainstorming

*Language*: Elements—phonemes, morphemes, syntax, semantics; surface and deep structure; understanding speech—top-down and bottom-up processing; language acquisition stages—babblings, one word, telegraphic two-word sentences, longer sentences; theories of acquisition—conditioning, imitation, rules; biological bases—universal grammar, Chomsky; bilingualism; language and primates; culture, language, and thought—Whorf linguistic determinism

*History of intelligence tests*: Alfred Binet—age-graded items, mental age, chronological age; Terman—Stanford-Binet, intelligence quotient; WWI and group tests

*Modern intelligence tests*: Components—verbal comprehension, perceptual reasoning, working memory, processing speed, fluid reasoning, knowledge, quantitative reasoning; scoring—percentile

*Aptitude vs. achievement tests*: Potential vs. learning

*Test qualities*: Reliability—test–retest, alternate forms, split-half; validity—content, criterion, construct, predictive; culture free/culture fair

*Issues in intelligence*: Nature vs. nurture—genetics and heredity, twin studies, adoption studies, environment—preschool enrichment, teacher expectancies; group differences in IQ scores—socioeconomic differences, ethnic differences; giftedness, mental retardation, learning disabilities

*Approaches to intelligence*: Psychometric—general intelligence and special intelligences, fluid and crystallized intelligence; information processing—attention and speed of processing; triarchic theory (Sternberg)—analytical, creative, practical; multiple intelligences (Gardner)—linguistic, logical-mathematical, spatial, musical, body-kinesthetic, intrapersonal, interpersonal, naturalistic

*Other cognitive abilities*: Creativity—divergent thinking

## Some options for organizing the concepts

*By developmental stage*: Start with a discussion of the cognitive functioning of a newborn and continue through the stages of childhood and adolescence integrating cognitive processes, cognitive abilities, and language.

*By topic*: I introduce cognition immediately following the memory unit. I see learning → memory → cognition and language → cognitive abilities as having a natural progression and I integrate the concepts from all of the units.

# Teaching the Content

Remember that the ⦿ symbol means that a printable version is available on the web site (www.blackwellpublishing.com/lucas) and ⓤ means that the URL is available on the web site.

## Topics that many students will find difficult

### Mental chronometry

I discuss factors that influence reaction time: complexity, expectancy, stimulus–response compatibility, and speed–accuracy trade-off. When time permits, I use the Mental chronometry classroom learning activity, which adds complexity to the "shoulder squeeze" demonstration I used in the biological psychology unit (see p. 184).

### Event-related potentials (ERPs)

I take this opportunity to integrate sensation, perception, and cognition. I explain the idea of an N100 (100 milliseconds after a stimulus is presented the N100 shows that initial sensory processing is taking place); and P300 (which occurs 300 milliseconds after a stimulus is presented and represents when perception of the stimulus occurs). A large P300 shows that the stimulus has some personal significance. This connects cognition with brain function and demonstrates the minuscule timing differences between sensing a stimulus and perceiving it. Research on P300s is helping to solve the communication problems of "locked-in" individuals (those with intact intelligence, but with body paralysis leaving them no way to communicate). When a person's brain waves are monitored, communication can be achieved by the person concentrating on the letter needed to spell out their thoughts. The basic premise is that by concentrating on the particular letter, a large P300 is recorded when viewing that letter, thus allowing the person to spell their thoughts. Currently, the process is also being used as a predictor of recovery from coma.

See Farwell and Donchin (1988), Onofrj, Thomas, Paci, Scesi, and Tombari (1997), and Donchin, Spencer, and Wijesinghe (2000).

### Psychometrics of IQ tests

The "statistical" aspects of IQ tests often confuse students. They tend to understand the advantages of using tests—standardization, quantifiable scores, and an economical and efficient way of gathering information. But reliability and validity are difficult concepts.

Reliability—consistency. I equate reliability to a thermometer. You take your temperature and it is 98.6. You sit quietly and take your temperature 5 minutes later and it is 103.5. Obviously, the thermometer is not accurate—not consistent—therefore your temperature readings are not reliable.

- Test—retest, alternate form, and split half are all ways of assessing the reliability of the test.

Validity—measures what it is designed to measure.

- *Content validity*—the degree to which the test items are related to what the test is supposed to measure. If students encountered questions about driving a car on their psychology test, the test would lack content validity.
- *Construct validity*—the extent to which scores on the test are in accordance with one's theory about what is being tested. If you believe that intelligence improves with age, and 5-year-olds score higher on your test than 30-year-olds, your test lacks construct validity.
- *Criterion validity*—the extent to which test scores correlate with another direct and independent measure of what the test is supposed to assess. If you scored an A+ on your test of Spanish speaking, but could not have a basic conversation with a native Spanish speaker, your test lacked criterion validity. If the criterion is a later measure it is often called *predictive validity*. If you score high on a college entrance exam, but then have failing grades your first semester, and no extraneous factors were at work, the entrance exam did not have predictive validity.
- *Concurrent validity*—sometimes new tests are "validated" against old tests—and this is called concurrent validity. If my new IQ test correlates highly with the WAIS-R, then it can be said to have concurrent validity.

Note that tests can be reliable but not valid—for example, if you have a broken thermometer that always gives a temperature of 99.9 it is consistent, but not measuring what it should. However, a test cannot be valid without being reliable; indeed validity can never exceed reliability. See Cohen and Swerdlik (2002), which describes validity and reliability as well as dedicating two entire chapters to intelligence tests. Eyal Reingold's (University of Toronto) web site ⓤ contains a *Scientific American* article on the evidence for a *g*-factor in intelligence and support for the idea that IQ tests are predictive of future successes. Eyal Reingold's course page ⓤ has information about the many things that IQ does predict.

## Other important topics

### Concepts, propositions, and mental models
These are the building blocks of thought. Formal concepts have nice boundaries and rules (What is a square?) while natural

concepts (What is clothing?) do not and often are best explained with a prototype (A shirt is clothing but is a hat?). Propositions express relationships between concepts. And mental models are visual images we use. So, when I ask students what color their house is, they almost always first bring up a mental picture of the house before answering the question. I also point out that I blame my lack of computer abilities on my poor mental model of a computer.

### Schemas and scripts
Schemas are discussed in development (Piaget), in memory (constructive memory), and in social psychology (stereotypes). I tie all of these uses of schemas together. Frederic Bartlett is often credited with developing the theory of schemas. See Bartlett (1932).

### Culture and cognitive style
There is research showing that cognition is based on environment—thus groups that grow up with round buildings are less likely to see the illusion in the Ames room than those growing up in an angular environment. This is important for students to understand, as they have a difficult time stepping out of their own culture. There has also been discussion of field dependence and field independence as a cultural style. For a discussion of that see Berry, Poortinga, Segall, and Dasen (2002, Chapter 5). The original "field dependence" article is Witkins and Goodenough (1977).

### Algorithms and heuristics
Because psychologists use the term "algorithm" differently than mathematicians, I spend time defining algorithm (a systematic formula or procedure that cannot fail to produce a correct solution, if there is one) and heuristics (mental shortcuts that usually work, but that are vulnerable to cognitive biases and errors). I use the example of playing Scrabble. Using an algorithm, you would put together all possible combinations of your tiles until you found the best combination—of course all the other players would have left long ago. But using a heuristic, you might separate vowels and consonants, for example. Three commonly used heuristics are anchoring, representativeness, and availability.

A good analogy for the anchoring heuristic is the idea of a boat anchor—once it is dropped the boat can only move a little bit either way. The typical example involves an original estimate that you have a 70% chance of being mugged on a visit to City Z. After reading an article that says that City Z is one of the safest to visit, you change your estimate to 60%, but not to 10%.

The *representativeness heuristic* relates back to the ideas of schemas and stereotypes. The Representativeness heuristic classroom learning activity (p. 187) demonstrates the fact that people tend to ignore base rate information and concentrate on what is most representative.

The *availability heuristic* involves fitting new information into existing schemas, a bit like Piaget's concept of assimilation. For example, during the anthrax scares a few years ago, people were receiving white powder contaminated with anthrax through the mail, and there was a lot of media attention surrounding it. When a white powder was found on the floor of my children's school, the cafeteria was evacuated—only to find that the white powder was sugar. Also, once a flu "epidemic" hits a community, your chances of being incorrectly diagnosed with flu when you are ill increase, as the flu model is the one most health professionals have.

### Biases in cognition

Daniel Gilbert (2006) discusses cognitive biases that tend to be universal, and presents a discussion of why we are poor predictors of our future. You can read a review of his book at the APS web site ⓤ. Gilbert also has a web site ⓤ.

### Problem solving

Helping students understand problem-solving strategies and providing them with a step-by-step guide for "rational" problem solving is important.

Strategies for problem solving include: incubation (I'll sleep on it); means–end analysis (I'll break these down into manageable parts); working backwards (this is the outcome I want, I'll start there and figure out how to get here); and using analogies (I had a similar problem last year—how did I approach that?).

For an excellent presentation on problem solving, including the Luchins water jar problem and the tower of Hanoi problem, see John Ackroff's PowerPoint slides ⓤ which he graciously grants public access to.

Difficulties in problem solving involve *mental sets* and *functional fixedness*. A mental set is the tendency for old patterns of problem solving to persist, even when they aren't useful. The Luchins jar problem is the classic demonstration of this. You may see the basic Luchins experiment at the National Academies Press web site Ⓤ. Functional fixedness, or not thinking of novel ways of using familiar objects, is easily demonstrated with the Functional fixedness classroom learning activity (pp. 188–9).

## Decision making

We all make decisions, but not always in a rational manner. Therefore, I walk my students through the model of evaluating options (I can major in psychology or accounting—what are the pros and cons of each major?) by comparing attributes of the options (a psychology major will take me 4 years to complete and I'll need to go to grad school, an accounting major will take 5 years, but I'll have a job when I graduate) and estimating the probability of each option (I failed math last semester, and I got an A in intro psychology) to provide a rational model of decision making.

Students are fascinated with the concept of loss aversion, the idea that people feel worse about losing a certain amount than they feel good about gaining the same amount. They are able to provide examples of loss aversion in their own lives. See Tversky and Kahneman (1991).

Gambler's fallacy—the idea that random events are influenced by previous events—is a difficult bias for students to understand.

## Language

Language organization includes phonemes, the smallest unit of sound that affects the meaning of speech; morphemes, the smallest unit of language that has meaning; words; syntax, the rules for combining words; and semantics, the rules governing the meaning of words and sentences.

Stages of language development proceed from babbling, to one-word speech, to telegraphic two-word sentences, to three-word and longer sentences. I talk about motherese, the tendency of adults to talk to infants in high-pitched voices, using exaggerated and elongated vowel sounds. We are rewarded for such behavior because infants attend to high pitches. I discuss Noam Chomsky's idea that we are all born with a language acquisition device (LAD) versus the behaviorist view that language is learned through rewards and punishments.

What is language? See *Cognition and Language* ⓤ (2001), a 30-minute video, for a discussion of what language involves and how human language differs from animal communication.

- Critical period—The story of Genie, a child raised in isolation for 13 years, tests the idea of a critical period for language development. Her story is compelling and is a powerful demonstration of language acquisition. See NOVA's *Secret of the Wild Child* ⓤ (60 minutes, 1994). An instructor's guide and a description of the video may be found at the PBS webpage ⓤ. See also Russ Rymer's (1992, 1993) study of Genie.

- Gender and language—Research has found that each gender uses language in a different manner and for different purposes. Women's "language culture" puts them at a disadvantage in the college classroom. See Hall and Sandler (1984) and Sandler and Hall (1986). Deborah Tannen has also written about this, although her work has come under fire from speech communication researchers. See Tannen (1990).

- Culture and language—The Sapir–Whorf hypothesis argued that language shapes our view of the world—that without the appropriate words, we couldn't have the appropriate thoughts. Although this theory is not widely held, I like to ask my students to ponder the implications of it. For a discussion of the hypothesis and its implications see Minnesota University at Mankato's e-museum web site ⓤ.

  For a more modern discussion of the influence of culture on communication, see *Cross-cultural communication: How culture affects communication* ⓤ (2005), a 20-minute DVD.

### What is intelligence? The nature/nurture controversy

Providing evidence for both views helps students understand that intelligence is a blend of genetics and environment.

Robert Sternberg's (1996a) article on 10 myths and counter-myths about IQ testing presents research regarding those claims. Even though it is an old article, the myths are still current.

For the environmental argument, I cite a very old study conducted by Harold Skeels in the 1930s. He removed two children from an orphanage and put them in a home for the mentally retarded because their behavior suggested they were mentally impaired. Later these two girls were shown to have average IQ and their behavior became "normal," all because they were loved and

nurtured by the mentally retarded patients in their new environment. Skeels then conducted an experiment, moving the children
who appeared the most "retarded" out of the orphanage and into
the home for mentally retarded. And once again these children
thrived socially and intellectually. For full details see Skeels,
Updegraff, Wellman, and Williams (1938). and Skeels (1966). A
more modern argument can be found in the research on the effects
of Project Head Start. Once touted as a way of increasing children's IQ and school performance, recent research has shown that
gains can be lost if the enrichment is not continued. See the U.S.
Department of Health and Human Services web site ⓤ for a listing
of papers on the effects of Head Start.

Sandra Scarr's transracial adoption study is often cited as classic in
research on environmental and genetic impacts on IQ. See Scarr and
Weinberg (1983). See also Duyme, Dumaret, and Tomkiewicz (1999).

## Approaches to intelligence

For a general resource, see Sternberg (2000).

The *psychometric approach* focuses on the products of intelligence,
not the process. Spearman's *g*, or the idea that there is a general
intelligence that underlies specific intelligences, is supported by
recent research on neural activity underlying intelligence tasks. See
Duncan et al. (2000). See also Haier, White, and Alkire (2003).

- See the American Association for the Advancement of Science's
  Science Magazine web site ⓤ for a discussion of general
  intelligence.
- Raymond Cattell's factor analytic studies showed two kinds of
  general intelligence, crystallized, which is specific knowledge, and
  fluid, which is the power of reasoning and problem solving. For
  information about Cattell, his theory, and some suggested references, see The Society for the Teaching of Psychology web site ⓤ.

The *information-processing approach* identifies the mental processes
involved in intelligence, not the traits. The emphasis is on processing speed, working memory, and attention.

Robert Sternberg's *triarchic theory*, proposes three different types of
intelligences—analytic (which is what is measured on traditional
IQ tests); creative (which is used in drawing a picture); and practical ("street smarts"). For a complete explanation of his theory
and examples of test items designed to test each type, see Sternberg
(1985, 1996b).

*Multiple intelligences* is the theory of Howard Gardner. He believes that people possess a number of intellectual abilities which draw on different skills. He has proposed that there are linguistic, logical-mathematical, spatial, musical, body-kinesthetic, intrapersonal, interpersonal, and naturalistic intelligences. See Gardner (1993). *Multiple Intelligences: Other Styles of Learning* Ⓤ is a 29-minute video highlighting "nontraditional intelligence."

## History of IQ testing

The original proponents of IQ testing had a hereditary perspective. Alfred Binet, often cited as the "father of modern IQ tests," developed his IQ test to identify mentally defective children and move them out of regular schools because he didn't think they could learn there. Francis Galton was one of the developers of eugenics theory—the idea that "selective breeding" could create a meritocracy, or a class of higher intelligence. And Henry Goddard believed that "feeble-mindedness" was genetic. Robert Yerkes and cohorts developed the original IQ tests in the United States to assess the intelligence, and thus best assignment, of recruits during World War I—the Army Alpha (for recruits who could read English) and the Army Beta (for recruits who did not read English). See Mark Holah's AS Psychology web site Ⓤ for examples of Beta test items. These tests were culturally biased and were also incorrectly used to "demonstrate" that immigrants from southern and eastern Europe had low intellect. These findings did have an impact on the passage of the Immigration Act of 1924 which severely restricted the number of immigrants allowed to enter the U.S. Excellent resources include Cianciolo and Sternberg (2004) and Privateer (2005). See *Intelligence & Creativity* Ⓤ (2001), a 30-minute video that discusses definitions of intelligence and the history of intelligence testing. See also Broad (1982): Chapter 11, "Failure of Objectivity," discusses fraud and "bad science" in IQ testing (Cyril Burt's research). See also Gould (1996).

## Intelligence and age

There is a perception that intelligence declines with age. Research shows that fluid intelligence, involving processing speed and manipulations of multiple data, does decrease fairly early in life (peaking about 30). However, crystallized intelligence and verbal abilities begin to decline later in life (50–60) and the decline is much more gradual. *Older Brains, New Connections: A conversation with Marian Diamond at 73* Ⓤ presents information about the "aging brain," refutes some myths surrounding aging and brain function, and discusses ways to maintain "brain health" as one ages.

Wisdom—Growing old can be associated with wisdom, defined as expert knowledge in the fundamental, practical aspects of life. See Sternberg (2003, 2005).

Terminal drop is the tendency for an individual's cognitive functioning to dramatically decrease in the few years before death. See Small and Baackman (1999).

## Giftedness

What is giftedness? Do gifted children just have "more" intelligence or do they have a different way of perceiving and processing information? For a discussion of these questions the following resources are helpful:

Sternberg and Davidson (2005). Chapter 1 by James Borland and Chapter 6 by Joan Freeman focus on what giftedness is.

Lewis Terman's study of gifted children introduced the concept of longitudinal research on intelligence. See Terman (1925) and Terman and Oden (1959).

For a discussion of Lewis Terman, his beliefs, and his study see the Stanford University Alumni Organization's web site ⓤ.

See the APA web site ⓤ for a description of current studies on gifted children.

See also the *BMJ Journal's* web site ⓤ for a paper that found a strong correlation between IQ and mortality—in other words, that those with higher IQs live longer.

## Mental retardation

While the terminology keeps changing, IQ scores of 90–110 are considered "average or normal," 80–90 is often called "dull normal," 70–80 "borderline," 55–70 "mild," 40–55 "moderate," 25–40 "severe" and anything below 25 "profound."

Mildly retarded children differ from those of higher intellect in that they perform certain mental operations more slowly, know fewer facts about the world, and are not good at using mental strategies.

Down syndrome, a genetic disorder, accounts for some instance of mental retardation. Environmental causes of mental retardation include birth traumas, drug or alcohol use by the mother while pregnant, and exposure to toxic chemicals. Familial retardation appears to have no genetic or environmental cause but tends to be observed in families of extremely low socioeconomic status.

## IQ and culture

Attempts to help members of the majority culture understand the cultural biases in most standard IQ tests resulted in the development of somewhat facetious IQ tests that are biased toward a minority culture. These included tests such as Adrian Dove's Dove Counterbalance Intelligence Test (often called the Chitling Test of Intelligence) and the Black Intelligence Test of Cultural Homogeneity.

The entire Dove test may be found in Haskins and Butts (1973, pp. 47–49), or a shorter version may be found at the Wilderdom web site ⓤ.

In 1972 Robert Williams developed the Black Intelligence Test of Cultural Homogeneity—again to demonstrate that children who can learn in their own subculture can learn in schools as well. For a short version of the BITCH test see Susan Ohanian's web site ⓤ. For Williams's paper see ERIC ED070799—The BITCH-100: A Culture-Specific Test. (Note: Both the Dove and Williams tests are out-of-date—something I use in my discussion of IQ tests.)

Raymond Cattell's Culture-Fair Intelligence Test was one of the first "standardized" attempts to develop an IQ test that was not dependent on culture. For a discussion of this test go to the Find Articles web site ⓤ.

For more modern discussions of culture and IQ, see Sternberg, Lautrey, and Lubart (2003).

For a current cultural perspective on intelligence see Chapter 5 of Berry et al. (2002).

## IQ in the classroom

Robert Rosenthal and Lenore Jacobson's famous study identified some of the ways that classroom teachers' interactions with their elementary school students increased student IQs. Although later studies did not replicate their dramatic findings, there is evidence that teacher behavior does have an impact on student behavior. See Rosenthal and Jacobson (1968), and Snow (1995).

Learning disabilities are quickly outpacing sensory disabilities in the classroom. This topic is an opportunity to tie learning concepts with intelligence and classroom performance. See O'Brien (2001,

2004). See also *Understanding Learning Disabilities* Ⓤ, a 16-minute video discussion what learning disabilities are and *Dyslexia: A Different Kind of Mind* Ⓤ, a 29-minute video discussing dyslexia and teaching techniques to help students with dyslexia to succeed.

### Stereotype threat
Claude Steele and his colleagues identified stereotype threat as "underperformance" on a cognitive task due to concern over negative stereotypes about the cognitive abilities of the group to which they belong. Recent research has questioned the strength of this impact. See Steele and Aronson (1995, 2000).

# Classroom Tips

## Stimulus questions for discussion

### Problem solving
What problem have you recently faced—for example, a disagreement with your roommate, deciding which classes to sign up for, performing poorly on your chemistry exams, or writing a term paper? How did you approach this problem? How did you solve it? What other ways could you have tried to solve this problem? (See Ⓦ Mini-assignment #2.)

### Language
How many of you speak a language other than English? Are you bilingual? When did you start learning the other language? How proficient are you in that language? If you could influence public school curricula, when would you introduce another language?

### Intelligence and biology
Are intelligent people just faster and more efficient processors? One study found that when people are learning to play a new video game, many areas of the brain are involved. But as they get better at the game, there is less brain activity. And the biggest decrease in activity (most efficient use?) occurs in people with the highest intelligence.

### Mental retardation and "rights."
There are many guidelines in place that protect the mentally ill from being "involuntarily committed." Those guidelines are not in place for the mentally retarded. Why?

### Identifying mental retardation

Some high school counselors comment that high school students who are in special classes for "low-IQ students" leave high school and "melt into the general population." How can you explain the difference in their status in school vs. their status in "real life"?

### IQ and income

One of the assertions of the controversial book *The Bell Curve* (Herrnstein and Murray, 1994) is that IQ determines income. What data would you need to test this idea? What evidence supports this assertion? What evidence disputes this assertion?

## Some suggested classroom learning activities

### Reaction time and cognitive complexity

(10–30 minutes) Go back to the Mental chronometry and speed of neural transmission classroom learning activity in the biological psychology unit (pp. 85–6). Repeat that simple demonstration first, but add cognitive components to subsequent trials. For example, give each student four letters that they have to memorize. They close their eyes, and a large stimulus letter is written on the blackboard so all will be able to see it when they open their eyes. On a signal from their neighbor, the student opens his or her eyes, looks at the letter on the board, decides if it is one of the letters they were to memorize and if it is they poke the neighbor's arm with their index finger; if it wasn't they poke their neighbor's arm with their middle finger. The neighbor doesn't know which finger it was, but the experimenter can watch to make sure no errors occur. Because cognitive processes are necessary, these trials will take much more time than the previous, simple reaction time trials. A simpler demonstration uses the shoulder squeeze, but if your right shoulder was squeezed, you have to squeeze the next person's left shoulder. Or, to make it even more complicated, if your right shoulder is squeezed once, you squeeze the next person's left shoulder once, who then squeezes the next person's right shoulder twice, and so forth. The results are the same—adding the cognitive component takes time—thinking takes time.

*Source for activity: Rozin and Jonides (1977) or Ware and Johnson (1996, pp. 38–41). See also Scripture (1895).*

### Schemas/Doing laundry

(5–10 minutes) I put the following paragraph on the overhead and ask students to write down what they think is happening. Then we talk about it and I ask them if having the title, *Doing Laundry*, would have made a difference. This is a good demonstration of how important schemas are in organizing information for us.

> Ⓦ The procedure is actually quite simple. First you arrange things into different groups depending on their makeup. Of course, one pile may be sufficient depending on how much there is to do. If you have to go somewhere else due to lack of facilities that is the next step, otherwise you are pretty well set. It is important not to overdo any particular endeavor. That is, it is better to do too few things at once than too many. In the short run this may not seem important, but complications from doing too many can easily arise. A mistake can be expensive as well. The manipulation of the appropriate mechanisms should be self-explanatory, and we need not dwell on it here. At first the whole procedure will seem complicated. Soon, however, it will become just another facet of life. It is difficult to foresee any end to the necessity for this task in the immediate future, but then one can never tell.

*Source for activity: Bransford and Johnson (1972, p. 722).*

## Schemas/Playing hooky
(2–3 minutes to read the handout, 10 minutes for the demonstration)

I have three different handouts. Each handout contains the same story, but has different instructions. One set of instructions asks students to read the story from the point of view of a burglar, another from the point of a home buyer, and one just says that this is a story about two boys playing hooky. I alternate the sheets before class and simply hand them out face down in class, asking the students to read through the handout once quickly, and then put the story away. I proceed with class until only about 10 minutes are left and then ask the students to write down everything they remember about the story, without looking at it again. I give them a couple of minutes to do this, and then as they provide information, I write it on the board in three columns, one for each set of instructions. Because only about one third of the class remembers any particular piece of information, they become suspicious and I reveal the three different sets of instructions, leading to a discussion about the influence of schemas on our organization and memory. As a follow-up, I often ask students two weeks later to write down what they remembered about the story. Most of the students will still remember the parts of the story which were relevant to their original schema.

> Ⓦ Instructions: This story is about two boys playing hooky from school.

🅦 Instructions: You are a residential burglar. You have been watching a large house for over a week. This house is discussed in the story below. Use the information to your advantage.

🅦 Instructions: You are in the market for a new house. Below is a story giving you information about one house that you have been considering. Use this information to your advantage.

🅦 Story:

The two boys ran until they came to the driveway. "See, I told you today was good for skipping school," said Mark. "Mom is never home on Thursday," he added. Tall hedges hid the house from the road so the pair strolled across the finely landscaped yard. "I never knew your place was so big," said Pete. "Yeah, but it's nicer now than it used to be since Dad had the new stone siding put on and added the fireplace."

There were front and back doors and a side door which led to the garage which was empty except for three parked 10-speed bikes. They went in the side door, Mark explaining that it was always open in case his younger sisters got home earlier than their mother.

Pete wanted to see the house so Mark started with the living room. It, like the rest of the downstairs, was newly painted. Mark turned on the stereo, the noise of which worried Pete. "Don't worry, the nearest house is a quarter of a mile away," Mark shouted. Pete felt more comfortable observing that no houses could be seen in any direction beyond the huge yard.

The dining room, with all the china, silver, and cut glass, was no place to play so the boys moved into the kitchen where they made sandwiches. Mark said they wouldn't go to the basement because it had been damp and musty ever since the new plumbing had been installed.

"This is where my Dad keeps his famous paintings and his coin collection," Mark said as they peered into the den. Mark bragged that he could get spending money whenever he needed it since he'd discovered that his Dad kept a lot in the desk drawer.

There were three upstairs bedrooms. Mark showed Pete his mother's closet which was filled with furs and the locked box which held her jewels. His sisters' room was uninteresting except for the color TV which Mark carried to his room. Mark bragged that the bathroom in the hall was his since one had been added to his sisters' room for their use. The big highlight in his room, though, was a leak in the ceiling where the old roof had finally rotted.

*Source for activity: Pichert & Anderson, 1977. By permission of Houghton Mifflin.*

## Scripts

(5 minutes) I read the following sentences and ask students to explain what is going on. Because of the script, they have an easy time, even with minimal information.

"Amy heard the bell outside. She ran to her piggy bank and then outside to get a popsicle" (source unknown). I then ask: Why did she get her piggy bank? Where did she get the popsicle? What season is it? How old is Amy? For other scripts see Schank and Abelson (1977) and Minsky (1977).

## Representativeness heuristic

(5–10 minutes.) To demonstrate this heuristic I divide the class in half. Group 1 closes their eyes and Group 2 reads the following information on the overhead display:

ⓦ *A panel of psychologists interviewed a sample of 70 engineers and 30 lawyers, summarizing their impressions in thumbnail descriptions of those individuals. The following description has been drawn at random from the sample of 70 engineers and 30 lawyers:*

Then Group 2 closes their eyes and Group 1 read the following information:

ⓦ *A panel of psychologists interviewed a sample of 30 engineers and 70 lawyers, summarizing their impressions in thumbnail descriptions of those individuals. The following description has been drawn at random from the sample of 30 engineers and 70 lawyers:*

Finally, both groups read the following description and are asked to immediately write down their probability.

ⓦ *John is a 39-year-old man. He is married and has two children. he is active in local politics. The hobby that he most enjoys is rare book collecting. He is competitive, argumentative, and articulate.*

*What is the probability that John is a lawyer rather than an engineer?*

Most students rate the probability that John is a lawyer as very high—no matter what base rate information they were given. This leads to a great discussion of using "stereotypes" or using the representativeness heuristic.

*Source for activity: By permission of Houghton Mifflin.*

## Biases in cognition

(5 minutes) I use Eliot Hearst's article (Hearst, 1991). It is difficult for us to notice when something is missing—but easy to notice when something is added. Hearst has a couple of easy examples that I put on transparencies and use as a "lead in" to this phenomenon. I ask students if they have ever noticed when they go home that something has been added—a lamp, a flower arrangement, or whatever. Most of us easily know when something is added. Then ask them if they have ever had something taken away—for example, when a friend shaved a beard (it took me two days to realize that my husband had shaved his mustache off!) or something was removed from a familiar room or a tree was cut down in a familiar place. This is more difficult; we have a sense that something is different, but we do not always know what that is.

## Mental sets

(2–5 minutes to unscramble the words, 5 minutes for discussion.) I have two sets of scrambled words. I give one row of students Set 1, the next row Set 2, and so on. Then I give them two minutes to unscramble the words. The last scrambled word is the same, but a mental set (either flower or dishes) should have been created so that the last word, which is the same letters, is unscrambled differently. The answer key is also provided.

Set 1

◍ As quickly as possible, unscramble the words in the list of six words provided below. Take each word in order, and unscramble it before moving to the next one. Write your answer on the line provided.

| | | |
|---|---|---|
| NYPAS | _____ | (PANSY) |
| FELA | _____ | (LEAF) |
| KTALS | _____ | (STALK) |
| DUB | _____ | (BUD) |
| LOBSOMS | _____ | (BLOSSOM) |
| LTEPA | _____ | (PETAL) |

Set 2

◍ As quickly as possible, unscramble the words in the list of six words provided below. Take each word in order, and unscramble it before moving to the next one. Write your answer on the line provided.

| | | |
|---|---|---|
| FINEK | _____ | (KNIFE) |
| OPONS | _____ | (SPOON) |
| KROF | _____ | (FORK) |
| PUC | _____ | (CUP) |
| ECUSAR | _____ | (SAUCER) |
| LTEPA | _____ | (PLATE) |

*Source for activity: By permission of Houghton Mifflin.*

## Functional fixedness

(20 minutes: 5 minutes for instruction and distribution of materials, 10 minutes for group work, 5 minute discussion.) Assemble an array of items including a sewing kit, a pad of $8^1/_2 \times 11$ paper, a roll of transparent tape, a sharpened pencil, and a phonograph record. To make the problem more difficult, add a tennis ball, a tool kit, an apple, and any number of other interesting and diverse items. You can divide the class into groups and provide the same materials to each group, or you can do this as a whole group exercise. Tell students that they have to play the phonograph record so that the class can hear it, using only the materials displayed.

Because none of the items available—except the record—are normally associated with record-playing, it may take a while for the students to think of the following solution: Take a sheet of paper, roll it from one corner to form a cone, and tape the edge to hold that shape. Then tape a needle from the sewing kit to the outside surface of the narrow end of the paper cone so that its sharp point extends an inch or so beyond the cone. Now push the pencil firmly into the hole in the record so that, by resting the eraser end on a firm surface, the record can be turned clockwise in a level plane. Now, while turning the record in this way, grasp the edge of the large end of the paper cone between thumb and forefinger and let the needle rest on the turning record. It won't be high fidelity or stereo, but the sound will be amplified enough for everyone to hear.

This problem-solving task becomes more difficult as the CD and MP3 era students have no experience with phonographs, and thus if you have older students in the class, their experience might make them more expert.

*Variation.* To demonstrate the effect of stress on problem solving, you might want to set a time limit on the task or, better yet, divide the class into several competing groups with a reward for the group that solves the problem first.

*Source for activity: Bernstein and Goss Lucas (1999).*

## Surface and deep structure in language

(I just incorporate these into my language lecture—they take minimal time.) The fact that a sentence can have one grammatical structure, but more than one meaning is a concept students understand and enjoy. Below are some headlines that I have accumulated from many resources over the years. I pick a few of them and then ask the students to provide the multiple deep structures. I also ask students to watch for such headlines themselves and share them with the class.

Research hindered by lack of brains.
Dog for sale: Eats anything and is fond of children.
3-year-old teacher needed for pre-school. Experience preferred.
For sale: Antique desk suitable for lady with thick legs and large drawers.
Used cars: Why go elsewhere to be cheated? Come here first.
Wanted: Man to take care of cow that does not smoke or drink.
Tired of cleaning yourself? Let me do it.
We do not tear your clothing with machinery. We do it carefully by
    hand.
Bake cookies with your children.
Grandmother of eight makes hole in one.
Deaf mute gets new hearing in killing.
Farmer bill dies in house.
Iraqi head seeks arms.
Safety experts say school bus passengers should be belted.
William Kelly was fed secretary.
Two convicts evade noose, jury hung.
Queen Mary having bottom scraped.
Prostitutes appeal to Pope.
Panda mating fails—veterinarian takes over.
Dr. Ruth to talk about sex with newspaper editors.
Eye drops off shelf.
Miners refuse to work after death.
Two sisters reunite after eighteen years at checkout counter.
Squad helps dog bite victim.
Dealers will hear car talk at noon.

## What is intelligence?

(30 minutes to prepare) I collect ^Mini-assignment #4 the class before I begin to discuss intelligence. I compile all of the responses (no names, of course) and copy some of them onto transparencies (you could put them in PowerPoint) and then I begin my discussion of

intelligence with student definitions. This "hooks" students into the topic both because they struggled with doing the assignment well and they are curious as to what their classmates had to say.

### Culture free/culture fair tests
(40 minutes to compile.) Once again, I compile the answers to this question from ⓦ Mini-assignment #4. I often put this together as a real "test" and ask students to complete the test in class. They object to some items, leading to a nice discussion of culture's impact on intelligence testing.

## Possible mini-assignments (written or groups)

### ⓦ Mini-assignment #1
Write a letter to a high school friend describing a fictitious auto accident you had while driving. Your letter should incorporate what you know about errors in information processing.

### ⓦ Mini-assignment #2
(Could be an in-class activity as well) You think you have been studying very hard, but you realize that you are failing your Chemistry class. How would you solve this problem? Make a list of what you would do and *why* you would use that strategy. What problem-solving method did you use? What other method could you have used?

### ⓦ Mini-assignment #3
You have been a student, sitting in classrooms for at least 13 years of your life. By this point in time you know teacher behaviors and styles that are positive for you, that help you learn, and those that do not help you. Make a list of three behaviors or activities that help you learn and tie those to concepts from both the Cognitive and Cognitive Abilities chapters (e.g., schemas, responses to questions).

### ⓦ Mini-assignment #4
Please complete this assignment before you read the Cognitive Abilities chapter.

Write a definition of intelligence.
Develop one item that could be used on a culture free/fair IQ test.

Ⓦ *Mini-assignment #5*
Take an IQ test on line. You may access a directory of on-line IQ tests at http://www.2h.com/iq-tests.html. After you have taken the test, answer the following questions.

1.  What was your experience taking the test?
2.  Do you think this is a valid test? Why or why not? How could you assess the validity of the test?
3.  Do you think this is a reliable test? Why or why not? How could you assess the reliability of the test?

## Handouts

Ⓦ Handout #1 IQ Scores and Mental Abilities

## References

Bartlett, F. (1932). *Remembering: A study in experimental and social psychology.* Cambridge, UK: Cambridge University Press.

Bernstein, D., & Goss Lucas, S. (1999). Functional fixedness in problem solving. In L. Benjamin, B. Nodine, R. Ernst, & C. Blair Broeker (Eds.), *Activities handbook for the teaching of psychology, Vol. 4* (pp. 216–217). Washington, DC: American Psychological Association.

Berry, J., Poortinga, Y., Segall, M., & Dasen, P. (2002). *Cross-cultural psychology: Research and applications* (2nd ed.). Cambridge, UK: Cambridge University Press.

Bransford, J., & Johnson, M. (1972). Contextual prerequisites for understanding: Some investigations of comprehension and recall. *Journal of Verbal Learning and Verbal Behavior, 11,* 717–726.

Broad, W. (1982). *Betrayers of the truth.* New York: Simon and Schuster.

Cianciolo, A., & Sternberg, R. (2004). *Intelligence: A brief history.* Oxford: Blackwell Publishing.

Cohen, R., & Swerdlik, M. (2002). *Psychological testing and assessment: An introduction.* New York: McGraw-Hill.

Donchin, E., Spencer, K. M., & Wijesinghe, R. (2000). The mental prosthesis: Assessing the speed of a P300-based brain-computer interface. *IEEETransaction on Rehabilitation Engineering, 8*(2), 174–179.

Duncan, J., Seitz, R., Kolodny, J., Bor, D., Herzog, H., Ahmed, A., Newell, F., & Emslie, H. (2000). A neural basis for general intelligence. *Science, 289*(5478), 457–459.

Duyme, M., Dumaret, A., & Tomkiewicz, S. (1999). How can we boost IQs of "dull children"?: A late adoption study. *Proceedings of the National Academy of Science, USA, 96,* 8790–8794.

Farwell, L., & Donchin, E. (1988). Talking off the top of your head: Toward a mental prosthesis utilizing event-related brain potentials. *Electroencephal Clinical Neurophysiology, 70,* 510–523.

Gardner, H. (1993). *Multiple intelligences: The theory into practice.* New York: Basic Books.

Gilbert, D. (2006). *Stumbling on happiness.* New York: Alfred A. Knopf.

Gould, S. J. (1996). *The mismeasure of man* (revised ed.). New York: Norton.

Haier, R., White, N., & Alkire, M. (2003). Individual differences in general intelligence correlate with brain function during nonreasoning tasks. *Intelligence, 31*(5), 429–441.

Hall, R., & Sandler, B. (1984). *Out of the classroom: A chilly campus climate for women?* Washington, DC: Project on the Status and Education of Women, Association of American Colleges.

Haskins, J., & Butts, H. (1973). *The psychology of black language.* New York: Barnes & Noble Books.

Hearst, E. (1991). Psychology and nothing. *American Scientist, 79*(5), 432–443.

Herrnstein, R., & Murray, C. (1994). *The bell curve.* New York City: The Free Press.

Minsky, M. (1977). Frame-system theory. In P. N. Johnson-Laird & P. C. Wason (Eds.), *Thinking: Readings in cognitive science* (pp. 355–376). Cambridge, UK: Cambridge University Press.

O'Brien, G. (2001). Defining learning: What place does intelligence testing have now? *Developmental Medicine and Child Neurology, 43,* 570–573.

O'Brien, G. (2004). Learning disability. *Medicine, 32*(8), 59–60.

Onofrj, M., Thomas, A., Paci, C., Scesi, M., & Tombari, R. (1997). Event-related potentials recorded in patients with locked-in syndrome. *Journal of Neurology, Neurosurgery, & Psychiatry, 63*(6), 759–764.

Pichert, J., & Anderson, R. (1977). Taking a different perspective on a story. *Journal of Educational Psychology, 69*(4), 309–314.

Privateer, P. (2005). *Inventing intelligence: A social history of smart.* Oxford: Blackwell Publishing.

Rosenthal, R., & Jacobson, L. (1968). *Pygmalion in the classroom.* New York: Holt, Rinehart & Winston.

Rozin, P., & Jonides, J. (1977). Mass reaction time: Measurement of the speed of the nerve impulse and the duration of mental processes in class. *Teaching of Psychology, 4*(2), 91–94.

Rymer, R. (1992). A silent childhood, Part I April 13, *New Yorker* 41–81; Part II April 20, 43–77.

Rymer, R. (1993). *Genie: A scientific tragedy.* New York: HarperCollins.

Sandler, B., & Hall, R. (1986). *The campus climate revisited: Chilly for women faculty, administrators, and graduate students.* Washington, DC:

Project on the Status and Education of Women, Association of American Colleges.

Scarr, S., & Weinberg, R. (1983). The Minnesota adoption studies: Genetic differences and malleability. *Child Development, 54*(2), 260–267.

Schank, R., & Abelson, R. (1977). *Scripts, plans, goals, and understanding: An inquiry into human knowledge structures.* Hillsdale, NJ: Erlbaum.

Scripture, E. W. (1895). *Thinking, feeling, and doing.* New York: Chautauqua-Century Press.

Skeels, H. (1966). Adult status of children with contrasting early life experiences. *Society for Research in Child Development Monograph, 31*(3) Serial #105, 1–65.

Skeels, H., Updegraff, R., Wellman, B., & Williams, H. (1938). A study of environmental stimulation: An orphanage preschool project. *Studies in Child Welfare: XV*(4), 1–191.

Small, B., & Baackman, L. (1999). Time to death and cognitive performance. *Current Directions in Psychological Science, 8,* 168–172.

Snow, R. (1995). Pygmalion and intelligence? *Current Directions in Psychological Science, 4,* 169–171.

Steele, C., & Aronson, J. (1995). Stereotype threat and the intellectual test performance of African Americans. *Journal of Personality and Social Psychology, 69*(5), 797–811.

Steele, C., & Aronson, J. (2000). Stereotype threat and the intellectual test performance of African Americans. In C. Strangor (Ed.), *Stereotypes and prejudice: Essential readings* (pp. 369–389). Philadelphia: Psychology Press/ Taylor & Francis.

Sternberg, R. (1985). *Beyond IQ: A triarchic theory of human intelligence.* Cambridge, UK: Cambridge University Press.

Sternberg, R. (1996a). Myths, counter-myths, and truths about intelligence. *Educational Researcher, 25*(2), 11–16.

Sternberg, R. (1996b). *Successful intelligence.* New York: Simon & Schuster.

Sternberg, R. (Ed.) (2000). *Handbook of intelligence.* Cambridge, UK: Cambridge University Press.

Sternberg, R. (2003). *Wisdom, intelligence, and creativity synthesized.* Cambridge, UK: Cambridge University Press.

Sternberg, R. (2005). Older but not wiser? The relationship between age and wisdom. *Ageing International, 30*(1), 5–26.

Sternberg, R., & Davidson, J. (Eds.) (2005). *Conceptions of giftedness* (2nd ed.) New York: Cambridge University Press.

Sternberg, R., Lautrey, J., & Lubart, T. (2003). *Models of intelligence: International perspectives.* Washington, DC: American Psychological Association.

Tannen, D. (1990). *You just don't understand: Women and men in conversation.* New York: Morrow.

Terman, L. (1925). *Studies of genius, vol. 1: Mental and physical traits of a thousand gifted children.* Stanford, CA: Stanford University Press.

Terman, L., & Oden, M. (1959). *The gifted group in the midlife: Thirty years follow-up on the superior child.* Genetic Studies of Genius, 4, Stanford, CA: Stanford University Press.

Tversky, A., & Kahneman, D. (1991). Loss aversion in riskless choice: A reference dependent model. *Quarterly Journal of Economics, 106,* 1039–1061.

Ware, M., & Johnson, D. (Eds.) (1996). *Handbook of demonstrations and activities in the teaching of psychology, vol. III.* Mahwah, NJ: Erlbaum.

Witkins, H., & Goodenough, D. (1977). Field dependence and interpersonal behavior. *Psychological Bulletin, 84*(4), 661–689.

## Additional Suggested Readings for Instructors

Broad, W. (1983). *Betrayers of the truth.* New York: Simon and Schuster.

Shurkin, J. (1992). *Terman's kids: The groundbreaking study of how the gifted grow up.* Boston: Little Brown.

Tannen, D. (2001). *I only say this because I love you: How the way we talk can make or break family relationships throughout our lives.* New York: Random House.

Tannen, D. (2005). *Conversational style: Analyzing talk among friends.* New York: Oxford University Press.

Tannen, C. (2006). *You're wearing that? Understanding mothers and daughters in conversation.* New York: Random House.

# Chapter 10

# Health, Stress, Coping, and Personality

## Getting Started

Stress is inevitable—to live is to experience stress. But student perceptions of stress are narrow. Thus I spend some time explaining stress, stressors, and stress mediators. I want my students to understand that their perception of stress actually mediates the impact. So adopting a more positive viewpoint can make stressors less intense.

I also want my students to be able to change dangerous health behaviors, such as excessive alcohol consumption, unsafe sexual practices, and smoking. So I talk about models for modifying such behaviors as well as presenting the research showing the long-term impact of them.

I introduce the diathesis-stress theory (an integration of nature or genetic predispositions with environment or stress) in this unit. I will use it later in the mental disorders unit—tying the units together.

I want my students to understand that psychologists use the term "personality" differently than the popular culture. No psychologist would say, "He has no personality." I want them to see their personality from a variety of theoretical perspectives and to understand that temperament, which we discussed in the development unit, is early personality and tends to predict later personality traits.

I want them to be skeptical of astrology and magazine "personality tests," and to understand that the issues surrounding personality tests are similar to those of intelligence—validity, reliability, and use of results.

## My outline for teaching (3 days—75 minute classes)

*Day 1*

Directions on board: Pick up a blank piece of paper from the front and draw a person. No names, please. (Draw-a-person classroom learning activity—pp. 216–18)

Questions from previous class (5 minutes)

Practice questions over material (5 minutes)

Administrivia (5 minutes)

  I.  Stress, stressors, stress reactions (10 minutes)

 II.  Major psychological stressors (10 minutes)

III.  Stress responses (10 minutes)

     Physical

     Psychological

       Emotional

       Cognitive

     Behavioral

       Burnout

       Post-traumatic stress disorder

 IV.  Interactions between people and stress/stress mediators (Ask the class to provide these) (15 minutes)

     Predictability

     Control

     Cognitive interpretation

     Social support

     Coping skills

  V.  Diathesis-stress theory (5 minutes)

     Predisposition toward mental illness/problems

     Stress in the environment

 VI.  Coping strategies (10 minutes)

*Day 2*

Questions from previous class (5 minutes)

Practice questions over material (5 minutes)

Administrivia (5 minutes)

  I.  Introduction: Personality is the unique pattern of enduring psychological and behavioral characteristics by which each

person can be compared and contrasted with other people.
(10 minutes)

Phrenology: An early attempt to assess personality

II.   Four basic theories

Trait (25 minutes)

Read obituaries: Tend to illustrate the trait approach.

Trait theory: Your horoscope and the Barnum effect (Classroom learning activity—pp. 214–17)

Hippocrates and Sheldon's body types: Difference between trait and type theory

Allport's theory

Biological trait theories: Eysenck, Gray's BIS and BAS

Big 5—valid across many cultures

Evaluation of theory: Weaknesses and strengths

Psychodynamic (25 minutes)

Freud the person

Basic assumption: Psychic determinism, unconscious

Structures of personality: Id, ego, superego

Defense mechanisms

Stages in development

Freud on Seuss Classroom learning activity (pp. 217–18)

Evaluation of theory: Weaknesses and strengths

Object relations theory

*Day 3*

Questions from previous class (5 minutes)

Practice questions over material (5 minutes)

Administrivia (5 minutes)

I.    Four basic theories of personality (cont'd)

Social cognitive approach (behavioral) (15 minutes)

Definition: Emphasis on situational specificity

Rotter's Locus of control classroom learning activity (p. 218)

Reciprocal determinism: Bandura

Skinner: Functional analysis of behavior

Evaluation of theory: Weakness and strengths

Humanistic/phenomenological (10 minutes)

Definition: Emphasis on personal uniqueness, personal perception of reality

Concepts: Positive regard, self-concept, conditions of worth, deficiency vs. growth orientation

Evaluation of theory: Weaknesses and strengths

II.   Ⓦ Mini-Assignment #5, Theories of personality (15 minutes)

III. Personality assessment (20 minutes)
Life outcomes
Situational tests
Observer ratings
Self-report
    Interview: Open-ended vs. structured
    Objective personality tests
    Projective personality tests
- Draw-a-person Classroom learning activity (pp. 216–18)
- Rorschach
- TAT—Henry Murray

## My transitions

I typically precede stress, coping, and health psychology with the motivation and emotion unit. I think that there is a smooth segue from emotions to stress. I also follow stress, coping, and health psychology with personality. I emphasize the approaches in personality and use the approaches to segue into mental disorders and therapies.

## Topics typically included in this unit

*Health psychology*: Behavioral medicine, lifestyle, and illness

*Stress and stressors*: Psychological stressors—life changes and strains, catastrophic events, chronic stressors, daily hassles; measuring stressors—life-change units (LCUs), Social Readjustment Rating Scale, Life Experiences Survey (LES)

*Stress responses*: Physical/Selye and general adaptations syndrome (GAS)—alarm, resistance, exhaustion, diseases of adaptation; psychological—emotional responses, cognitive responses—ruminative thinking, catastrophizing, mental sets, functional fixedness; behavioral responses—burnout and post-traumatic stress disorder

*Stress mediators*: Appraisal; predictability; perception of control; coping resources—problem-focused, emotion-focused; social support; personality—disease-resistant, dispositional optimism, gender

*Stress, illness, and the immune system*: Leukocytes—B-cells, T-cells, natural killer cells; macrophages; stressors and the suppression of the immune system; social support as a moderator of immune function; heart disease and hostility

*Health-endangering behaviors*: Smoking; alcohol; unsafe sex; obesity

*Promoting healthy behaviors*: Health-belief model; changing health behaviors (Prochaska model)—precontemplation, contemplation, preparation, action, maintenance

*Coping strategies*: Cognitive—cognitive restructuring; emotional—support; behavioral—time management; physical—progressive relaxation, exercise, meditation, drugs

*Psychodynamic approach*: Structure of personality—id, ego, superego; defense mechanisms—repression, rationalization, projection, reaction formation, sublimation, displacement, denial, compensation; stages of development—oral, anal, phallic/Oedipus and Electra complex, latent, genital; Jung—introversion and extraversion, collective unconscious; Adler—striving for superiority; Horney—womb envy; contemporary object relations and attachments

*Trait approach*: Trait vs. types; Allport—central and secondary traits; Big Five—openness to experience, conscientiousness, extraversion, agreeableness, neuroticism; Eysenck's biological theory—introversion–extraversion and emotionality–stability; Gray's approach-inhibition theory—behavioral approach system (BAS) and behavioral inhibition system (BIS)

*Social-cognitive approach*: Skinner—functional analysis; Rotter's expectancy theory—internal and external locus of control; Bandura—reciprocal determinism, self-efficacy; Mishel's cognitive/affective theory—cognitive personal variables

*Humanistic theory*: Phenomenological approach; Rogers' self theory—self-concept, positive regard, conditions of worth; Maslow's growth theory—deficiency and growth orientation

*Culture and personality*: Independent self-system and interdependent self-system; well-being—having positive attributes vs. having no negative attributes

*Assessing personality*: Life outcomes; situational tests; observer ratings; self-reports; interviews—open-ended and structured; objective personality tests—NEO-PI-R, MMPI-2; projective personality tests—thematic apperception test (TAT), Rorschach inkblot test

## Some options for organizing the concepts

*By approach*: You could teach the personality section early in the course—emphasizing the approaches to personality and continuing that "thread" throughout the rest of the course.

*By topic*: Many textbooks have health, stress, and coping as a "lead-in" chapter to personality. This is the way I organize the material in my own course. I teach these two units and then the mental disorders, therapies, and social units. However, the health, stress, and coping unit is very self-contained, so this unit could be taught immediately before the demands of midterm assignments, so that students are given some information about handling their stress at that time of the semester. This chapter could also be taught early in the semester, for the same reason.

# Teaching the Content

Remember that the ⓦ symbol means that a printable version is available on the web site (www.blackwellpublishing.com/lucas) and ⓤ means that the URL is available on the web site.

## Topics that many students will find difficult

### *Physiological components of stress*
I begin my discussion with Hans Selye's general adaptation syndrome (GAS). The GAS "makes sense" to most students and thus adding in the physiological details of each stage and introducing the terminology (catecholamines, corticosteroids, sympathoadrenomedullary system, hypothalamic-pituitary-adrenocortical system) has a structure. Mayo Clinic has a succinct description of the physiological stress response at their web site ⓤ. See *Stressed to the Limit: Stress and Health* ⓤ (2006) a 30-minute DVD discussing the physiology of stress. See also *Psychobiology of Stress* ⓤ, a 10-minute DVD.

### *Gray's approach–inhibition theory of personality*
Jeffrey Gray believes there are two basic systems: the behavioral approach system (BAS) and the behavioral inhibition system (BIS). These systems involve brain regions that are sensitive to rewards (BAS) and punishments (BIS). Gray relates these systems to Eysenck's emotional–stable and introverted–extraverted dimensions. He believes that extraverts have a more sensitive BAS, whereas introverts have a more sensitive BIS. Students struggle with this biological personality theory. The Wilderdom web site ⓤ provides a simple explanation of this com-plicated theory, as well as presenting other biological theories of personality.

## Other important topics

### *Stress, stressors, and stress reactions*
Students often incorrectly use these terms interchangeably so I provide the definitions at the beginning of this unit. I emphasize that stress is a process; stressors are events or situations; and stress reactions are physical, psychological, cognitive, and behavioral responses to stressors.

## Sources of stress

Different textbooks classify stressors differently. I ask students to provide sources of their stress and then I classify them as life changes, catastrophic events, daily hassles, or chronic stressors. You could also classify psychological stressors as frustration—obstacles to the goal; pressure—requirement to do too much in too short a time; boredom—understimulation for a long time; trauma—a shocking physical or emotional experience; conflict—both externally as interpersonal disputes or internally; and change. Students often do not think of boredom or change as stressors.

## Measuring stress

The Holmes and Rahe Social Readjustment Rating Scale has been one classic way of measuring life stressors. However, because this scale has limited applicability to college students, there is another scale for college students (ICSRLE). It's important to emphasize the difficulty inherent in "measuring" stress. See Holmes and Rahe (1967), Renner and Mackin (1998), Cohen (1994, p. 166).

For other stress inventories see Alpert and Haber (1960) and Brantley, Waggoner, Jones, and Rappaport (1987).

## Mediators of stress

Stress mediators include predictability, control, interpretation, and social support.

Predictability—Predictable stressors typically have less impact than unpredictable ones. However, knowing that a stressor might occur, but not knowing whether or not it will, increases stress.

Control—People who feel in control of their stressors experience less stress. This is true even when they perceive control, but they actually do not have control. I tie this concept to learned helplessness (learning and memory unit). People who feel they have no control over their life stressors give up trying to deal with them.

Interpretation—People who interpret their stressors as challenges rather than catastrophes experience less stress. Interpreting stressors in a more positive light can reduce stress.

Social support—Having a support network helps alleviate the effects of stress. However, having too much social support, or support of the wrong kind (enablers), can be as harmful as having no social support. Married people have been thought to be happier and healthier than unmarried people. However, recent research finds that both husbands and wives in bad marriages face serious health problems. See Barnett, Steptoe, and Gareis (2005).

## Coping skills

I distinguish between problem-focused skills and emotion-focused skills and I stress that there are times when both are appropriate responses. For instance, when faced with a stressor you have no control over—death of a loved one for example—emotion-focused skills (calming thoughts or emotional detachment) might be the best option. When faced with the stress of failing a class, problem-focused skills might be best.

Coping with Stress ⓤ is a 30-minute video discussing the link between stress and illness, along with the positive aspects of stress, and ideas for managing stress.

## Diathesis-stress theory

Because I use the nature/nurture interaction "thread" throughout my course, I introduce the idea of diathesis-stress—that environmental stress can be mediated by genetics *and* vice-versa. I pick up this idea in the next unit I teach, mental disorders. I illustrate this theory using famous cases of loving mothers who "snap" after experiencing extreme environmental stressors. You can get the details on the Susan Smith and Andrea Yates cases at the Court TV Crime Library web site ⓤ.

## Physical stress responses/Hans Selye and the GAS

I introduce the physical stress responses by talking about Hans Selye and his general adaptation syndrome theory. As a medical student, Selye observed that although patients had a diversity of illnesses, they had similar symptoms. He first called this the "syndrome of just being sick." After research he changed it to "syndrome produced by various nocuous agents" and finally realizing that stress was the tie, "general adaptation syndrome" or GAS. See Selye (1952).

The Science of Stress ⓤ is a 50-minute Discovery Channel video discussing the links between stress and illness. Stress: The Body and the Mind ⓤ focuses on stress and physiological responses.

## Behavioral stress responses

It's important to note that some behavioral stress responses are positive and some are negative. Road rage is a good negative example of aggression as a response to stress. Alcohol and drug use are also negative behavioral stress responses. For an interesting paper on the connection between stress hormones and aggression, see Kruk, Meelis, Halasz, and Haller (2004).

I illustrate burnout by talking about social workers who deal with difficult situations every day, often having little control. Another example is air traffic controllers who have thousands of lives in their hands every day.

Post-traumatic stress disorder is familiar to many students—primarily as reported in the media about soldiers returning from war zones. However, there are other examples including students who experienced the Virginia Tech shootings or people who have been assaulted or raped.

See the Neuroscience for Kids web site ⓤ for a description of post-traumatic stress disorder and for a list of popular movies demonstrating the disorder (along with a guide pointing out what to look for in each movie).

## Psychological stress responses

Psychological stress responses are divided into emotional and cognitive. Emotional stress responses include distress, depression, anxiety disorders, and helplessness. Cognitive stress responses include "cognitive flooding"—a sudden temporary inability to think, catastrophizing—the proverbial making a mountain out of a molehill, and possibly Freudian defense mechanisms (although I discuss these in the personality unit).

## Lifestyle behaviors that affect the leading causes of death

It is an eye-opener for many students to understand that the leading causes of death—heart disease, cancer, stroke, lung disease, and accidents and injury—are often the product of lifestyle choices. Thus the abuse of alcohol, smoking, a poor diet, lack of exercise *and* excessive stress, all contribute to these causes of death.

## Changing health behaviors

Stages of readiness: James Prochaska and colleagues present stages of readiness to change health behaviors. These are precontemplation—before perception of a health problem, contemplation—awareness of the health problem and serious consideration of changes, preparation—a strong intention to change and taking some preliminary steps, action—maintaining the behavior change for at least six months, and maintenance—using skills learned to prevent relapse. See Prochaska and DiClemente (1992).

## What is personality?

When I introduce the topic of personality, I relate it back to the idea of temperament (from development).

I also trace early ideas of personality, including Franz Joseph Gall's theory of phrenology. You can read a short description of Gall's theory along with a map of his "faculties" at the Phrenology homepage ⓤ. For a picture of a psychograph (used to graph these faculties) and a listing of other phrenology resources see the web site of Bob McCoy (an international expert on medical quackery and health fraud and the founder of the Museum of Questionable Medical Devices) ⓤ.

See *Personality Theories* ⓤ (2001), a 30-minute overview of the psychodynamic, social-cognitive, and humanistic personality theories. *Theories of Personality* ⓤ (1994), a 20-minute DVD, explains trait, psychodynamic, social-learning, cognitive, and humanistic theories.

## Trait approach to personality (dispositional theory)

Most students use the trait theory when trying to describe their personality or that of friends. I introduce this topic by reading aloud some obituaries—paid obituaries provide lots of details about an individual's traits—and asking students to describe the person's personality based on their obituary.

Allport's theory of cardinal, central, and secondary traits is a good introduction to trait theory.

The Big Five theory, that there are five factors that describe personality across many cultures—openness, conscientiousness, extraversion, agreeableness, neuroticism—is an easy theory for most students to grasp. The mnemonic of OCEAN (created by taking the first letter of each factor) helps them remember the factors.

For a discussion of culture's impact on personality see Chapter 4 of Berry, Poortinga, Segall, and Dasen (2002, pp. 86–113).

To differentiate type theory from trait theory I talk about Hippocrates' theory of the four humors in the body and their influence on personality. Students also like Sheldon's physiognomy theory of body types. For a great web site that lists most of the major type theories see the Wilderdom web site ⓤ.

## Birth order

Alfred Adler is credited with first hypothesizing that birth order could have an impact on personality. Students are intrigued with the idea that first-borns are conscientious, orderly, and leaders; last-borns are sociable, charming, and attention-seeking; while middle children are mediators, get along well with others, but have less defined characteristics than first- or last-borns. Summaries of birth order research can be found Nyman (1995) and Leman (2000).

Dr. Benjamin Spock talked about the effect of birth order, primarily how parents treat first-borns differently, in his famous parenting book. See Spock (1961, pp. 61–80). For a review of the interaction between birth order and IQ see Zajonc and Mullally (1997).

## Psychodynamic approach to personality

I spend time talking about Freud's theories, but in the context of the era in which he lived. I present the basic premises from Masson (1984) and the counterarguments (which are numerous). I ask students to think about the issue from a critical perspective. See Allen Esterson's web site ⓤ for a rebuttal to Masson (or his original article, Esterson, 1998).

See the chapter on psychoanalysis in Benjamin (1997, pp. 488–523). See also Freud's 1901 book, *The Psychopathology of Everyday Life*, which focused on how everyday "errors"—such as slips of the tongue—could provide information about a person's personality. This can also be found at Christopher Green's Classics in the History of Psychology web site ⓤ.

See *Freud: Hidden Nature of Man* ⓤ (1970), a 29-minute video discussing Freud's stages of development and structure of personality. Also *History of Psychology II: Freud, Jung, and Psychoanalysis* ⓤ (2006), a 30-minute DVD presenting the psychoanalytic theory and application to personality and mental disorders.

Defense mechanisms—I talk about the most common defense mechanisms and assign ⓦ Mini-assignment #3. For a nice listing of defense mechanisms with examples, go to the AllPsych Online web site ⓤ.

I am seldom able to cover Carl Jung, Alfred Adler, or Karen Horney's theories, but I ask students to read them. I do talk about the more modern psychodynamic theory, object relations, and relate it back to attachment theory from the developmental chapter. See Cristobal (2003).

## Social-cognitive approach to personality
## (social learning or behavioral)

I use the approaches to psychology as a common "thread" throughout the course. Thus I refer back to the behaviorists from the learning unit, and the idea that personality is merely behavior that is shaped by punishments and rewards. I talk about the idea of situational specificity as a contrast to the trait theory.

Julian Rotter's idea of locus of control can be introduced by asking students to fill out Rotter's scale, without giving students the cue of locus of control. (See Locus of control classroom learning activity, p. 218.)

Albert Bandura's theory of reciprocal determinism makes sense to most students. I ask students for examples from their own lives. See *Bandura's Social Cognitive Theory: An Introduction* Ⓤ (2003), a 30-minute DVD focusing on Bandura's theories and providing original footage of his Bobo doll experiments.

B. F. Skinner's functional analysis of behavior explores personality from the perspective of the person's rewards and punishment patterns.

## Humanistic or phenomenological approach to personality

The main concepts are that people are innately good, inclined towards goodness and creativity, and all behavior is meaningful to the person displaying it. Each person's unique perception of reality shapes not only their behavior, but their individual construct of the world. For a quick overview of humanistic psychology see the AllPsych Online web site Ⓤ or the Psi Café web site Ⓤ. See also Carl Rogers' classic paper "Some Observations on the Organization of Personality" found at Christopher Green's Classics in the History of Psychology web site Ⓤ.

Carl Rogers' self theory is the idea that we need the approval of others, or positive regard, and that our self-concept is the way we think about ourselves. When our self-concept is not in synch with our ideal self, we experience psychological discomfort. I talk about "conditions of worth" from a childrearing perspective, the idea that children come to view their value based only on displaying the attitudes and behaviors that their caregivers consider correct. According to Rogers, a behavior, not a person, should be evaluated.

Abraham Maslow's idea of a deficiency orientation or a growth
  orientation makes sense to students and is a great discussion starter.
I prompt students that we will revisit the humanists again when we
  talk about psychotherapies.

### Personality assessment
I think it is important that students understand that personality can
be assessed without using tests. So I talk about using life outcomes,
observer ratings, interviews, and self-reports. But I also take this
opportunity to reinforce the concepts of test validity and reliability
that I introduced in the cognitive abilities unit. See Russell Dewey's
Psych Web Resources web site ⓤ for a list of many online personality
tests. Students can click on the test and be directed to the web site
where they can take the test and have it scored.

### Objective personality tests
Objective personality tests are paper and pencil (or on the computer),
include specific questions or statements, and are scored objectively
by being compared with norms. I talk about rational norming, items
that seem appropriate (content/face validity), vs. empirical norming,
items that are answered differently by people with the characteristic
and those without. I emphasize that often it is a pattern of response,
not just a response to a particular question that is most relevant. We
talk about the MMPI, Cattell 16PF, and the NEO-PI-R as examples
of objective personality tests.

### Projective personality tests
Validity and reliability are lower for projective than objective
personality tests. However, the acquiescence and social desirability
problems are lessened in projective tests. *Scientific American* ⓤ recently
released the results of a study showing that projective tests are not
useful in diagnosing mental disorders.

TAT—I begin discussion of projective tests by putting a picture on
  the overhead. (I choose pictures from magazines of a person
  engaged in an activity or interacting with others.) I give students a
  couple of minutes to write about what is happening in the picture.
  When we talk about their stories I incorporate Henry Murray's
  needs, and introduce the Thematic Apperception Test. (The TAT
  manual lists the needs and what to look for in the stories—e.g.,
  who the person identifies with and what that person's wishes,
  strivings, and conflicts are. See Murray, 1943; also online at The

University of Auckland, New Zealand's web site ⓤ.) For a discussion of the images that Murray used and more tips on scoring the TAT see Morgan (1995).

Rorschach—Most students will know of the "ink blot" test, even if they don't know that it is the Rorschach. All of the pictures, along with scoring tips, can be found (strangely enough) at the Separated Parenting Access and Resource Center (SPARC) web site ⓤ.

# Classroom Tips

## Stimulus questions for discussion

### Stress and your immune system
Researchers found "valium" receptors on cells of the human immune system (which defends again infectious disease and cancer). How could this link between an antianxiety substance in the brain and the immune system explain why moods affect physical health or psychosomatic illness?

### Reducing stress
One study found that when patients having cataracts removed (they did not receive general anesthesia) were allowed to listen to "soft" music before and during their surgery they lowered their stress level, as measured by heart rate and blood pressure. How can you explain this from the perspective of stress mediation? See Allen et al. (2001).

### Lifestyle and health
The evidence is overwhelming that people's lifestyle decisions—diet, exercise, smoking, drinking alcohol, and so forth—has a major impact on their health. The research has been well publicized in the popular media, yet it has been ineffective in getting people to change their lifestyle behaviors. How can people be convinced to change?

### Locus of control
There is some evidence that people with an internal locus of control tend to do better in school and have a hardy or stress-resistant personality. How do you explain these outcomes? Are there other ways to explain them that don't involve the idea of locus of control?

### Personality tests
Do you believe that personality tests are valid? Why or why not? Who should have access to the results? Your family? Your employer?

The government? How could the results of personality tests be misused?

## Some suggested classroom learning activities

### Stress inventories
(Students complete the inventories outside of class—minimal time) I use as many stress inventories as I can find (see previous suggestions) and then I ask students to fill them out and judge their validity. This leads into a discussion, relevant to both the stress and personality units, about whether or not their agreement with their test results makes the test valid, or conversely, if their disagreement makes the test invalid.

### Adjusting the Social Readjustment Rating Scale
(15 minutes to design the instruments, 2–3 minutes per group to present) I assign students to small groups and provide them with blank transparencies, pens, and a copy of Holmes and Rahe's SRRS. Their task is to develop an SRRS that is more appropriate for their age and living situation. They develop the instrument—copying their questions onto the transparencies—and then present them to the class. An alternative is to ask each group to develop their "stress instrument," collect them, and then copy each one for students for the next class. This could also be used as an introduction to the unit—allowing the instructor to categorize the items.

Another alternative is to have students take the College Life Inventory (Renner and Mackin, 1998) and compare it with the SRRS.

### Type A/B behavior patterns
(The online inventory is completed before class—minimal time) An old concept that many students will know about is the idea of Type A and Type B personalities. I give the students a Type A/Type B test adapted from Friedman and Rosenman (1974), and I have them score their own. I tell them that recent research has found that it's the hostility, not so much the "hurryness," that leads to heart disease. Friedman and Rosenman (1974, pp. 82–86) has a description of Type A psychological and behavioral characteristics (e.g., you may be Type A if you always move, walk, and eat rapidly) and a description of Type B (e.g., you may be Type B if you can relax without guilt).

Students can take an online modified-for-college-students version of the Type A/B test at Paula Goolkasian's (University of North Carolina, Charlotte) web site Ⓤ.

*Achievement anxiety test*

(Completed prior to class—minimal time) I do spend time discussing the outcomes of this test, and the idea that there is debilitating and facilitating anxiety. Students' anxiety has an impact on their academic performance, and sometimes this is an indicator for students to seek further help to alleviate their anxiety level.

Students can take the online version of this test at Paula Goolkasian's (University of North Carolina, Charlotte) web site Ⓤ.

*Change an unhealthy behavior*

(15–25 minutes) After discussing Prochaska and colleagues' model for changing a behavior, I ask students to privately write down one health-endangering behavior that they engage in. I then ask them to take the perspective of a person at each stage of Prochaska's model and to describe what that person would be doing at each stage. My hope is that this exercise will help students move more quickly along the "readiness" scale. Most students will develop a plan to deal with smoking, alcohol abuse, overeating, lack of exercise, and so forth.

*Cognitive restructuring*

(10–20 minutes) I divide the class into groups and give each group one of the negative thoughts (listed below). I then ask them to provide a rational replacement thought which responds to the stressor as a challenge rather than a threat. Then I ask each group to develop one novel example of a negative thought and corresponding rational replacement thought. This provides students with experience engaging in cognitive restructuring.

Ⓦ Negative thought #1: "I should know exactly what I want to do with my life by now."
Rational replacement thought #1:
Negative thought #2: "I must be perfectly competent."
Rational replacement thought #2:
Negative thought #3: "Everyone is smarter than I am."
Rational replacement thought #3:
Negative thought #4: "It will be so awful if I don't know the answers."
Rational replacement thought #4:

*Source for activity: Adapted from an activity by Sylvia Puente, University of Illinois at Urbana-Champaign. Permission Houghton Mifflin.*

*Progressive relaxation*
(20–25 minutes) The objective of progressive relaxation is to tense and then relax specific muscle groups so that one becomes more aware of what muscular tension and relaxation feels like, and thus can better control the process through repeated practice. Each muscle group is tensed and relaxed separately until the whole body has been covered.

Read the following directions to the class. Speak slowly in a clear, calm voice. Take time to let students feel the sensations of each step.

*Clear all books and bags away from your laps. Sit centered in your chair with both feet resting flat on the floor. Rest each hand comfortably on each of your knees. Close your eyes and remain quiet.*

*Slowly take in a deep breath through your nose, fully inflating your lungs. Concentrate on the feeling of air rushing in, forcing your lungs open. Then exhale slowly through your mouth. Feel the air leave your lungs rushing out of your body.* [Repeat this two more times for a total of three deep breaths.]

*Make a fist with both of your hands. Tense the hand muscles tightly and hold them in a fist. Concentrate on the feeling of the taut muscles and the blood being forced from your hands. Count one . . . two . . . three. Now, let your hands fully relax, still and motionless, as if you had no muscles in your hands at all. Focus on the feeling of the blood returning to the tissues in the hand. Concentrate on this feeling.*

*Now, bend your arms at the elbows, flexing your biceps muscle as much as possible. Squeeze your arm muscles as much as you can so that your arm is maximally flexed at the elbow. Feel the tension in your arm muscles as the circulation slows down. Hold this position as you count one . . . two . . . three. Now, let your arms completely relax, falling limp, as if you had no motor control in them anymore. Concentrate on the feeling of the blood revitalizing the starved tissues. Feel the sensation returning.*

*Slowly take in a deep breath, again through your nose, fully inflating your lungs. Feel the air rushing in, forcing your lungs open. Then exhale slowly through your mouth. Feel the air leave your lungs and your breathing muscles relax.* [Repeat this two more times for a total of three deep breaths.] *At the count of three you will open your eyes feeling calm and relaxed. One . . . two . . . three.*

Point out that in a complete session one would proceed in similar fashion for all muscle groups throughout the body. After the exercise concludes, ask students to comment upon their experiences. What did they notice? Would this be a difficult therapy to undertake with people? Why or why not? Would it be helpful? When and for what?

*Source for activity: Broota and Sanghvi (1994), Carlson and Bernstein (1995), Lehrer and Carr (1997). By permission of Houghton Mifflin.*

## Trait theory: Your horoscope and the Barnum effect

(If you provide an individual "result" to students, the "test" must be given during one class period (5–10 minutes) and "results" distributed in the next.) Forer (1949) showed that some personality evaluations (e.g., horoscopes) are so general and vague that they seem to describe almost everyone—the so-called Barnum effect. Forer developed a class demonstration to make two points. First, some personality characteristics are almost universally valid. Second, personality evaluation or measurement is not valid solely based on client agreement. In other words, a personality instrument does not have validity just because the person being assessed agrees with the evaluation. The following exercise can be used to encourage critical thinking.

*Option 1.* For the purposes of this classroom exercise, any personality test will do. A sample test is provided. Have students complete the tests, collect them, but don't score them. Next class, give everyone a personality profile (see below for two samples) scrambling the results so they look different. Write each student's name on one paper and hand the results out individually. Tell students that the information is "personal" and that they should not look at their neighbors' sheets.

*Option 2.* Have students complete the test and score their own (adding points). Photocopy the personality sketch (two samples are offered below) on four different colors of paper with each color having a scrambled version of the same traits. Then ask students to raise their hands if they scored between certain points, say, 80 and 100, 60 and 79, 40 and 59, less than 40, and hand out the sketches of one color to each range of scores until all have been distributed. Ask students to raise their hands if they thought the personality sketch was 100% accurate. Continue with 90% accurate, 80% accurate . . . all the way to totally inaccurate. Most students find the profile to be at least 80% accurate. Read a "sample" personality sketch (the one everyone received) and ask students if they found anything similar to their own sketches. Begin a discussion about the accuracy of horoscopes, astrology, tea-leaf reading, palm reading, and so on. You also may want to discuss what is needed for a personality test to be considered valid.

### ⓦ The G-B Personality Profile

Answer the questions that follow as honestly as you can using the following scale. Write your responses in the blank to the left of each statement.

| Never | | | | Always |
|---|---|---|---|---|
| 1 | 2 | 3 | 4 | 5 |

1. \_\_\_\_\_ I am a shy person.
2. \_\_\_\_\_ I get anxious taking tests.
3. \_\_\_\_\_ I resent my parents.
4. \_\_\_\_\_ It is difficult for me to talk in front of a large group of people.
5. \_\_\_\_\_ I am usually persuaded by arguments made by experts.
6. \_\_\_\_\_ Children and animals like me.
7. \_\_\_\_\_ I have difficulty getting to know people of the opposite sex.
8. \_\_\_\_\_ I enjoy parties.
9. \_\_\_\_\_ Life is serious and difficult to cope with.
10. \_\_\_\_\_ My goals in life are easily attainable.
11. \_\_\_\_\_ I would prefer to take a walk in the rain alone rather than attend a formal dance.
12. \_\_\_\_\_ I am very critical of myself.
13. \_\_\_\_\_ People think that I am a better person than I really am.
14. \_\_\_\_\_ I prefer something new and exciting to something old and familiar.
15. \_\_\_\_\_ I tend to "slide by" rather than really applying myself.
16. \_\_\_\_\_ Even though I appear self-confident on the outside, inside I am very insecure.
17. \_\_\_\_\_ I have difficulty revealing the "true me" to other people.
18. \_\_\_\_\_ I defer to authority figures.
19. \_\_\_\_\_ I prefer one really good friend to several casual friends.
20. \_\_\_\_\_ I am more a "thinking" person than a "feeling" person.

*Sources for activity: By permission of Houghton Mifflin.*

### ⓦ The G-B Personality Profile B1

1. You have a great need for other people to like and admire you.
2. You have a tendency to be critical of yourself.

3. You have a great deal of unused capacity that you have not turned to your advantage.
4. Although you have some personality weaknesses, you are generally able to compensate for them.
5. Your sexual adjustment has presented problems for you.
6. Disciplined and self-controlled outside, you tend to be worrisome and insecure inside.
7. At times you have serious doubts as to whether you have made the right decision or done the right thing.
8. You prefer a certain amount of change and variety and become dissatisfied when hemmed in by restrictions and limitations.
9. You pride yourself on being an independent thinker and do not accept others' statements without satisfactory proof.
10. You have found it unwise to be too frank in revealing yourself to others.
11. At times you are extraverted, affable, sociable; at other times you are introverted, wary, reserved.
12. Some of your aspirations tend to be pretty unrealistic.
13. Security is one of your major goals in life.

*Source for activity: By permission of Houghton Mifflin.*

Ⓦ The G-B Personality Profile B2

Factor A

Security is one of your major goals in life.
You pride yourself on being an independent thinker and do not accept others' statements without satisfactory proof.
You prefer a certain amount of change and variety and become dissatisfied when hemmed in by restrictions and limitations.
You have a great deal of unused capacity that you have not turned to your advantage.

Factor B

You have a great need for other people to like and admire you.
Your sexual adjustment has presented problems for you.
Disciplined and self-controlled outside, you tend to be worrisome and insecure inside.
At times you have serious doubts as to whether you have made the right decision or done the right thing.

At times you are extraverted, affable, sociable; at other times you are introverted, wary, reserved.

Some of your aspirations tend to be pretty unrealistic.

Factor C

You have a tendency to be critical of yourself.

Although you have some personality weaknesses, you are generally able to compensate for them.

You have found it unwise to be too frank in revealing yourself to others.

*Source for activity: By permission of Houghton Mifflin.*

## *Projective personality tests/Draw a person*

Students draw a person before this unit begins. For ethical reasons, I either exchange pictures between classes (if I'm teaching two classes) or I use a previous year's pictures. I ask the class to interpret the pictures "cold" and start a discussion of what to look for in the pictures. I always begin by pointing out that I am *not* a clinician. After analyzing the pictures we discuss the validity of projective personality tests—which is very low. I put up a picture and ask students a series of questions:

Does the drawing show a head on a body, or just a floating head?

Is the body a stick figure or is it drawn with details? What unusual details are drawn?

Are there body parts missing from the drawing (e.g., no feet)?

Is the person drawn standing on a surface of some kind, or drawn on an otherwise plain page, as if unanchored and "floating" in space?

Does the person's body appear properly proportioned, or are some features overemphasized or underemphasized?

What facial expressions are shown?

Is the person doing anything, and if so, what?

If there are eyes on the person's face, are there any pupils? Where do the eyes appear to be looking?

Is the person wearing clothes? What is the person's style of dress?

Are there other people in the drawing and if so how are they interacting with each other?"

Then I offer some interpretations and explain some of the symbols.

Arm extensions (including cleaning instruments/weapons): need to control the environment

Elevated figures: a dominant figure or striving for dominance in the family

Erasures on figures: related to conflicts about self or interactions with others

Hanging, falling, or precarious positions: tension

Omission/distortion of body parts: conflicts

Rotated figures (in relation to other figures): feelings of being different

Covered/obscured figures: anxiety; internalization

Balls: competition between figures; libido; jealousy; inability to compete (bouncing ball)

Intertwined/close/touching figures: harmony; love

Dangerous objects: anger; aggression

Heat, light, or warmth: love and/or anger; need for love or warmth; passive-aggressiveness

Lack of barriers between figures: unreserved and natural love; closeness; trust

Lining at the bottom of the page: attempts to stabilize a seemingly unstable world

Standing (no action) and stick figures: defensiveness

Symbols:


Beds: sexual or depressive themes

Bikes (overemphasized): significant masculine strivings

Cats: dominant symbol; conflict in identification with mother (i.e., preoccupation with cats)

Dirt, digging, shoveling: negative connotations or feelings; dirty thoughts

Drums: displaced anger

Flowers: love of beauty; growth

Kites: attempts to escape restricting or threatening family or environment

Ladders: tension; precarious balance

Leaves: dependency; unmet needs

Rain or water (overemphasized): depressive tendencies

Vacuums: power; controlling tendencies

*Source for activity: Burns and Kaufman (1972), Goodenough (1926), Hammer (1958, 1968). By permission of Houghton Mifflin.*

## Freud on Seuss

Students read Dr. Seuss's *Cat in the Hat* (found in every public library) before coming to class. In class, I ask them to "become Freudians" and to look at the book from a Freudian perspective. I have some pages of the book copied onto transparencies and I put them up and ask students to apply Freudian terminology to the action taking place. At the end, I share Josh LeBeau's ⓦ *Freud on Seuss*, in which he interprets *Cat in the Hat* from a Freudian perspective. Students love this exercise and they begin to read children's fiction from a different perspective.

## Rotter's Locus of Control

Rotter's idea of locus of control is easily demonstrated by using his scale. I ask students to "Choose the item of the pair that you more strongly believe." I use a subset of items taken from Rotter (1971). However, there are more items available (and scoring directions) at the University of Ballarat, Australia web site ⓤ. After all have filled out the scale, we talk about locus of control and its relevance to first-borns, honor students, and so forth.

## Possible mini-assignments (written or groups)

### ⓦ *Mini-assignment #1*

Write down one stressor that you are encountering in your life right now. This could be pressure from your family, disagreements with roommates, not enough time to complete assignments. Follow the outline provided to evaluate your stressor and develop a plan to deal with it.

1.  What is the real source of my stress and how is that affecting me?
2.  List my stressors and my stress responses.
3.  Make a plan for specific steps I will take to deal with my stressor and/or change my response.
4.  How could I implement my plan?
5.  How could I evaluate how my methods are helping or not helping me cope with my stressor?

### ⓦ *Mini-assignment #2*

(Could be an in-class activity as well)

Bella B. is having trouble adjusting to the various stressors in her life. She is holding down a full-time job, going to school part-time, and raising three children as a single parent. Bella comes to you and asks, "What can I do to handle the stress in my life more adaptively?" Based on what you know about adaptively handling stress, give Bella four pieces of advice to help her *mediate* her stress.

## ⓦ *Mini-assignment #3*
(Could be an in-class activity as well) Fill out Rotter's scale, following the directions given. Analyze your results as indicated at the end of the scale. Do the results fit your view of your personality? If so, how? If not, how do they differ? Do you think the questions on Rotter's scale are valid? How would you assess the validity of this test?

## ⓦ *Mini-assignment #4*
Pick three of Freud's defense mechanisms. Describe how each defense mechanism works and provide an example of each. If possible, provide personal examples.

## ⓦ *Mini-assignment #5*
(This is a group, in-class assignment)

1. Pick a famous person that most people in the class will know.
2. Pick one of the four major theories of personality (psychodynamic, trait, social-cognitive, or phenomenological). Using this theory, write a profile of the famous person's personality (e.g., Trait approach: Madonna: extrovert, attention-seeking, artistic, impulsive, imaginative, emotional, sexual).
3. Write the name of the person you are discussing at the top of the page, *but do not use the person's name in your profile.*
4. Read your personality profile to the rest of the class to see if it allows others to identify the person profiled.
5. Have all members of your group sign this sheet before it is handed in.

## Handouts

ⓦ Handout #1 Prescription for Stress or How to Make Yourself a Complete Basket Case in Four Easy Steps
ⓦ Handout #2: The 10 Irrational Commandments
ⓦ Handout #3: Coping Strategies

# References

Allen, K., Golden, L., Izzo, J., Ching, M., Forrest, A., Niles, C., Niswander, P., & Barlow, J. (2001). Normalization of hypertensive responses during ambulatory surgical stress by perioperative music. *Psychosomatic Medicine*, *63*, 487–492.

Alpert, R., & Haber, R. (1960). Anxiety in academic achievement situations. *Journal of Abnormal and Social Psychology*, *61*(2), 207–215.

Barnett, R., Steptoe, A., & Gareis, K. (2005). Marital-role quality and stress-related psychobiological indicators. *Annals of Behavioral Medicine*, *30*(1), 36–43.

Benjamin, L. (1997). *History of psychology* (2nd ed.). New York: McGraw-Hill.

Berry, J., Poortinga, Y., Segall, M., & Dasen, P. (2002). *Cross-cultural psychology* (2nd ed.). Cambridge, UK: Cambridge University Press.

Brantley, P., Waggoner, C., Jones, G., & Rappaport, N. (1987). A daily stress inventory: Development, reliability and validity. *Journal of Behavioral Medicine*, *10*, 61–74.

Broota, S., & Sanghvi, C. (1994). Efficacy of two relaxation techniques in examination anxiety. *Journal of Personality & Clinical Studies*, *10*(1–2), 29–35.

Burns, R., & Kaufman, S. (1972). *Actions, styles, and symbols in kinetic family drawing (K-F-D): An interpretive guide*. Oxford: Psychology Press.

Carlson, C. R., & Bernstein, D. A. (1995). Relaxation skills training: Abbreviated progressive relaxation. In W. O'Donohue & L. Krasner (Eds.), *Handbook of psychological skills training: Clinical techniques and applications* (pp. 20–35). Boston: Allyn & Bacon.

Cohen, R. (1994). *Psychology and adjustment*. Boston: Allyn & Bacon.

Cristobal, R. (2003). The psychoanalytic process in the light of attachment theory. In M. Cortina & M. Marrone (Eds.), *Attachment theory and the psychoanalytic process* (pp. 335–355). London: Whurr.

Esterson, A. (1998). Jeffrey Masson and Freud's seduction theory: A new fable based on old myths. *History of the Human Sciences*, *11*(1), 1–21.

Forer, B. (1949). The fallacy of personal validation: A classroom demonstration of gullibility. *Journal of Abnormal and Social Psychology*, *44*, 118–123.

Friedman, M., & Rosenman, R. (1974). *Type A behavior and your heart*. New York: Knopf.

Goodenough, F. L. (1926). *Measurement of intelligence by drawings*. Yonkers, NY: World Book Co.

Hammer, E. F. (1958). *The clinical application of projective drawings*. Springfield, IL: Thomas.

Hammer, E. F. (1968). Projective drawings. In A. I. Rabin (Ed.), *Projective techniques in personality assessment* (pp. 366–393). New York: Springer.

Holmes, T., & Rahe, R. (1967). The social readjustment scale. *Journal of Psychosomatic Research, 11*(2), 213–218.

Kruk, M., Meelis, W., Halasz, J., & Haller, J. (2004). Fast positive feedback between the adrenocortical stress response and a brain mechanism involved in aggressive behavior. *Behavioral Neuroscience, 118*(5), 1062–1070.

Lehrer, P., & Carr, R. (1997). Progressive relaxation. In W. T. Roth (Ed.), *Treating anxiety disorders* (pp. 83–116). The Jossey Bass Library of Current Clinical Technique. San Francisco: Jossey Bass.

Leman, K. (2000). *The new birth order book: Why you are the way you are.* Minnesota: Baker Books.

Masson, J. (1984). *The assault on truth: Freud's suppression of the seduction theory.* New York: Farrar, Straus, Giroux.

Morgan, W. (1995). Origin and history of the thematic apperception test images. *Journal of Personality Assessment, 65*(2), 237–254.

Murray, H. (1943). *Thematic apperception test manual.* Cambridge, MA: Harvard University Press.

Nyman, L. (1995). The identification of birth order personality attributes. *Journal of Psychology Interdisciplinary & Applied, 129*(1), 51–60.

Prochaska, J., & DiClemente, C. (1992). Stages of change in the modification of problem behaviors. In M. Hersen, R. Eisler, & P. Miller (Eds.), *Progress in behavior modification* (pp. 184–214). Sycamore, IL: Sycamore Press.

Renner, M., & Mackin, R. (1998). A life stress instrument for classroom use. *Teaching of Psychology, 25*(1), 46–48.

Rotter, J. (1971). External control and internal control. *Psychology Today, 5*(1), 37.

Selye, H. (1952). *The story of the adaptation syndrome.* Montreal, Quebec: Acta Inc.

Spock, B. (1961). *Dr. Spock talks with mothers.* Cambridge, MA: Riverside Press.

Zajonc, R., & Mullally, P. (1997). Birth order: Reconciling conflicting effects. *American Psychologist, 52*(7), 685–699.

## Additional Suggested Readings for Instructors

Carver, C., & Scheier, M. (2004). *Perspectives on personality* (5th ed.). Boston: Allyn Bacon.

Feist, J., & Feist. G. (2002). *Theories of personality* (5th ed.). New York, McGraw-Hill.

Joshi, V. (2005). *Stress: From burnout to balance.* Thousand Oaks, CA: Sage.

Kemeny, M. (2003). The psychobiology of stress. *Current Directions in Psychological Science, 12*, 124–129.

Mischel, W. (2002). *Introduction to personality* (7th ed.). Fort Worth, TX: Harcourt Brace.

Selye, H. (1976). *Stress in health and disease.* Boston: Butterworths.

Selye, H. (1978). *The stress of life* (revised ed.). New York: McGraw-Hill.

# Chapter 11

# Mental Disorders and Therapies

## Getting Started

Students find this unit inherently interesting. In fact, for many students, this content is what they thought introductory psychology was all about. The easiest way to dampen their interest is to teach this unit as though it were a "laundry list" of disorders. You have to find an integrating principle. The history of diagnosing disorders and their treatment helps me to put each disorder into an historical and cultural perspective. One of my major goals for this unit is to have my students understand that culture has an impact on how mental disorders are diagnosed, how the general population views them, and how they are treated.

I also want them to understand that views of mental disorders have shifted dramatically, beginning with the idea of "special" powers or demonic possession, to a psychological illness with characteristics similar to physical illness, to learned patterns of behavior, to a search for the neurological and neurodevelopmental underpinnings.

Looking at the statistics I know that many of my students have either received psychotherapy or will in their lifetime. Thus I want them to be knowledgeable about the techniques and emphasis of each type of psychotherapy.

Finally, I want my students to feel compassionate about people with mental disorders. Thus, I treat this unit very seriously and I don't make jokes or funny asides about the disorders or treatments.

## My outline for teaching (3 days—75 minute classes)

*Day 1*
Collect ⓦ Mini-assignment #1
Questions from previous class (5 minutes)
Practice questions over material (5 minutes)
Administrivia (5 minutes)
 I.  Mental disorders: What is abnormal? (10 minutes)
     Results of ⓦ Mini-assignment #1
     Approaches
        Infrequency/statistical
        Personal suffering
        Norm violation
        Practical approach: Content/ context/ consequences of the behavior
     Cultural and historical influences
 II.  Models of psychological disorders (10 minutes)
     Demonological
     Biopsychosocial: Biological factors; psychological processes; sociocultural context
     Diathesis-stress
 III.  Schizophrenia (20 minutes)
     Symptoms—video clip
     Types
     Target populations
     Causes
 IV.  Anxiety disorders (20 minutes)
     Phobias—video clip
     Generalized anxiety disorder
     Panic disorder
     Obsessive-compulsive disorder
     Causes

*Day 2*
Questions from previous class (5 minutes)
Practice questions over material (5 minutes)
Administrivia (5 minutes)

I. Mood disorders (20 minutes)
Depressive disorders
Bipolar disorder
Causes
II. Dissociative disorders (20 minutes)
Fugue/amnesia/dissociative identity disorder
Causes
III. Diagnoses—Diagnosing mental disorders classroom learning
activity, pp. 237–40 (20 minutes)

*Day 3*
Questions from previous class (5 minutes)
Practice questions over material (5 minutes)
Administrivia (5 minutes)
I. Therapies: Introduction/statistics (10 minutes)
II. Psychodynamic (10 minutes)
III. Social-cognitive/behavioral (15 minutes)
IV. Humanistic (10 minutes)
V. Biological treatments (15 minutes)

## My transitions

Although the topics of mental disorders and treatment could be taught almost anywhere in the curriculum, I teach them after personality and before social psychology. I want my students to develop a more "informed" view of mental disorders and treatments: thus I integrate principles from other units—biological psychology and learning in particular. This also follows my ordering of the introductory material from the cell to social interaction with others.

## Topics typically included in this unit

*Defining psychological disorder*: Criteria—infrequency, norm violation, personal suffering; practical approach—content, context, and consequences of the behavior, impaired functioning; *Diagnostic and Statistical Manual of Mental Disorders* (DSM)
*Explaining psychological disorders*: Biopsychosocial model—biological factors, medical model, Hippocrates and the four humors; neurobiological model; psychological processes—psychodynamic, social-learning, humanistic; sociocultural context—gender, age, marital status, social status, economic status, culture; diathesis-stress

model—diathesis or biological predisposition plus stress or environmental impact

*Classifying psychological disorders*: DSM-IV—Axis I major mental disorders; Axis II personality disorders; Axis III medical conditions; Axis IV cognitive, emotional, or behavior problems; Axis V rating (1–100) of current level of functioning

*Anxiety disorders*: Phobias—simple, social, agoraphobia; generalized anxiety disorder; panic disorder; obsessive-compulsive disorder; causes—biological, psychological

*Somatoform disorders*: Conversion disorder, somatization disorder, pain disorder

*Dissociative disorders*: Amnesia, fugue, dissociative identity disorder (multiple personality disorder)

*Mood disorders*: Depressive disorders—major depressive disorder, dysthymic disorder, suicide and depression, bipolar I, mania, cyclothymic disorder; biological factors—genetics, neurotransmitters; other factors—culture, gender, negative attributional style, learned helplessness, distracting coping style

*Schizophrenia*: Symptoms—neologisms, loose associations, clang associations, word salad, delusions (grandeur, persecution), ideas of reference, thought broadcasting, thought blocking or withdrawal, thought insertion, hallucinations, flat affect, movement disorder, poor social skills, inability to function in everyday life, lack of personal hygiene; classifying schizophrenia by positive and negative symptoms; categories—paranoid, disorganized, catatonic, undifferentiated, residual; causes—biological and genetic, dopamine, diathesis-stress

*Personality disorders*: Paranoid, schizoid, schizotypal, dependent, obsessive-compulsive, avoidant, histrionic, narcissistic, borderline, antisocial

*Psychological disorders of childhood*: Conduct disorders, attention deficit hyperactivity disorder (ADHD), separation anxiety disorder, autistic spectrum disorders

*Substance-related disorders*: Alcohol use disorder, heroin and cocaine dependence

*Mental illness and the law*: Mental incompetence to stand trial; not guilty by reason of insanity—M'Naughton rule and irresistible impulse

*Basic features of treatment for psychological disorders*: Client/patient, therapist, inpatients and outpatients; psychiatrists, psychologists, clinical social workers, licensed professional counselors;

ethics—rules and rights in the therapeutic relationship, client–therapist relationship privileged

*Psychodynamic psychotherapy*: Psychoanalysis—free association, working through, latent and manifest content of dreams; transference; modern psychoanalysis—ego analysis, short-term dynamic psychotherapy, object relations therapy, interpersonal therapy

*Humanistic psychotherapy*: Rogers' client-centered therapy—unconditional positive regard, empathy, congruence; Perls' Gestalt therapy—body language, role play

*Behavior therapy*: Systematic desensitization—progressive relaxation and desensitization hierarchy; modeling—assertiveness training and social skills training; positive reinforcement—contingencies; extinction—flooding; aversion therapy—aversion conditioning; punishment

*Cognitive-behavior therapy*: Ellis's rational-emotive behavior therapy (REBT), Beck's cognitive therapy

*Group, family, couples therapy*: Self-help therapy, structural family therapy

*Effectiveness of psychotherapy*: Eysenck's meta-analysis, clinical vs. statistical significance, appropriate therapy for specific problems, the ultimate question ("what treatment, by whom, is most effective for this individual with that specific problem, under what set of circumstances?"), empirically supported therapies, cultural factors

*Biological treatments*: Electroconvulsive therapy (ECT); psychosurgery; psychoactive drugs—neuroleptics, antidepressants, anxiolytics

*Community psychology*: Prevention emphasis, community mental health movement

## Some options for organizing the concepts

*By approach:* Taking each approach and explaining its view of what a mental disorder is and methods of treatment (e.g., the behavioral approach, how behaviorists would view the specific disorders and available treatment methods) provides a unifying theme to these two chapters.

*By topic:* It is easy to take each mental disorder and discuss it as a separate concept. However, it's important that some unifying thread be used, if not approaches, then maybe prevalence rates, presenting the most common disorders first, or presenting treatment methods first and discussing which disorders would respond to which treatments. I choose to present mental disorders first, and treatments later, but these two chapters could be integrated as well.

# Teaching the Content

Remember that the ⓦ symbol means that a printable version is available on the web site (www.blackwellpublishing.com/lucas) and ⓤ means that the URL is available on the web site.

## Topics that many students will find difficult

### Personality disorders
Students have a difficult time understanding that people with personality disorders do not choose to be the way they are, for example, narcissistic or lacking a "conscience." The National Mental Health Association web site ⓤ contains a fact sheet that outlines what is and is not a personality disorder. See *Personality Disorders* ⓤ, a 1997 26-minute video.

## Other important topics

### What is abnormal?
Before I begin this unit I ask students to complete ⓦ Mini-assignment #1, observing abnormal behavior. I then categorize their examples under the headings: statistical/infrequency, valuative/norm violation, and personal suffering. I summarize by presenting the practical approach (which I call "the 3 Cs"), evaluating the content, context, and consequences of a behavior, before deciding whether it is abnormal.

The role of history, gender, age, and so forth is important in the diagnosis of mental disorders. It's important for students to understand how behaviors become viewed as disorders and how similar behaviors, in different circumstances or different eras or performed by different people, will be labeled differently. See Stimulus question Cultural/historical/ethnicity impact in diagnosing mental disorders (pp. 235–6).

This is a good point to present the ideas of Thomas Szasz, that mental illness is just a myth based on labeling people instead of labeling behavior, thus creating self-fulfilling prophesies. You can access his classic 1960 paper at Christopher York's Classics in the History of Psychology web site ⓤ.

### Mental disorders and culture
It's important that students understand that some disorders are culture-specific (e.g., koro (or genital retraction syndrome), *susto*—see

the Hispanic Center of Excellence Premedical Honors College Program web site ⓤ, anorexia nervosa), while others seem to be pervasive across cultures (schizophrenia, affective disorders).

See Berry, Poortinga, Segall, and Dasen (2002, p. 433) for an explanation of "culture bound syndrome." The entire "Health Behavior" chapter (pp. 423–455) is an excellent resource.

The World Health Organization has developed an International Classification of Mental and Behavioral Disorders (ICD-10) for disorders that seem to be pervasive across many cultures. The general categories of disorders included are: organic, substance use, schizophrenia, affective, neurotic-anxiety, physiological dysfunction, anorexia, personality disorders, mental retardation, development, childhood (Berry et al., 2002, p. 428). See the World Health Organization web site ⓤ for a description of these disorders.

## Models of psychological disorders

Along with discussing the models of disorder, I try to give students a sense of how disorders have been defined, diagnosed, and treated in past times. Thus I present the demonological model—prevalent in the Middle Ages and the colonial period in American history. Many mentally ill people were executed as witches during those times. The "guidebook" to hunting witches, the *Malleus maleficarum* (1438), can be accessed online at the Malleus Maleficarum organization web site ⓤ.

Hippocrates was important in the development of the *biological model*, even though his "humors" theory has not stood the test of time. The biological model has progressed from a medical model to a more neurobiological one.

The *psychological model* is most familiar to students—including the psychodynamic, social-cognitive (old behaviorists), and humanistic views of mental disorders.

The *sociocultural model* has become more important as we become aware of cultural and social contexts of mental disorders.

I am a big believer in the *diathesis-stress model*, combining genetic and environmental factors. So I present this model (from the health, stress and coping unit) again in the context of mental disorders.

## Anxiety disorders

I reassure students that all of us have periods of anxiety, that all of us have "songs in our heads that won't go away," and we all experience mild panic at some point in time. However, this does not mean that we have a mental disorder. Stressing the severity of anxiety disorders is important. See the video *Circuits of Fear: Anxiety Disorders* ⓤ.

Many people have phobias—however, for most people these do not cause major disruptions of their lives. For vignettes of people whose phobias do cause disruption of their lives see *Simple and Social Phobias* ⓤ (2003) and *Phobias: Living in Terror* ⓤ (1998) videos.

The National Institute of Mental Health web site ⓤ provides a list of symptoms and possible treatments of agoraphobia. The Internet Mental Health web site ⓤ provides an American and European description of agoraphobia as well as links to mental health resources.

Obsessive-compulsive disorder (OCD) is often misunderstood, because students believe that the person with OCD can just decide to end the obsessions or compulsions. I show a short video clip from the beginning of *As Good As It Gets* ⓤ, for a pretty accurate view of living with OCD. See also the videos *Obsessive-Compulsive Disorder* ⓤ and *Obsessive-Compulsive Disorder: The Tyranny of Rituals* ⓤ.

Panic attacks are more pervasive than students believe and they are more severe. For information about panic attacks see the Mayo Clinic web site ⓤ and the video *Panic Attacks* ⓤ.

## Mood disorders

I try to reintroduce ideas from previous chapters in this unit. For example, I point out that depressed people often experience learned helplessness, a self-blaming attributional style, and experience the "sadder but wiser" effect (happy people are overly optimistic and think things are better than they are, while depressed people tend to be more realistic in their appraisals).

*Mood disorders/depression.* Depression seems to be a cross-cultural disorder. Because the rates of depression are high and it is probable that at least one of my students is on antidepressants, I try to be especially sensitive when discussing this topic.

I remind students that we've all "been blue" but major depression involves a much more severe disruption of life. Dysthymia is a milder form of depression expressed for at least two years.

Depression does increase the risk of suicide. The Mental Health Association in Boone County (IN) web site ⓤ provides statistics about suicide. The National Institute of Mental Health web site Ⓤ provides frequently asked questions about suicide.

Seasonal affective disorder is depression associated with variations in seasonal light. Many people suffering from this disorder experience depression during the winter months, when there are low levels of light. For information about this disorder see the National Mental Health Association's web site Ⓤ. There are many commercial products that are marketed as helping with seasonal affective disorder.

*Mood disorders/bipolar disorder.* Students will often know this disorder by its old name, manic depression. They will need help understanding the severity of this disorder and that cyclothymia is a milder form of the disorder occurring over a period of years. Kay Redfield Jamison is a psychologist who has bipolar disorder, and her book, *An Unquiet Mind* (1997), provides a good picture of the disorder. See also *Flight from Despair: Depression and Mania* and *Depression and Manic Depression* Ⓤ (featuring Mike Wallace and Kay Redfield Jamison), a 2001 52-minute video; *Mood Disorders* Ⓤ, a 1997 45-minute video; and *Bipolar Disorders* Ⓤ, a 2001 29-minute video. See also the video, *Kay Redfield Jamison: Surviving Bipolar Disorder* Ⓤ.

## Schizophrenia

Misconceptions abound about schizophrenia. Students first must understand that schizophrenia is *not* the same as "split personality" (dissociative identity disorder, or multiple personality disorder) and that it is not "one disorder" but a spectrum of related disorders. Schizophrenia is another cross-cultural disorder. I begin with the statistics—1% of the world population is affected by schizophrenia, equal numbers of men and women, early onset, and so forth. (For a very nice general outline of schizophrenia see the Neuroscience for Kids web site Ⓤ. Symptoms of, possible causes of, and treatments for schizophrenia are discussed. It also contains links to other sources of information, including the NIMH and the National Alliance for the Mentally Ill web sites.) Following these statistics I show a short video clip of two schizophrenic patients (I don't know the source of my clips, but you may use clips from *Dark Voices: Schizophrenia* Ⓤ, a 2001 52-minute video, and *Understanding Mental Illness and Schizophrenia* Ⓤ, a 2004 27-minute video). Then we begin a general discussion of the symptoms and types of disorders.

*Symptoms*: Any abnormal psychology textbook can provide examples of disorders of thought. I use Davidson and Neale (2001). You can also find information about symptoms of schizophrenia at the British Columbia Schizophrenia Society web site ⓤ. This web site also discusses treatments, the effect of schizophrenia on families, and frequently asked questions. A great illustration of schizophrenic patients' perceptual distortions is a series of drawings of cats demonstrating the artist Louis Wain's progression into schizophrenia. See the pictures at the Neuroscience Art Gallery web site ⓤ.

*Types*: Differentiating between disorganized, paranoid, and catatonic is easier if you can show students the differences. I use a short video clip from *One Flew Over the Cuckoo's Nest* ⓤ—the scene where McMurphy (the character played by Jack Nicholson) tries to get "the chief" to play basketball. I ask the students if "the chief" is displaying any schizophrenic symptoms—and we talk about catatonia and "the chief" having his hands molded into position by McMurphy.

*Causes*: There is no one cause of schizophrenia—so I talk about research studies pointing to dopamine as being important in schizophrenia. Another neurochemical component includes overactivity of protein kinases C (PKC). I also talk about the neurodevelopmental model, the idea that schizophrenia is a developmental disorder, with prenatal roots. One study found that infants born with obstetric complications, and thus low Apgar scores, were four times more likely to develop schizophrenia, especially displaying negative symptoms, than those without obstetric complications. See Kotlicka-Antczak, Gmitrowicz, Sobow, and Rabe-Jablonska (2001). See also Rapoport, Addington, Frangou, and Psych (2005).

## Dissociative disorders

Students are fascinated with dissociative disorders, often knowing dissociative identity disorder (DID) by its older name of multiple personality disorder. I begin this section by asking students if they believe that multiple personality disorder exists (see Stimulus question Dissociative identity disorder, p. 236). For a skeptical view of the disorder see the Skeptic's Dictionary web site ⓤ. This can lead to a discussion of diagnoses in general and a therapist's influence on a client.

Information differentiating between dissociative amnesia, fugue, and identity disorder may be found at the Merck web site ⓤ. Several popular movies do a decent job of presenting DID. I especially like

*The Three Faces of Eve* ⓤ, an old black and white movie—there is an especially interesting scene when Eve is taken to see a therapist by her husband and two "personalities" emerge. I follow up on this clip by referring students to Chris Sizemore's book (Sizemore & Pittillo, 1977) which disputes the idea that she had only two personalities and that she got "better" with therapy. See Thigpen and Cleckley (1957).

### Somatoform disorders

Students often misuse the term "hypochondriac" so discussing these disorders can be informative for them. I present conversion disorder and talk about Freud calling the disorder "hysteria." I talk about hypochandriasis, that people are not "faking it," as well as pain disorder. For information about somatoform disorders see Vincent Hevern's (LeMoyne College) webpage ⓤ and the National Institute of Health web site ⓤ.

### Diagnosing mental disorders

Although I think the details of the DSM-IV go beyond what most introductory students need to know, I do talk about the five axes of the DSM. And I have an exercise where students use Axis I (major mental disorders) to make a diagnosis when presented with case studies (see Diagnosing mental disorders classroom learning activity, pp. 237–40).

### Therapy basics

I present the statistic that 1 out of every 10 people will receive treatment for a psychological disorder at some time in their life. I point out the differences between a psychiatrist and a psychologist. And I emphasize that the best therapists, regardless of orientation, listen, accept their clients, and are supportive. I talk about the proliferations of psychotherapists in the last several decades, about the fact that most psychologists work with clients in the general population (not institutionalized or incarcerated populations), and that statistics show that therapy does have a positive impact.

APA has a series of videos about psychotherapy, *Systems of Psychotherapy* ⓤ. These include client-centered therapy, cognitive therapy, and cognitive-behavior therapy. While intended for potential therapists, these clips might help students understand the differences between different psychotherapies. See the Psi Café web site ⓤ for links to discussions of the major psychotherapies.

## Therapies and culture

The approach to treating mental disorders is influenced by a culture's view of what mental disorders are and what causes them. There are indigenous psychotherapies that would not translate across cultures. For example, Berry et al. (2002, pp. 438–439) discuss Morita therapy practiced in Japan. The goal of this therapy is to have patients accept the realities of life, rather than trying to change reality to match their needs, which would be the prevalent Western approach. Psychotherapy must be sensitive to the cultural background of clients. See Reynolds (1998).

## Therapies (psychoanalytic/psychodynamic)

I begin discussing specific therapies with the psychodynamic model because this model is what most students think of when talking about therapies. I talk about the goals and the specific techniques, such as free association, interpretation of dreams, analysis of everyday behavior including Freudian slips, giving interpretations, and analysis of transference.

For information about psychoanalytic methods of therapy see the Answers.com web site ⓤ.

Discussion of neo-Freudians who emphasized the ego over the id, and object relations therapy "modernizes" students' views of psychoanalysis. See the Object Relations Organization's web site ⓤ.

## Therapies (behavioral)

It is important to relate behavior therapies back to learning theories. If students understand the behavioral approach, they will see characteristics of behaviorism in treatments such as systematic desensitization, modeling, positive reinforcement, extinction, aversive conditioning, and punishment. The movie and book, *A Clockwork Orange* ⓤ (novel by Anthony Burgess, 1962/movie by Stanley Kubrick, 1971), are excellent at showing aversive conditioning, although both are extremely violent.

For a listing and brief discussion of behavioral therapy techniques see the Alter-ABC company web site ⓤ.

A good article from the U.S. Governments' Department of Veteran Affairs ⓤ describes how "exposure therapies" work. See also Boston University's Center for Anxiety and Related Disorders web site ⓤ. And see Hebert (2006; also at APS web site ⓤ.)

## Therapies (cognitive-behavioral)

The two most famous cognitive therapies are Beck's cognitive therapy and Ellis's rational-emotive behavior therapy (REBT). I spend some time discussing Ellis's idea of self-defeating thoughts and cognitive restructuring. I also talk about Beck's idea that psychological disorders can be traced to clients' errors of logic and cognitive distortions—quite a different picture of mental disorder from Freud's.

For more information about Albert Ellis's REBT, see the Counseling Resource web site ⓤ. (Although this is a commercial web site, it does contain good information.)

For more information about Aaron Beck's cognitive therapy, see the College of Integrated Therapies web site ⓤ.

## Therapies (humanistic)

The humanistic (phenomenological) approach to personality is probably best known for its contribution to psychotherapy. The humanists first called those seeking help "clients" rather than "patients," and this distinction is salient. Carl Rogers' client-centered approach introduced the ideas of unconditional positive regard, empathy, congruence, and reflection.

For a nice discussion of Rogers, his theories and therapy see George Boeree's (Shippensburg University) web site ⓤ. See also Rogers (1951).

Fritz Perl's theory of Gestalt therapy is often mentioned in introductory textbooks. For a description of its development and basic techniques see the Association for the Advancement of Gestalt Therapy's web site ⓤ.

## Therapies (group, family, and couples)

I do not discuss this topic in any depth. I primarily talk about the advantages of group therapy—that the therapist can see the client interacting with others, that it helps clients know they aren't alone and bolsters their self-confidence, and that it allows clients a supportive environment to try new skills. For a comparison of group and individual therapies see the Web4Health web site ⓤ.

## Biological treatments

I make the case that biological treatments presuppose a physiological basis for mental disorders. This often leads to an interesting discussion about the connection between theories of mental disorders and their treatments. I present Hippocrates as one of the first to propose that psychological problems have physical causes. Included in biological treatments are drug therapy, psychosurgery, and electroconvulsive therapy (ECT).

The story of the evolution of ECT is truly one of serendipity. I want my students to understand that therapies are developed and refined over many years. This leads to a discussion of ethics and whether those who are mentally ill can provide "informed" consent for their treatment. See Valenstein (1986) and Fink (1984).

I follow the same historical presentation with drug therapies, discussing the appropriate use of neuroleptics, anxiolytics, and anti-depressants. I discuss Prozac (fluoxetine) in more detail because some of my students may be taking this drug. For more information see the NIH web site ⓤ. See also Taravosh-Lahn, Bastida, and Delvill (2006; also available on line at APA's web site ⓤ).

Trephining (early psychosurgery) might actually have helped some people by opening their skull to allow for swelling of the brain. However, psychosurgery seems to be forever associated with pre-frontal lobotomies and Walter Freeman. I discuss Freeman's work in the context that it is possible that at some time in the future resear-chers will look back at the therapies and treatments that we use today with the same abhorrence and disbelief with which we now view prefrontal lobotomies. See Brain and Mind Electronic Magazine on Neuroscience's web site ⓤ for an excellent discussion of the history of psychosurgery and modern advances. See also El-Hai (2005).

# Classroom Tips

## Stimulus questions for discussion

### Mental health literacy

What people know and believe about mental disorders has an impact on their recognition of a disorder and how they decide to treat it. An international study of mental health literacy (Jorm, 2000) found that many people did not correctly recognize mental disorders and did not understand the meaning of psychiatric terms. Negative attitudes about medications for mental disorders and the belief that they only "treat the symptom, not the disease" leads to less stringent adherence to prescribed psychotropic medications. Do you think this study is accurate? How can the public be better educated about mental disorders?

### Cultural/historical/ethnicity impact in diagnosing mental disorders

In the mid-1800s Samuel Cartwright found two types of mental disorders common in slaves: drapetomania and dysathesia aethiopica. There was one symptom for drapetomania—the slave ran away. Dysathesia aethiopica had symptoms including destroying plantation property, talking back to the master, and refusing to work (Bronstein & Quina, 1998, p. 39). Are these mental disorders? Why or why not? What criteria did you use for evaluation? Are there any modern disorders that you think history will view similarly?

### Dissociative identity disorder

Do you believe that dissociative identity disorder is a legitimate mental disorder? Why or why not? What evidence would be helpful in answering this question, in other words, what would convince you that the disorder either exists or does not exist?

### Therapies

Do you think that drugs or surgery are appropriate treatments for disorders? If yes, then are mental disorders biological in nature? If not, why not? What treatments are effective? What model of mental disorders would be addressed by this treatment?

## Some suggested classroom learning activities

### Being sane in insane places

(Students complete the work outside of class, 20 minutes to present)
In 1973 David Rosenhan selected eight associates as "pseudopatients," people with no diagnosed mental disorders, who attempted to be admitted to different mental institutions. All eight of them were admitted and took notes on how they were treated in the institution. He published the results in *Science*. Titled *On Being Sane in Insane Places*, the research can be found online on the Walnet web site ⓤ. I have used this highly accessible paper as a learning activity in one of two ways.

1. Assign all students ⓦ Mini-assignment #2. Have the students meet in small groups, assigning each group to present information about one of the questions to the entire class.
2. Assign different seminal papers in psychology to be presented by small groups of students throughout the semester. This is one paper that I have used for that assignment. Each group has

20 minutes to present the paper to the class and is asked to follow these guidelines when presenting:
- A summary of the article/study.
- Analysis of the study, including problems, flaws, or ethical concerns with the study.
- How this study relates to the material we are covering in the textbook/class.
- What is the importance of understanding this study/topic for understanding psychology?
- Three to five points that you want the class to remember about this research study.

## Diagnosing mental disorders

(5 minutes for group diagnosis, 15 minute class discussion) Students have a better understanding of the difficulty in diagnosing mental disorders when they are asked to do so. Doug Bernstein and I developed/ adapted these case studies so that they have very straightforward diagnoses. I break students into small groups and assign each group one case study. When we meet back as a whole class, we discuss each case study with the group assigned that case acting as experts. Each group is asked to identify the symptoms, make a primary diagnosis, a secondary diagnosis, and talk about a treatment plan.

ⓦ *Case 1: Andrew.* A 30-year-old accountant had a 6-month history of recurrent bouts of extreme fear accompanied by sweating, shortness of breath, palpitations, chest pain, headache, muscular tension, and the thought that he was going to die. No physical abnormalities could be found.

The patient, married for five years, had no children. He had earned a master's degree in business administration and was quite successful and well liked at his firm. He and his wife, a teacher, generally got along well and had several couples with whom they enjoyed going out.

Because of the episodes, which occurred in a variety of situations, the patient started to avoid driving his car and going into department stores, lest he have an episode in these situations. He began to coax his wife to accompany him on errands, and during the last month he felt comfortable only at home with his wife. Finally he could not face the prospect of leaving home to go to work, and took a medical leave of absence.

When asked about the onset of the episodes, the patient said that he and his wife had been discussing buying a house and moving from their apartment. He admitted that the responsibilities of home ownership intimidated him and related the significance of the move to similar concerns his mother had had that prevented his parents from ever buying a house.

⍟ *Case 2: Belinda.* A 24-year-old, single, copy editor was admitted to a psychiatric hospital for the first time. Her admission followed an accident in which she had wrecked her car while driving at high speed late at night when she was feeling "energetic" and that "sleep was a waste of time." The episode began while she was on vacation, when she felt "high" and on the verge of a "great romance." She apparently took off all of her clothes and ran naked through the woods. On the day of admission she reported hearing voices telling her that her father and the emergency-room staff were emissaries of the devil, out to "get" her for no reason that she could understand.

When meeting with the psychiatrist she was calm and cooperative and talked of the voices she had heard in the past, which she now acknowledged had not been real. She realized she had an illness, but was still somewhat irritated at being hospitalized.

⍟ *Case 3: Carol.* A 46-year-old housewife was experiencing "attacks of dizziness" accompanied by slight nausea, four or five nights a week. During the attacks, the room around her would take on a "shimmering" appearance, and she would have the feeling that she was "floating" and unable to keep her balance. Inexplicably, the attacks almost always occurred at about 4:00 p.m. She usually had to lie down on the couch and often did not feel better until 7:00 or 8:00 p.m. After recovering, she generally spent the rest of the evening watching TV, and more often than not, she would fall asleep in the living room, not going to bed in the bedroom until 2:00 or 3:00 a.m. A physical exam could find nothing wrong.

When asked about her marriage, the patient described her husband as a tyrant, frequently demanding and verbally abusive of her and their four children. She admitted that she dreaded his arrival home from work each day, knowing that he would comment that the house was a mess and the dinner, if prepared, not to his liking. Recently, since the onset of her attacks, when she was unable to make dinner he and the four kids would go to McDonald's or the local pizza parlor. After that, he would settle in to watch a ballgame in the bedroom, and their conversation was minimal. In spite of their troubles, the patient claimed that she loved her husband and needed him very much.

Ⓦ *Case 4: Marcia.* Marcia, a 32-year-old housewife, began to have doubts about whether she had made the dessert correctly at a family Christmas party. This doubt was accompanied by fear that she might have harmed her children and guests, and soon spread to other areas. Marcia became unable to give her children vitamins for fear of making a mistake and injuring them, and she could not cook for fear that she would poison someone. She gave up driving the car, plagued by the thought that she might kill someone. She repeatedly checked locks, faucets, the fireplace, and her husband's tools as possible sources of danger. She began to bathe as often as six times a day, particularly if she happened to brush against something that carried germs—like the garage door—before she would touch things in the house. Her hands became swollen from repeated washings.

Ⓦ *Case 5: Dirk.* A 26-year-old migratory farm worker suddenly appeared in a judge's chamber and demanded to be put to death because he felt he was responsible for the production of evil and violence in the world. He was put in jail where he was agitated, easily angered, suspicious, and guarded. His speech was disorganized, and often incoherent. He stated that he could not eat meat or terrible violence and evil would be unleashed on the world. He also described a plot by the California Mafia to keep him from working, and he spoke of voices that told him what to do and that "must be obeyed."

Ⓦ *Case 6: Edward.* Edward was a 46-year-old sheriff who, on three separate occasions, "came to" and found himself as far as 200 miles from his home. He would immediately call his wife who told him that he had just suddenly disappeared. He could not completely recall what he did when he was on these trips, some of which had lasted for several days.

However, after some treatment he remembered that during the trips he adopted an alias, drank heavily, mingled with a rough crowd, and went to brothels and wild parties.

## Answer key

### Case 1: Andrew

Diagnosis: Agoraphobia with panic attacks

Keys: recurrent unexpected panic attacks present, concern about having additional attacks, anxiety about being in places or situation from which escape might be difficult or embarrassing or in which help might not be available in the event of an attack

*Case 2: Belinda*
Diagnosis: Bipolar disorder, mania
Keys: Distinctive period of abnormality and persistently elevated, expansive, or irritable mood; inflated self-esteem or grandiosity; decreased need for sleep; more talkative than usual or pressure to keep talking; flight of ideas or subjective experience that thoughts are racing; distractibility; excessive involvement in pleasurable activities that have a high potential for painful consequences (foolish business investments, etc.)

*Case 3: Carol*
Diagnosis: Conversion disorder
Keys: Symptoms suggesting a neurological or general medical condition, symptoms not intentionally produced, symptoms not explained medically
Specific: Occur at same time each day, associated with husband's arrival, enable her to avoid her husband and preparing evening meals, no evidence she is voluntarily producing symptoms

*Case 4: Marcia*
Diagnosis: Obsessive-compulsive disorder/anxiety disorder
Keys: Recurrent and persistent thoughts, impulses, or images which are not just excessive worries about real-life problems; realizes they are excessive or unreasonable

*Case 5: Dirk*
Diagnosis: Paranoid schizophrenia
Keys: Preoccupation with one or more delusions or frequent auditory hallucinations, *no* disorganized speech, *no* disorganized or catatonic behavior, *no* flat or inappropriate affect

*Case 6: Edward*
Diagnosis: Dissociative fugue
Keys: Sudden, unexpected travel away from home or place of work with inability to recall one's past; confusion about personal identity or assumption of new identity

*Role plays of therapy sessions*
(The time depends on the number of role plays involved. Students without a script will need 10 minutes, those with a script 5 minutes)
Many instructors write their own role plays to simplify the therapy situation, making it easier for students to see the major techniques of each approach. If you do this, I think it is important that you yourself play the client or that both roles are scripted. There are

some class role plays that you may find at the University of West Virginia's Robert C. Byrd's Health Sciences Center web site Ⓦ. You may find a similar activity, for a group therapy simulation, including sample scripts, in Rudisill (1999).

Wesley and Schira provide a "game" demonstration in which students are divided into five groups, each representing one therapeutic perspective (humanistic, biomedical, cognitive, behavioral, and psychoanalytic). The authors provide 11 case studies. Each team has a representative who chooses one of the case studies, reads it to the class, provides a diagnosis and then provides a treatment based on their group's perspective. For the specific guidelines and case studies see Wesley and Schira (1999).

## Possible mini-assignments (written or groups)

### Ⓦ *Mini-assignment #1*
Please complete this assignment before you read the mental disorders chapter.

1. Observe people around you.
2. Write down one instance of abnormal behavior that you observe. (You could write about behavior that you have observed in the past.) Describe the behavior, the context, and explain why you think it is abnormal.
3. Write a definition of mental abnormality.

### Ⓦ *Mini-assignment #2*
Read David Rosenhan's article, *On Being Sane in Insane Places*, on the Walnet web site Ⓦ. After you have read this paper, please answer the following questions.

1. What were the main points of this experiment?
2. What were the results of the experiment?
3. Are there ethical questions to be addressed in this experiment?
4. Explain how confirmation bias and the anchoring heuristic are demonstrated.

### Ⓦ *Mini-assignment #3*
(This assignment is worth more points.)

Watch a movie that attempts to portray a mental disorder. Clear the movie with me before you begin this assignment but some possible movies include: *As Good As It Gets*, *The Aviator*, *Awakenings*, *The Bell Jar*, *Fight Club*, *Harvey*, *I Never Promised You a Rose*

*Garden, One Flew Over the Cuckoo's Nest, Rain Man, Sybil, Three Faces of Eve.* Then answer the following questions.

1. What disorder does the movie portray and how does it portray the disorder?
2. How does your textbook describe this disorder?
3. Compare the movie's portrayal of the disorder and your textbook's description.
4. How could the movie be changed to be more accurate?

🐦 *Mini-assignment #4*
Psychotherapy is often viewed in a negative light because people in the general population seldom know how individual therapies work or which therapy is appropriate for which disorder. In two or three paragraphs tell me what general information about psychotherapy you learned in this unit. Has this changed your perspective on psychotherapy? (It's OK to say no.) Why or why not?

🐦 *Mini-assignment #5*
(Note: This is a group assignment with individual accountability.) Please read carefully, and understand the therapeutic approach assigned to your group. Write down some key concepts important to this therapeutic approach. Your group will be the "experts" on this approach and will teach the basics of this therapy to the class.

Group 1: Psychoanalytic
Group 2: Behavioral
Group 3: Cognitive
Group 4: Humanistic/client-centered
Group 5: Humanistic/Gestalt

## References

Berry, J., Poortinga, Y., Segall, M., & Dasen, P. (2002). *Cross-cultural psychology* (2nd ed.). Cambridge, UK: Cambridge University Press.

Bronstein, P., & Quina, K. (Eds.). (1998). *Teaching a psychology of people: Resources for gender and sociocultural awareness.* Washington, DC: American Psychological Association.

Davidson, G., & Neale, J. (2001). *Abnormal psychology.* New York: John Wiley.

El-Hai, J. (2005). *The lobotomist: A maverick medical genius and his tragic quest to rid the world of mental illness.* New York: Wiley.

Fink, M. (1984). Meduna and the origins of convulsive therapy. *American Journal of Psychiatry, 141,* 1034–1041.

Hebert, R. (2006). We love to be scared at Halloween but fears and phobias are no laughing matter. *APS Observer, 19*(10), 14–19.

Jamison, K. R. (1997). *An unquiet mind.* New York: Vintage Books.

Jorm, A. (2000). Mental health literacy. *British Journal of Psychiatry, 177,* 396–401.

Kotlicka-Antczak, M., Gmitrowicz, T., Sobow, M., & Rabe-Jablonska, J. (2001). Obstetric complications and Apgar score in early-onset schizophrenic patients with prominent positive and prominent negative symptoms. *Journal of Psychiatric Research, 35*(4), 249–257.

Rapoport, J., Addington, A., Frangou, S., & Psych, M. (2005). The neurodevelopmental model of schizophrenia: Update 2005. *Molecular Psychiatry, 10,* 434–449.

Reynolds, D. (1998). *Flowing bridges, quiet waters: Japanese psychotherapies, Morit and Naikan.* Albany, NY: State University of New York.

Rogers, C. (1951). *Client-centered therapy.* Boston: Houghton Mifflin.

Rudisill, J. (1999). Diagnosis of psychological disorder: A group therapy simulation. In L. Benjamin, B. Nodine, R. Ernst, & C. Blair Broeker (Eds.), *Activities handbook for the teaching of psychology, vol. 4* (pp. 384–392). Washington, DC: American Psychological Association.

Sizemore, C., & Pittillo, E. (1977). *I'm Eve.* New York: Jove.

Taravosh-Lahn, K., Bastida, C., & Delvill, Y. (2006). Differential responsiveness to fluoxetine during puberty. *Behavioral Neuroscience, 120*(5), 1084–1092.

Thigpen, C., & Cleckley, H. (1957). *The three faces of Eve.* New York: McGraw-Hill.

Valenstein, E. (1986). *Great and desperate cures.* New York: Basic Books.

Wesley, A., & Schira, C. (1999). The doctor is in: How to treat psychological disorders. In L. Benjamin, B. Nodine, R. Ernst, & C. Blair Broeker (Eds.), *Activities handbook for the teaching of psychology, vol. 4* (pp. 397–401). Washington, DC.: American Psychological Association.

## Additional Suggested Readings for Instructors

Kramer, P. (1993). *Listening to Prozac.* New York: Penguin Books.

Schreiber, F. (1974). *Sybil.* New York: Warner Books.

Styron, W. (1992). *Darkness visible: A memoir of madness.* New York: Basic Books.

Urban, H., & Ford, D. (1998). *Contemporary models of psychotherapy: A comparative analysis.* Hoboken, NJ: Wiley.

U.S. Surgeon General's first report on Mental Health. http://www.surgeongeneral.gov/library/mentalhealth/home.html, Released in December, 1999, it provides a comprehensive overview of mental illnesses and resources in the United States.

# Chapter 12

# Social Psychology

## Getting Started

Social psychology, of course, is an entire course on its own. You will have to pick the topics that you think are most important and/or those in which you have the most interest. I give my students a choice of topics to discuss—and interpersonal attraction/love is always the Number 1 interest. Social norms, attitudes, attribution, prejudice and stereotypes, deindividuation, and obedience, conformity and compliance are other popular topics. I teach the concepts that I believe have the most relevance in students' lives.

Beyond student interest, I incorporate the idea of culture—that many social concepts differ between cultures. Attributions and social norms (e.g., distance between two people interacting) are two examples. I also focus on the idea of social norms—that they are so ingrained that we often don't think about them, but when we violate them we are embarrassed or uncomfortable.

I also want students to understand that all of us obey—that the setting and/or the situation determines our obedience. Thus I want them to understand that any one of us could have reacted the way Milgram's subjects did. I also want them to talk about the ethics of psychological research—and the Milgram study is a great stimulus.

I want my students to understand the concept of deindividuation. I want them to realize what happens when individual identities merge into a mob identity. And I want them to think about that the next time they find themselves in such a situation.

Finally, I want my students to understand that much of what we know about ourselves we learn from others—often from evaluating ourselves by others' standards. We have reference groups that we check with in deciding if we are doing OK or if we have a problem.

## My outline for teaching (3 days—75 minute classes)

*Day 1*

Collect deindividuation responses handed out at previous class
 (Deindividuation classroom learning activity—pp. 263–4)
Questions from previous class (5 minutes)
Practice questions over material (5 minutes)
Administrivia (5 minutes)
  I.  Social comparison (5 minutes)
      Temporal comparison
      Relative deprivation
 II.  Social norms (15 minutes)
      Descriptive and injunctive
      The reciprocity norm
      Results of ^Mini-assignment #1
III.  Attitudes (10 minutes)
      Structure (cognitive, behavioral, affective)
      Forming attitudes—Learning and the mere-exposure effect
 IV.  Cognitive dissonance (10 minutes)
      Cognitive dissonance classroom learning activity (pp. 256–7)
  V.  Persuasion (10 minutes)
      Elaboration likelihood model: Central vs. peripheral route
      Foot-in-door, door-in-face, low-ball
 VI.  Attribution (10 minutes)
      Fundamental attribution error
      Actor–observer bias
      Self-serving bias
      Attribution classroom learning activity

*Day 2*

Questions from previous class (5 minutes)
Practice questions over material (5 minutes)

Administrivia (5 minutes)
  I.   Reactance (10 minutes)
  II.  Deindividuation (20 minutes)
       Deindividuation classroom learning activity (pp. 263–4)
       Clip from *To Kill a Mockingbird*
  III. First impressions (10 minutes)
       First impressions classroom learning activity (pp. 264–5)
  IV.  Interpersonal attraction (20 minutes)
       Environment
       Evolutionary/sociobiological theory
       Romanticism scales
       Biology of romantic love
       Faithful attraction
       Marriages fail/divorce
       Marital and global happiness
       Sternberg's triangular theory of love

*Day 3*
Questions from previous class (5 minutes)
Practice questions over material (5 minutes)
Administrivia (5 minutes)
  I.   Bystander intervention (15 minutes)
  II.  Conformity, compliance, obedience (15 minutes)
       Video clip *Conformity and Independence* ⓤ
       Video clip *Obedience: A Reenactment* ⓤ
  III. Aggression (10 minutes)
       Theories
  IV.  Prejudice and stereotypes (20 minutes)
       Contact hypothesis
       Jigsaw
       Video clip *Eye of the Storm* ⓤ

## My transitions

I use the social psychology unit as the final unit of material in the course. I like to end the course talking about how people influence each other. And I like to use the final unit to integrate as many concepts learned throughout the course as possible. Also, students find the social psychology material to be especially relevant to their lives, and thus end the course applying the concepts they have learned to their everyday lives. Hopefully they will continue to apply the psychological concepts they have learned, well after the course has ended.

## Topics typically included in this unit

*Social influence on self*: Social comparison—reference groups; relative deprivation; social identity theory; schemas; first impressions; self-fulfilling prophecy

*Attribution*: Sources—consensus, consistency, distinctiveness; cultural influence; biases in attribution—fundamental attribution error, actor–observer bias, self-serving bias

*Self-protective functions*: Unrealistic optimism, unique invulnerability

*Attitudes*: Structure—affective, cognitive, behavioral; forming attitudes—learning, mere-exposure effect; changing attitudes—elaboration likelihood model; central and peripheral routes, cognitive dissonance theory; self-perception theory

*Prejudice and stereotypes*: Theories—motivational, cognitive, learning; reducing prejudice—contact hypothesis, jigsaw technique

*Interpersonal attraction*: Why?—physical proximity, similarity, physical attractiveness, balanced and imbalanced relationships; intimate relationships and love—interdependence, commitment, Sternberg's triangular theory—passion, intimacy, commitment; marriage

*Social norms*: Descriptive and injunctive, reciprocity, deindividuation

*Motivation and presence of others*: Social facilitation, social impairment, social loafing

*Conformity and compliance*: Public conformity vs. private acceptance; why conform?—ambiguity of situation, unanimity and size of majority, minority influence, gender; inducing compliance—foot-in-the-door, door-in-the face, low-ball

*Obedience*: Milgram's experiment; factors affecting obedience—experimenter status, presence of others who disobey; authoritarian personality; ethics of Milgram's experiment

*Aggression*: Why?—thanatos, genetics, testosterone, learning, culture; when?—frustration-aggression, excitation transfer, environmental influences—pollution, heat, crowding

*Altruism and helping behavior theories*: Arousal: cost-reward—clarity of need for help, presence of others, bystander effect and diffusion of responsibility, personality of helper; empathy-altruism; evolutionary

*Cooperation, competition, and conflict*: Social dilemmas—prisoner's dilemma, resource dilemmas; tit-for-tat; zero-sum game; bargaining; superordinate goals/identity

*Group processes*: Group leadership—task-oriented vs. person-oriented; groupthink

## Some options for organizing the concepts

*By student interest*: I teach social psychology at the end of the course, after having traced how we are alike (biological, sensation, etc.), how we differ (personality) and now how others influence us. I make a list of the traditional topics in social psychology and before we get to this unit I have students rank order the topics in terms of what they are most interested in. I always teach basics—norms and attribution, for example—but I also spend varying amounts of time on other content areas, based on student interest.

*Social cognition vs. social influence*: Some textbooks divide the social psychology content into social cognition (how we perceive and react to others) and social influence (how our behavior is affected by other people).

# Teaching the Content

Remember that the ⓦ symbol means that a printable version is available on the web site (www.blackwellpublishing.com/lucas) and ⓤ means that the URL is available on the web site.

## Topics that many students will find difficult

### Cognitive dissonance

Students will understand hypothetically that you will change your appraisal of a behavior in order to make your behavior and attitude compatible—but specific examples are more difficult. Especially troubling to students is the idea that if you are adequately rewarded for engaging in the behavior you do not have to change your attitude—that you are more likely to change your attitude if you engage in the behavior without an adequate reward. There are several classic studies, including Festinger's "peg turning" experiment (Festinger & Carlsmith, 1959) and Phil Zimbardo's grasshopper study (Zimbardo, Weisenberg, Firestone, & Levy, 1965). Also, see the Cognitive dissonance classroom learning activity, pp. 256–7.

Daryl Bem's (1967) self-perception theory attempts to explain the same behavior as cognitive dissonance. Bem says that when people are unsure of their attitudes, they look at their behavior and infer what their attitude must be.

## Attribution

Most students will understand the fundamental attribution error and the actor–observer bias. However they have a difficult time understanding how consistency, consensus, and distinctiveness are involved in the attribution. Thus I assign ⓦ Mini-assignment #3 for small group work and provide ⓦ Handout #1 to help them work through the Attribution classroom learning activity.

East Asian cultures are less likely to make the fundamental attribution error because they pay more attention to the situation or social context. See Choi, Nisbett, & Norenzayan (1999). This is a nice demonstration of the importance of culture in social cognition.

## Conformity, compliance, obedience

Students often have a difficult time distinguishing between these concepts. I present conformity as "going along with the group," compliance as a response to a direct request, and obedience as a response to a direct request from an authority figure. A great illustration is Bickman's (1974) study in which a confederate of the experimenter chose people at random and told them to put money in an expired parking meter that was not theirs. If the confederate wore a uniform, a much higher percentage of people did as "told" (92%) than if the person was dressed in normal street clothes (50%). The study is discussed in Cialdini (1993).

Students can see examples in their own lives of foot-in-door, door-in-the-face, and low-ball. Cialdini (1993) has an entire chapter on obedience and studies on obedience.

See also a 1975, 24-minute DVD, *Conformity and Independence* ⓤ, narrated by Stanley Milgram. *Obedience: A Reenactment* ⓤ is an 11-minute DVD presenting segments from Milgram's (1965) experiment. You can also read Milgram's description of his study that he wrote in 1974 for Harper magazine, *Perils of Authority*, available at the Age of the Sage web site ⓤ.

I also like Blass's discussion of the Milgram experiment (2000).

## Other important topics

## Social psychology general resources

*Candid Camera: Social Psychology* ⓤ (1994) is a 58-minute video illustrating conformity, compliance, construction of social reality, and persuasion.

## Social psychology and culture

Cross-cultural psychologists study cultural similarities and differences in social behavior. Berry, Poortinga, Segall, and Dasen (2002, pp. 55–56) provide a list of universals in social behavior, including regulation of affective expression, socialization, and control of disruptive behavior. This is a nice way to talk about how all societies are similar.

## Social comparison

That we evaluate ourselves using other people as the basis for comparison can also be related back to Maslow's deficiency and growth orientations in personality. I remind students that even statistics, such as their ACT or SAT score, are difficult to put into perspective without knowing means and standard deviations—reference to other scores. When talking about reference groups I ask students if they would evaluate themselves differently if they were using Nobel Prize winners as a reference group. This often leads to a discussion of "keeping up with the Joneses." I also point out that in the movie *Good Will Hunting* Ⓤ, part of Will's problem is that his reference group is "too low."

When we discuss relative deprivation I use a sports figure holding out for a multi-million dollar contract. (There is always one!) These players often feel they are underpaid relative to other sport figures of their caliber. However, their current salary is several times larger than the average person's salary.

## Social norms

Students do not really understand the pervasiveness of social norms. These seldom written, but powerful, rules are automatically followed and make our social situations less ambiguous. Pointing out the cultural aspect of norms as well as gender and age differences helps students be a bit more tolerant of people not like them. Be sure to differentiate injunctive and descriptive norms.

The powerfulness of the reciprocity norm can be demonstrated by asking students if they have ever received a gift from someone for whom they didn't have a gift and how they felt. This norm is so powerful that students remember incidents from their childhood. Marketers take advantage of the "free gift strategy"—for example, the Hare Krishna group used to give people a flower and then ask for a donation. Many mail solicitations for money now contain things like flower seeds, or a nickel, or greeting cards—trying to make you feel that you need to reciprocate with a monetary donation.

A great example of reciprocity is a study by Kunz and Woolcott (1976; cited in Cialdini, 1993). A university professor sent Christmas cards to a group of strangers and was surprised that over 20% of the strangers reciprocated by sending a card in return.

Violating a social norm often makes us feel uncomfortable. I have students complete ⦿ Mini-assignment #1, violating a social norm, and write about the experience. This always leads to a discussion of the power of norms and how a simple behavior, such as turning backwards in an elevator, can embarrass us.

## Reactance

Although this is an old psychological concept, my students readily relate to it. People who perceive that their freedom is being restricted react by resisting or opposing or contradicting whatever they feel caused the loss. A real example involved a group of parents who tried to ban a book that was on a high school recommended reading list. Bookstores sold out of the book as students wanted to read the book their parents didn't want them to read. I point out that two-year-olds and adolescents seem to exhibit the most reactance. Two-year-olds want to play with the toy that they are told they can't play with, and adolescents want to date people they have been forbidden to date (the Romeo and Juliet effect). See Brehm (1972), Cialdini (2000), and Driscoll, Davis, and Lipetz (1972).

## Deindividuation

Students understand "becoming submerged in the group" and a loss of a sense of individuality. They relate to people getting caught up in the moment at sporting events—trying to bring down a goal post or a basket. Not being individually identified, for example wearing a mask or costume, can accentuate this process—the Ku Klux Klan or the Halloween violence on campuses are great examples.

I talk about Ed Diener and colleagues' Halloween studies (Diener, Fraser, Beaman, & Kelem, 1976) that show that when a sign told kids to take only one candy and they could be identified, only 8% took more than one candy. When they were part of a group, and not individually identifiable, 80% took more than one candy.

I also show a clip of the movie, *To Kill a Mockingbird* ⓤ, in which a mob comes to lynch a defendant in jail and Scout changes the "mob" into identifiable people by addressing each one individually by name. The Deindividuation classroom learning activity (pp. 263–4) is excellent.

## Self-esteem

I like Carol Dweck's definition of self-esteem: "It is a way of experiencing yourself when you are using your resources well—to master challenges, to learn, to help others" (Dweck, 2000, p. 128). Research on how to foster self-esteem often seems counterintuitive to students. Dweck's work talks about praise "that backfires" (Chapter 16), and the idea that children need to view intelligence from a growth, mastery position and not as a finite quality helps students think about self-esteem and parenting from a different perspective.

## Attitudes

I focus on the fact that attitudes are learned, and that attitudes differ among social groups. See *Attitudes* ⓤ, a 30-minute video that also examines cognitive dissonance and stereotyping.

## Persuasion

The central and peripheral route to attitude change can easily be illustrated for students, especially during election years. If you have a "vested interest" in the situation, you are going to need more facts and information before being persuaded. If you have less of an interest, you are more likely to be convinced by celebrity endorsement, or more peripheral means.

## First impressions

Students are fascinated with the idea that first impressions are easily formed, difficult to change, and long-lasting. They also are interested that we tend to give others the benefit of the doubt and are predisposed to have a positive impression—but negative information is judged more important than positive information. The First impressions classroom learning activity is a quick and easy way to introduce the topic. For current research in the area of first impressions see the APS web site ⓤ.

## Self-fulfilling prophecy

Robert Merton's idea that something comes true because we expect it to happen, and unconsciously behave to make it happen, is a new idea for most students. I describe the four stages:

1. Adopt an attitude or make a decision.
2. Behave as though the decision or attitude is true.
3. Another person or people react to your behavior.
4. Your prophecy comes true.

I often term this the "blind date" phenomenon. Wikipedia ⓤ has a nice history and explanation of self-fulfilling prophecy and Merton's theories.

## Aggression

Understanding what aggression is or is not is important—because aggression means many different things. Ludy Benjamin's Aggression classroom learning activity is a great way to begin. Differentiating physical assault, verbal assault, competitiveness, and passive aggression is important. Typically intent—trying to hurt or injure another—is the important component.

Studies show that high testosterone and low serotonin levels are implicated in aggression (see Bernhardt, 1997). The hypothalamus and amygdala are also implicated in aggression.

For a discussion of the history of research on aggression see Gibbs (1997).

For a discussion of the influence of the media on aggression see Anderson et al. (2003).

See also Sternberg (2005) on the psychology of hate.

## Helping behaviors

I talk about the various theories of why we help: arousal, cost–reward, empathy-altruism, and evolutionary theory.

See *Silent Witnesses: The Kitty Genovese Murder* ⓤ, a 1999 50-minute video that discusses helping behavior.

For a nice explanation of the evolutionary perspective on helping behavior see Burnstein (2005).

A series of studies on helping behavior were conducted by John Darley and Bibb Latane in the 1960s. Some of the studies I use in my class are Darley and Batson (1973), Darley and Latane (1968a, 1968b), Latane and Darley (1968, 1970), Latane and Rodin (1969).

Other sources of information about helping behavior include Piliavin, Dovidio, Gaertner, and Clark (1981) and Steblay (1987).

## Interpersonal attraction

Proximity (absence does *not* make the heart grow fonder!), similarity of attitudes, and the matching hypothesis of physical attraction are explanations of why people are attracted to one another.

I often ask students to write a personal ad (see ⓦ Mini-assignment #2). This leads to a discussion of the evolutionary theory of mate selection. See Campbell and Ellis (2005) for a nice discussion of this theory.

There are several romanticism scales that I use (see Romanticism scales classroom learning activity, pp. 261–3). Rather than having them fill out the scales, I sometimes ask my students to look at Hobart's scale from 1956 and Rubin's scales from the 1980s and compare the gender roles in both. I also ask them to develop questions for a more modern scale.

*The chemistry of falling in love.* Michael Lieboritz explored this question in the 1980s. For a discussion of this research and the neurophysiology of love see Fisher (1994). See also *Falling in Love* ⓤ, a 2001 52-minute video exploring research on love and the neurochemistry of falling in love, and *Being in Love* ⓤ, a 2001 51-minute video.

*Attachment and romantic relationships.* There is current research linking an individual's attachment style as a child, and their relationship with a romantic partner as an adult. In other words, the form of your attachment in childhood may be reflected in your adult relationship. For an overview of this theory and research see R. Chris Fraley's web site ⓤ.

*Marriage.* John Gottman has ongoing research on why marriages succeed or fail (Gottman & Levenson, 1992). He has a summary of his research in the form of tips on his web site ⓤ, where students may also take a relationship quiz, and has also written a book for the general public (Gottman, 1994).

I think it's important for students to understand that marriages have cycles: I like to use the falling in love → settling down → bottoming out → beginning again cycle to try to have students see that falling in love and the "high" of that cannot possibly be maintained long term. This is also a good time to introduce Robert Sternberg's triangular theory of love. See Sternberg (1988, 1998a, 1998b).

For statistics on marriages, divorces, and remarriages in the United States, see the National Center for Health Statistics web site ⓤ.

I talk about Greeley (1992), because it presents a more optimistic view of marriage—including statistics that 90% report being faithful throughout their present marriage, three-fifths of people in the survey say their marriage is "very happy," three-quarters say their spouse is their best friend, and so forth.

I also talk about being in a happy marriage having a positive impact on subjective well-being. See Dush and Amato (2005).

## Stereotypes, prejudice, and discrimination

I point out that we all use stereotypes and often in a good way. I present the contact hypothesis, emphasizing that the groups must interact on an equal basis to decrease prejudice, stereotypes, and discrimination.

Jigsaw, a technique developed by Eliot Aronson to ease the tensions invoked by school desegregation, is an excellent classroom technique as well as a social technique. The basic premise is that everyone's input into a group project is essential for the entire group to succeed. For the particulars, see Aronson's excellent web site ⓤ that provides the history of the jigsaw technique as well as tips for implementing it.

*Prejudice: Eye of the Storm* ⓤ is a powerful 25-minute video (1970) showing Jane Elliott's attempt to create prejudice and stereotypes in her homogenous third-grade classroom. Frontline, a PBS video, shows a 15-year reunion of Jane Elliott and her students. *A Class Divided* ⓤ was broadcast in 1985. The PBS web site allows you to watch the program ⓤ and read the script ⓤ, providing a discussion outline and teacher's manual. The web site also relates some of the ideas to more current theories (e.g., Claude Steele's idea of stereotype threat). You may also read about this experiment in Peters (1987).

## Social dilemmas

Resource dilemmas include not picking flowers on public property or all flowers would disappear, not paying for PBS and the station ceases to exist, people using water to hose down their homes during a fire, decreasing water pressure and making it less likely to extinguish the fire.

Prisoner's dilemma, zero-sum games, and strategies such as tit-for-tat are also concepts that students can find examples of in their everyday lives. See the Game theory.net web site ⓤ for a description of zero-sum games and a list of articles describing such games.

# Classroom Tips

## Stimulus questions for discussion

### Aggression

More males are arrested for violent crimes and imprisoned than women. What are some possible explanations for this phenomenon? Does violence in the media—TV, video games, movies, and so forth have an effect on the viewer's level of aggression? Explain.

### Helping behavior

When was the last time that you helped someone? Was it a relative, friend, or stranger? Why did you help? Do you think there is a "helping personality"? If so, what are the characteristics? If not, why do people help?

### Persuasion

Think of a time when you wanted to try to change someone's mind. How did you go about persuading them? What techniques did you use?

### Obedience

Whom do you obey? Why do you obey that person? Whom would you not obey? Why would you not obey that person?

## Some suggested classroom learning activities

### Cognitive dissonance

Feldman and Lafleur (1999) explain cognitive dissonance from the perspective of Mark Twain's *Tom Sawyer*. In one passage Tom persuades another boy, Ben, to paint the fence Tom is supposed to paint. He is able to do this by framing "fence painting" as fun. Once Ben begins to paint he has to reconcile his belief that fence painting is work with the fact that he is painting the fence for free. He decides that fence painting is fun. Ask students what would happen if Tom paid Ben to paint the fence? Would Ben experience cognitive dissonance?

⟪ Tom surveyed his last touch with the eye of an artist, then he gave his brush another gentle sweep and surveyed the result, as before. Ben ranged up alongside of him. Tom's mouth watered for the apple, but he stuck to his work. Ben said:

"Hello, old chap, you got to work, hey?"

Tom wheeled suddenly and said:

"Why, it's you, Ben! I warn't noticing."

"Say—I'm going in a-swimming, I am. Don't you wish you could? But of course you'd druther work—wouldn't you? Course you would!"

Tom contemplated the boy a bit, and said:

"What do you call work?"

"Why, ain't that work?"

Tom resumed his whitewashing, and answered carelessly:

"Well, maybe it is, and maybe it ain't. All I know, is, it suits Tom Sawyer."

"Oh come, now, you don't mean to let on that you like it?"

The brush continued to move.

"Like it? Well, I don't see why I oughtn't to like it. Does a boy get a chance to whitewash a fence every day?"

That put the thing in a new light. Ben stopped nibbling his apple. Tom swept his brush daintily back and forth—stepped back to note the effect—added a touch here and there—criticised the effect again—Ben watching every move and getting more and more interested, more and more absorbed. Presently he said:

"Say, Tom, let me whitewash a little."

Tom considered, was about to consent; but he altered his mind:

"No—no—I reckon it wouldn't hardly do, Ben. You see, Aunt Polly's awful particular about this fence—right here on the street, you know—but if it was the back fence I wouldn't mind and she wouldn't. Yes, she's awful particular about this fence; it's got to be done very careful; I reckon there ain't one boy in a thousand, maybe two thousand, that can do it the way it's got to be done."

"No—is that so? Oh come, now—lemme just try. Only just a little—I'd let you, if you was me, Tom."

"Ben, I'd like to, honest injun; but Aunt Polly—well, Jim wanted to do it, but she wouldn't let him; Sid wanted to do it, and she wouldn't let Sid. Now don't you see how I'm fixed? If you was to tackle this fence and anything was to happen to it—"

"Oh, shucks, I'll be just as careful. Now lemme try. Say—I'll give you the core of my apple."

"Well, here—No, Ben, now don't. I'm afeard—"

"I'll give you all of it!"

Tom gave up the brush with reluctance in his face, but alacrity in his heart. And while the late steamer Big Missouri worked and sweated in the sun, the retired artist sat on a barrel in the shade close by, dangled his legs, munched his apple, and planned the slaughter of more innocents. (*Tom Sawyer*, Chapter 2. You may download this passage for free at the Carnegie Mellon School of Computer Science web site. ⓤ)

## Persuasion

Vivian Makosky (1996) has students explore techniques of persuasion by bringing advertisements into the classroom and analyzing which level of Maslow's hierarchy of needs was "met" by that product. She also has students bring in the first five ads from an expensive magazine (*Vogue*) and the first five ads from an inexpensive magazine (*Family Circle*) and compare which of Maslow's levels the advertisements were aimed at. You could also ask students to identify ads using a central route and those using a peripheral route to change attitudes.

## Aggression

Give students a copy of the Aggression Questionnaire (Benjamin, 1994) and have them mark the statements that they believe are examples of aggression. Tell them to respond personally, not how they think they should respond. Collect the questionnaires, shuffle them, and redistribute them, so students aren't reading their own. This leads to a discussion of what aggression involves—whether intent is necessary, whether it has to be committed by a human being, whether it must be behavior or can be verbal, whether it must be directed at a human being or an animal or an inanimate object, whether it has to be an action or whether it can be an inaction.

ⓦ Aggression Questionnaire

1. A spider eats a fly.
2. Two wolves fight for the leadership of the pack.
3. A soldier shoots an enemy at the front line.
4. The warden of a prison executes a convicted criminal.
5. A juvenile gang attacks members of another gang.
6. Two men fight for a piece of bread.
7. A man viciously kicks a cat.
8. A man, while cleaning a window, knocks over a flowerpot which, in falling, injures a pedestrian.
9. A girl kicks a wastebasket.
10. Mr. X, a notorious gossip, speaks disparagingly of many people of his acquaintance.
11. A man mentally rehearses a murder he is about to commit.

12. An angry son purposely fails to write to his mother, who is expecting a letter and will be hurt if none arrives.

13. An enraged boy tries with all his might to inflict injury on his antagonist, a bigger boy, but is not successful in doing so. His efforts simply amuse the bigger boy.

14. A man daydreams of harming his antagonist, but has no hope of doing so.

15. A senator does not protest the escalation of bombing to which he is morally opposed.

16. A farmer beheads a chicken and prepares it for supper.

17. A hunter kills an animal and mounts it as a trophy.

18. A dog snarls at a mail carrier, but does not bite.

19. A physician gives a flu shot to a screaming child.

20. A boxer gives his opponent a bloody nose.

21. A Girl Scout tries to assist an elderly woman, but trips her by accident.

22. A bank robber is shot in the back while trying to escape.

23. A tennis player smashes his racket after missing a volley.

24. A person commits suicide.

25. A cat kills a mouse, parades around with it, then discards it.

## Attribution

Foster-Fishman (1996) presented an exercise she used with her community psychology class to demonstrate the concept of blaming the victim (although the story is one that has been used before). Valeri Werpetinski from the University of Illinois adapted this exercise to emonstrate external and internal attributions. The story goes like this:

Ⓦ As he left for a visit to his outlying districts, the jealous baron warned his pretty wife, "Do not leave the castle while I am gone, or I will punish you severely when I return." But as the hours passed, the young baroness grew lonely, and despite her husband's warning she decided to visit her lover, who lived in the countryside nearby. The castle was situated on an island in a wide, fast-flowing river. A drawbridge linked the island to the mainland at the narrowest point in the river. "Surely my husband will not return before dawn," she thought and ordered her servants to lower the drawbridge and leave it down until she returned. After spending several pleasant hours with her lover, the baroness returned to the drawbridge, only to find it blocked by a gateman wildly waving a long, cruel knife. "Do not attempt to cross this bridge, baroness, or I will have to kill you," he cried. "The baron has ordered me to do so." Fearing for her life, the baroness returned to her lover and asked him for help. "Our relationship is only a romantic one," he said. "I will not help." The baroness then sought out a boatman on the river, explained her plight to him and asked him to take her across the river in his boat. "I will do it, but only if you pay me my fee of five marks." "But I have no money with me!" the baroness protested. "That is too bad. No money, no ride," the boatman said flatly. Her fear growing, the baroness ran crying to the home of a friend and after explaining her desperate situation, begged for enough money to pay the boatman his fee. "If only you had not disobeyed your husband, this would not have happened," the friend said. "I will give you no money." With dawn approaching and her last resource exhausted, the baroness returned to the bridge in desperation, attempted to cross to the castle, and was slain by the gateman.

Rank order the six characters in this story (baron, baroness, lover, gateman, boatman, friend) in terms of their responsibility for the baroness's death. (Foster-Fishman, 1996, pp. 11–12)

Students then get into groups of five or six and share their rank orders and create one list, and then write their final list on the chalkboard. Many students will blame the baroness for her own death—creating an internal attribution—the baroness was bad and "got what she deserved." However, at some point in the discussion, raise the question, "If the baroness was visiting her dying mother, whom the baron forbade her to visit, who would be the most responsible for the baroness's death?" Usually, students will say, "the baron," making an external attribution for her death. This can lead to a discussion of how attributions are made. A "twist" to this activity is to devise two stories^, substituting the dying mother for the lover. Again the students receiving the original story are most likely to blame the baroness, an internal attribution, while those receiving the "dying mother" story are most likely to blame the baron, an external attribution.

### Stereotypes

Students often read about stereotypes and prejudice but believe that such issues apply to "other" people, not to them. It is important that students realize that *all* people use stereotypes in one way or another. The following activity helps demonstrate this point.

Distribute the directions and list of 12 people below. Be sure to speak softly in a nonaccusing tone as you explain the exercise. The list describes 12 people. Students must choose seven of these people as the only ones to enter a protected bomb shelter with them as the rest of the world is being destroyed in some disaster. Students should be prepared to defend the reasoning behind their choices.

After students have made their choices, begin a discussion by asking students to reveal their selections and the reasons for them. Ask students to comment on each other's choices. Link the responses to the concepts of *stereotypes*, *prejudice*, and *discrimination*.

Ⓦ Directions

It is the end of the world. You have been put in charge of deciding who will go into a protected bomb shelter to be the only survivors. You must select seven of the following people to go into the shelter with you. Be prepared to defend your choices.

1. A 31-year-old judge, refuses to be separated from her husband (#2)
2. A 29-year-old botanist, a former mental patient, refuses to be separated from his wife (#1)
3. A 27-year-old second-year medical student, recovering alcoholic (sober two years)
4. A 36-year-old college student, former prostitute, "retired" for eight years, has one teenage child
5. A 42-year-old historian, author, Iranian
6. A 30-year-old mechanical engineer, female, lesbian
7. A biochemist, male, Asian, amputee
8. A 16-year-old female, high school dropout, pregnant
9. An Olympic track athlete, African
10. A carpenter, born-again Christian fundamentalist
11. A 45-year-old physician, female, unable to have children
12. A 40-year-old rabbi, talented musician

*Source for activity: Adapted from an activity by Nancy Briton, Northwestern University. By permission of Houghton Mifflin.*

## Romanticism scales

This activity allows students to see how romanticism scales are constructed, as well as to appreciate how changing economic conditions and sex roles have had an impact on the conception of romantic love. Ask students what items they would change or add, or they could create their own romanticism scale. You could collect and analyze the class data and compare it to that of previous researchers.

Romanticism, long considered the province of poets, has become the subject of scientific investigation in the last 50 years. Hobart (1958), while revising a romanticism scale first developed by Gross (1944), was surprised to find that men scored higher, and thus were considered more romantic than women on his scale. This finding, that women are less idealistic about love than men, has been empirically replicated (Dion & Dion, 1973; Hatkoff & Lasswell, 1979; Hong, 1986).

Hobart's Romanticism Scale and Rubin's Love Scale are both presented here, as is the scoring for each scale.

Ⓦ Hobart Romanticism Scale

|  |  | Agree | Disagree |
|---|---|---|---|
| 1. | Lovers ought to expect a certain amount of disillusionment after marriage. | ___ | ___ |
| 2. | True love should be suppressed in cases where its existence conflicts with the prevailing standards of morality. | ___ | ___ |
| 3. | To be truly in love is to be in love for ever. | ___ | ___ |
| 4. | The sweetly feminine "clinging vine" girl cannot compare with the capable and sympathetic girl as a sweetheart. | ___ | ___ |
| 5. | As long as they at least love each other, two people would have no trouble getting along together in marriage. | ___ | ___ |
| 6. | A girl should expect her sweetheart to be chivalrous on all occasions. | ___ | ___ |
| 7. | A person should marry whomever he loves regardless of social position. | ___ | ___ |
| 8. | Lovers should freely confess everything of personal significance to each other. | ___ | ___ |
| 9. | Economic security should be carefully considered before selecting a marriage partner. | ___ | ___ |
| 10. | Most of us could sincerely love any one of several people equally well. | ___ | ___ |
| 11. | A lover without jealousy is hardly to be desired. | ___ | ___ |

12. One should not marry against
    the serious advice of one's parents.     _____     _____

*Scoring the Hobart Romanticism Scale.* On items 3, 5, 6, 7, 8, 11, students should give themselves one point for each *agree* response. On items 1, 2, 4, 9, 10, 12, students should give themselves one point for each *disagree* response. The total is the romanticism score.

Rubin's Love Scale

The [ . . . . . . ] in each question should be thought of as your boyfriend/girlfriend/lover. Write the appropriate number from the scale below in the space provided before each statement. Feel free to use the entire scale. The anchors of the scale are 1 = Not at all or Disagree completely; 5 = Moderately true; 9 = Definitely true or Agree completely.

1          2          3          4          5          6          7          8          9
Not at all                       Moderately true                    Definitely true
Disagree completely                                                 Agree completely

1. _____ If [ . . . . . . ] were feeling badly, my first duty would be to cheer him (her) up.
2. _____ I feel that I can confide in [ . . . . . . ] about virtually everything.
3. _____ I find it easy to ignore [ . . . . . . ]'s faults.
4. _____ I would do almost anything for [ . . . . . . ].
5. _____ I feel very possessive toward [ . . . . . . ].
6. _____ If I could never be with [ . . . . . . ], I would feel miserable.
7. _____ If I were lonely, my first thought would be to seek [ . . . . . . ] out.
8. _____ One of my primary concerns is [ . . . . . . ]'s welfare.
9. _____ I would forgive [ . . . . . . ] for practically anything.
10. _____ I feel responsible for [ . . . . . . ]'s well-being.
11. _____ When I am with [ . . . . . . ], I spend a good deal of time just looking at him (her).
12. _____ I would greatly enjoy being confided in by [ . . . . . . ].
13. _____ It would be hard for me to get along without [ . . . . . . ].

*Scoring Rubin's Love Scale.* Students should total all of the numbers they have circled. The mean in Rubin's studies is 81. Steck, Levitan, McLane, and Kelley (1982) have grouped Rubin's questions into the three categories of care, need, and trust. *Care*: questions 1, 4, 8, and 10. *Need*: questions 5, 6, 7, and 13. *Trust*: questions 2, 3, 9, and 12. (Permission Houghton Mifflin)

See also Sternberg and Grajek (1984) on the nature of love.

## Deindividuation

This exercise illustrates *deindividuation* and reveals "that even 'normal, well-adjusted' college students are capable of highly inappropriate, antisocial behavior, given certain social and situational conditions" (Dodd, 1985, p. 89). In the class session before you are discussing deindividuation, give each student a handout with the following question: "♦ No names please! If you could do anything humanly possible with complete assurance that you would not be detected or held responsible, what would you do?" Collect the responses and for the next class period, categorize and rate each response for its content and social desirability, according to Dodd's two categories.

- ♦ Scale 1 (Social desirability): Prosocial—intending to benefit others, antisocial—injuring others or depriving them of their rights, nonnormative—violates social norms but does not help or hurt others, and neutral—not in the other three categories.
- ♦ Scale 2 (Content): 1. Aggression, 2. Charity, 3. Academic dishonesty, 4. Crime, 5. Escapism, 6. Political activities, 7. Sexual behavior, 8. Social disruption, 9. Interpersonal spying and eavesdropping, 10. Travel, 11. "Other."

Dodd compared college student responses with those of students who were taking college courses while incarcerated in prisons. He found that the responses of the imprisoned samples and those of the nonimprisoned samples did not differ significantly on either the social desirability scale or in terms of content. Thirty-six percent of the responses were antisocial, 19% nonnormative, 36% neutral, and only 9% prosocial. The most frequent responses were criminal acts (26%), sexual acts (11%), and spying behaviors (11%). The most common single response was "rob a bank," which accounted for 15% of all responses. Compute your students' percentages and compare to the percentages of Dodd's incarcerated samples. Also, read a sample of responses from as many categories as you have. Students are typically surprised that their responses do not vary significantly from those of prisoners.

## First impressions

This exercise demonstrates the impact of first impressions, even when we know they are based on unreliable information. You can also use this demonstration to show how top-down processing and expectancy affects social cognition. Create handouts of the vignette that differ in the first descriptor with the questions at the bottom. Mix up copies of each handout version, passing them out so each student takes one and half the class receives "stubborn" and the remaining students receive "persistent." Tell the class to read the description and answer the questions. Students will answer questions differently because they interpreted the ambiguous paragraph on the basis of their initial impressions. Ask for a show of hands of students' responses to the questions as you discuss first impressions.

ⓦ Jim is rumored to be [stubborn/persistent]. We know the following information about Jim: Once he makes up his mind to do something, it is as good as done, no matter how long it might take or how difficult the going might be. Only rarely does he change his mind, even though it might have been better if he had.

Use a 5-point Likert scale, where 1 is Not at all and 5 is Extremely.

1. How likable is Jim?
2. Is he argumentative?
3. Would you like to have him as a roommate?

*Source for activity: Adapted from an activity by Chuck Carroll, University of Illinois at Urbana-Champaign, based on research conducted by Higgins, Bargh, and Lombardi (1985). By permission of Houghton Mifflin.*

See also Bargh and Pietromonaco (1982) and Higgins, Rholes, and Jones (1977).

## Obedience

Students are not always convinced by Milgram's obedience studies (Hunter, 1981). This demonstration is designed to give students a personal experience with the concept of *obedience*. Introduce one of your colleagues to the class as a guest lecturer on any topic. The guest lecturer should enter the classroom after students have arrived. If necessary, he or she should begin by requesting that everyone be seated and then continue with the following instructions:

> "Could I have everyone move up and fill the empty seats toward the front, please. I find it difficult to speak loudly enough to be heard in the back. [Pause until this request has been honored. If necessary, request individual students to move.] Thank you."

> "Now please remove everything from your desks and place your hands flat on the desk so that I can see when everyone is ready. [Pause.] Good. Thank you."

"Now could I have the first three people in this row exchange places with the last three people in that row? [Pause.] Yes, that's good. Now I'd like everyone with blond hair to stand for a moment. [If necessary, say, 'I'd call your hair blond, would you stand, please?' Pause.] Okay."

"And people who are wearing a watch, would you raise the hand your watch is on?" [Pause.]

"Now, those who are standing, turn and face the back. Those whose hands are up, stay as you are. Everyone else, give them a round of applause. [Start clapping; when it appears that all are clapping, stop and continue talking]. Thank you, now everyone be seated and relax." (Hunter, 1981, p. 149)

Begin discussion with the question, "Why did you do all of that?" Eventually, students will offer that they ascribed *authority* to the guest lecturer. Ask students why that person had authority. Other questions to pursue include: Why do you obey authority? Should you always obey people in authority? If not, what conditions warrant or justify disobedience? How does a person get authority? What would the world be like without authority? What would the world be like if everyone always obeyed authority? (Hunter, 1981). Introduce the Milgram studies (1963, 1965) and discuss the ethics of his work.

*Source for activity: By permission of Houghton Mifflin. See also Cartwright and Zander (1968) on group dynamics.*

## Possible mini-assignments (written or groups)

### ⓦ *Mini-assignment #1*
Violate a social norm. Do *not* do anything lewd, obscene, or illegal! Please listen to the suggestions given in class.

After you have violated a social norm, write the following:

1. What behavior you engaged in and why you picked it.
2. How other people reacted to your behavior.
3. How you felt violating that norm.
4. What you learned from this experiment (if anything).

### ⓦ *Mini-assignment #2*
Write a personal ad. Be sure to list the characteristics that you believe are most important in a potential mate.

◍ *Mini-assignment #3*

Your best friend, who has always been very open and positive with you, has suddenly told you that she/he no longer wants to be friends with you. Develop a plausible explanation for her/his behavior—first making an internal attribution, and then making an external attribution. (Be sure to use the terms consistency, consensus, and distinctiveness.)

◍ *Mini-assignment #4*

(Could also be a group exercise)

Describe a social dilemma that was not described in your textbook. Explain why it is a social dilemma and what would happen if all people acted in their own best interest.

◍ *Mini-assignment #5*

(Could also be a group exercise)

You are driving when your car breaks down. Explain, in detail, the situation in which you are most likely to receive help and why.

## Handout

Handout #1: Attributions

## References

Anderson, C., Berkowitz, L., Donnerstein, E., Huesmann, L., Johnson, J., Linz, D., Malamuth, N., & Wartella, E. (2003). The influence of media violence on youth. *Psychological Science in the Public Interest, 4*(3), 81–110.

Bargh, J., & Pietromonaco, P. (1982). Automatic information processing and social perception: The influence of trait information presented outside of conscious awareness on impression formation. *Journal of Personality and Social Psychology, 43*, 437–449.

Bem, D. (1967). Self-perception: An alternative interpretation of cognitive dissonance phenomena. *Psychological Science, 7*, 111–114.

Benjamin, L. (1994). Defining aggression. In M. Ware & D. Johnson (Eds.), *Handbook of demonstrations and activities in the teaching of psychology, Vol. III* (pp. 127–131). Mahwah, NJ: Lawrence Erlbaum.

Bernhardt, P. (1997). Influences of serotonin and testosterone in aggression and dominance: Convergence with social psychology. *Current Direction in Psychological Science, 6*(2), 44–48.

Berry, J., Poortinga, Y., Segall, M., & Dasen, P. (2002). *Cross-cultural psychology* (2nd ed.). Cambridge, UK: Cambridge University Press.

Bickman, L. (1974). The social power of a uniform. *Journal of Applied Social Psychology*, 4, 47–61.

Blass, T. (Ed.) (2000). *Obedience to authority: Current perspectives on the Milgram paradigm*. Mahwah, NJ: Erlbaum.

Brehm, J. (1972). *Responses to loss of freedom: A theory of psychological reactance*. Morristown, NJ: General Learning Press.

Burnstein, E. (2005). Altruism and genetic relatedness. In D. Buss (Ed.), *The handbook of evolutionary psychology* (pp. 528–551). Hoboken, NJ: John Wiley.

Campbell, L., & Ellis, B. (2005). Commitment, love, and mate retention. In D. Buss (Ed.), *The handbook of evolutionary psychology* (pp. 419–442). Hoboken, NJ: John Wiley.

Cartwright, D., & Zander, A. (1968). *Group dynamics: Research and theory* (3rd ed.). New York: Harper & Row.

Choi, I., Nisbett, R., & Norenzayan, A. (1999). Causal attribution across cultures: Variation and universality. *Psychological Bulletin*, 125(1), 47–63.

Cialdini, R. (1993). *Influence: The psychology of persuasion* (revised ed.). New York: Quill.

Cialdini, R. (2000). *Influence: Science and practice* (3rd ed.). New York: HarperCollins.

Darley, J., & Batson, D. (1973). "From Jerusalem to Jericho": A study of situational and dispositional variables in helping behavior. *Journal of Personality and Social Psychology*, 27, 100–108.

Darley, J., & Latane, B. (1968a). When will people help in a crisis? *Psychology Today*, 2, 54–57, 70–71.

Darley, J., & Latane, B. (1968b). Bystander intervention in emergencies: Diffusion of responsibility. *Journal of Personality and Social Psychology*, 8, 377–383.

Diener, E., Fraser, S., Beaman, A., & Kelem, R. (1976). Effects of deindividuation variables on stealing among Halloween trick-or-treaters. *Journal of Personality and Social Psychology*, 33, 178–183.

Dion, K., & Dion, K. (1973). Correlates of romantic love. *Journal of Consulting and Clinical Psychology*, 41, 51–56.

Dodd, D. (1985). Robbers in the classroom: A deindividuation exercise. *Teaching of Psychology*, 12(2), 89–91.

Driscoll, R., Davis, K., & Lipetz, M. (1972). Parental interference and romantic love: The Romeo and Juliet effect. *Journal of Personality and Social Psychology*, 24, 1–10.

Dush, C., & Amato, P. (2005). Consequences of relationship status and quality for subjective well-being. *Journal of Social and Personal Relationships*, 22(5), 607–627.

Dweck, C. (2000). *Self-theories: Their role in motivation, personality, and development*. Philadelphia: Psychology Press.

Feldman, A., & Lafleur, R. (1999). Tom Sawyer: The fence and social psychology. In L. Benjamin, B. Nodine, R. Ernst, & C. Blair Broeker (Eds.), *Activities handbook for the teaching of psychology, Vol. 4* (pp. 343–345). Washington, DC: American Psychological Association.

Festinger, L., & Carlsmith, J. (1959). Cognitive consequences of forced compliance. *Journal of Abnormal and Social Psychology, 58*, 203–210.

Fisher, H. (1994). The nature of romantic love. *The Journal of NIH Research, 6*, 59–64.

Foster-Fishman, P. (1996). Applying collaborative learning techniques in undergraduate community courses. *The Community Psychologist, 29*(1), 10–13.

Gibbs, W. (1997). Seeking the criminal element. *Scientific American Special Issue, 7*(1), 102–110.

Gottman, J. (1994). *Why marriages succeed or fail: And how you can make yours last.* New York: Fireside.

Gottman, J., & Levenson, R. (1992). Marital processes predictive of later dissolution: Behavior, physiology, and health. *Journal of Personality and Social Psychology, 63*, 221–233.

Greeley, A. (1992). *Faithful attraction: Discovering intimacy love and fidelity in American marriage.* New York: St. Martin's Press.

Gross, L. (1944). A belief pattern scale for measuring attitudes toward romanticism. *American Sociological Review, 9*, 463–472.

Hatkoff, T., & Lasswell, T. (1979). Male–female similarities and differences in conceptualizing love. In M. Cook & G. Wilson (Eds.), *Love and attraction* (pp. 221–227). Oxford: Pergamon Press.

Higgins, E., Bargh, J., & Lombardi, W. (1985). Nature of priming effects on categorization. *Journal of Experimental Psychology: Learning, Memory, and Cognition, 11*, 59–69.

Higgins, E., Rholes, W., & Jones, C. (1977). Category accessibility and impression formation. *Journal of Experimental and Social Psychology, 13*, 141–154.

Hobart, C. (1958). The incidence of romanticism during courtship. *Social Forces, 36*, 362–367.

Hong, S. (1986). Romantic love, idealistic or pragmatic: Sex differences among Australian young adults. *Psychological Reports, 52*, 922.

Hunter, W. (1981). Obedience to authority: Activity 61. In L. Benjamin, & K. Lowman (Eds.), *Activities handbook for the teaching of psychology: Vol. 1* (pp. 149–150). Washington, DC: American Psychological Association.

Kunz, P., & Woolcott, M. (1976). Season's greetings: From my status to yours. *Social Science Research, 5*, 269–278.

Latane, B., & Darley, J. (1968). Group inhibition of bystander intervention in emergencies. *Journal of Personality and Social Psychology, 10*, 215–222.

Latane, B., & Darley, J. (1970). *The unresponsive bystander: Why doesn't he help?* Englewood Cliff, NJ: Prentice-Hall.

Latane, B., & Rodin, J. (1969). A lady in distress: The effects of friends and strangers on bystander intervention. *Journal of Experimental Social Psychology, 5*, 189–202.

Makosky, V. (1996). Identifying major techniques of persuasion. In M. Ware & D. Johnson (Eds.), *Handbook of demonstrations and activities in the teaching of psychology, Vol. III* (pp. 242–244). Mahwah, NJ: Lawrence Erlbaum.

Milgram, S. (1963). Behavioral study of obedience. *Journal of Abnormal and Social Psychology, 67*, 371–378.

Milgram, S. (1965). Some conditions of obedience and disobedience to authority. *Human Relations, 18*, 57–76.

Peters, W. (1987). *A class divided: Then and now* (expanded ed.) New Haven, CT: Yale University Press.

Piliavin, J., Dovidio, J., Gaertner, S., & Clark, R. (1981). *Emergency intervention.* New York: Academic Press.

Steblay, N. (1987). Helping behavior in rural and urban environments: A meta-analysis. *Psychological Bulletin, 102*, 346–356.

Steck, L., Levitan, D., McLane, D., & Kelley, H. (1982). Care, need, and conceptions of love. *Journal of Personality and Social Psychology, 43*, 481–491.

Sternberg, R. (1988). *The triangle of love: Intimacy passion, commitment.* New York: Basic Books.

Sternberg, R. (1998a). *Cupid's arrow: The course of love through time.* New York: Cambridge University Press.

Sternberg, R. (1998b). *Love is a story: A new theory of relationships.* New York: Oxford University Press.

Sternberg, R. (Ed.) (2005). *The psychology of hate.* Washington, DC: American Psychological Association.

Sternberg, R., & Grajek, S. (1984). The nature of love. *Journal of Personality and Social Psychology, 47*, 312–329.

Zimbardo, P., Weisenberg, M., Firestone, I., & Levy, B. (1965). Communicator effectiveness in producing public conformity and private attitude change. *Journal of Personality, 33*, 233–255.

## Additional Suggested Readings for Instructors

Abelson, R., Frey, K., & Gregg, A. (Eds.) (2004). *Experiments with people: Revelations from social psychology.* Mahwah, NJ: Erlbaum.

Moghaddam, F., & Marsella, A. (Eds.) (2004). *Understanding terrorism.* Washington, DC: American Psychological Association.

# Chapter 13

# Ending Your Course, Reflecting on it, and Getting Ready for the Next Time

The best time to think about revising and improving your introductory psychology course is while you are actually teaching and immediately afterward. This is difficult to do the first time you teach, when you feel that you are barely keeping your head above water. However, over the years I've developed a system that has helped me. I make an individual folder for each day I teach and I label it by day and content, for example "Day 27/Social." In the folder I include my outline for the day, a master copy of any handouts I am using, a list of any ancillary materials I need to bring to class (such as a video clip, book, or equipment for a classroom demonstration), and a piece of paper for suggestions for revising that class next time.

## Reflections During the Semester

I set aside 30 minutes before I teach and 30 minutes after I teach to concentrate on that day's class. The pre-teaching time is devoted to reviewing my folder (this is not when I prep the class) and getting the content firmly in mind (Lowman, 1995).

The post-teaching time is when I make notes to myself to revise aspects of the class for next time. For example, I note when a video clip worked well or when it did not, whether a class activity worked well and how I could have improved it, whether I need to develop or find more relevant examples of concepts. I also note how much material I was able to actually cover and what I left out. And finally, I try to write one or two quiz or exam questions over the content I covered in that class. Or I at least make a note of specific concepts or ideas that should be included in my next quiz or exam.

## Incorporating student feedback

Throughout the term, I solicit and incorporate student feedback. This feedback helps me make revisions to my course as the semester progresses, as well as helping me make decisions about more far-reaching revisions for the next term. I gather student feedback in several ways.

Three weeks into the semester, and again at nine weeks into the semester, I ask students for anonymous feedback about the course. I emphasize that I am asking for these evaluations because I want to use the feedback to improve the course for them. I choose the three week mark because, by then, my students are somewhat familiar with me, my class presentations, and some graded assignments, but it is still early enough in the term for me to make any changes that I think might be appropriate. At nine weeks, they have experienced every aspect of the course and are able to assess the impact of changes I made as a result of their earlier feedback.

I keep my evaluation form simple. I ask them three questions: "What three things do you like most about this class? What three things do you like least about this class? What three things would you change in this class if you could?"

If you are interested in collecting more specific information, ask students to fill in incomplete sentences such as: "The textbook _____." "The teacher's ability to explain concepts is _____." "The organization of the course _____."

Cashin (1999) suggests that you ask students to "describe something that I did not do that you personally would have found helpful."

I don't always want to make the changes that students suggest (e.g., easier quizzes) and I'm not always able to follow their recommendations (e.g., start class at a later hour). However, after I have read and analyzed their comments, I always take a few minutes in class to thank my students for their comments, discuss their feedback, and explain any changes I will or will not be making, and, most importantly, why I made those decisions.

One-minute papers are also helpful in providing feedback. When a class has not gone the way I expected, I take the last three or four minutes and ask my students to anonymously jot down anything that confused them about the topic we discussed that day (Angelo & Cross, 1993). I then use these papers to decide what topics will need to be covered in a different way in the next class.

You could also ask students to write a one-minute paper about their reactions to the lecture or demonstration or activity that took place at the previous session. This would give them more time to reflect and give you information about how much they actually remembered. But as Zakrajsek (2004) points out, you must address the main points at the next class or students will be less likely to give you this feedback the next time you ask for it.

## Integrating new information

As the term progresses, and even when I am not teaching, if I find a relevant journal article, new video clip, an example from the media, or an illustrative cartoon, I put it, or a note about it, into the relevant day/content folder. When I prepare that class next term, I integrate the content with my revision ideas and the new information. I've taught introductory psychology so many terms now that I am able to put in the front of every folder a copy of the handouts and a list of materials that will be needed for the *following* class period. This allows me to always be working a day ahead.

When I prepare a class, I plan a week's worth at one time. While this involves a significant time commitment—and a block of time is often difficult to find—this allows me to differentiate the topics I believe *must* be covered from those I would like to present. After every day's class, I assess how well I met my goals and make minor revisions to the next class based on what still must be covered. This works well for me and allows me to be thinking more than just one class period ahead.

This system might not be of value to you, and you may already have a different way of collecting new information and integrating it into your teaching. Whatever system you use, remember that it is important to set aside time after every class to reflect on the positives and negatives of that class and on ways to "fix" the negatives and further improve the positives. In other words, you need to develop a structured revision plan for yourself so that you are making conscious decisions about the content you want to include rather than simply teaching the "default" content from a previous term.

Finally, at the end of the term, I try to find several hours to sit down and assess how that term went. I will say more about this reflective process in a moment, but first I want to say a few words about ending your course, and the particular importance of the last day of class.

## The Last Class Session

The last class session is often a bittersweet experience. My students and I are both sad to see the semester end, especially if the class has been a good experience, and yet happy to see another semester successfully completed. However, the last day of class often just "slips away" without much thought or planning. Yet I think it is important to provide closure on the course for you and your students.

Maier and Panitz (1996) make two suggestions for closing day activities: (1) review your course syllabus with your class and decide if most of the goals were met, or (2) ask your students, perhaps in a group activity, to develop flow charts or concept maps of the major concepts in the course, showing how they fit together.

Eggleston and Smith (2002) suggest that the instructor provide a course summary, similar in design to the chapter summaries of most textbooks. Another suggestion they have is to provide some memento of the course—such as certificates of achievement with a personal quote for each student or an acknowledgement of some meaningful accomplishment of each student. In a large class, you might distribute "fortunes" on slips of paper, each containing a summary of an important idea or lesson from the course or something interesting that happened in class. Or words of wisdom could be put on the overhead for the entire class.

Students could also write a letter that details their own learning in the course. If you used a pre-test at the beginning of the course to assess what students think that they intuitively know about psychology, you could spend the last class reviewing that test and discussing what has been learned since the first class. Or ask students, "What is psychology?" to help them summarize and integrate the information they have gained from your class. You can also ask students for their "Top 10" list of research studies or ideas that had an impact on the direction of psychology (Eggleston & Smith, 2002).

You could also ask them to write a letter to you at the end of the following semester telling you one thing they learned in your course that they use. Or they could write letters to the students who will take your course the next semester, to be sealed and randomly handed out to the newcomers (Maier & Panitz, 1996).

My colleague, Bob Hendersen (2002), ends his introductory course by asking his students what they think psychology will look like in 50 years and sharing information about where psychology was 50 years ago.

## Staying in touch with students

It is important to me to continue the classroom rapport after class has officially ended. I encourage my students to stay in touch, providing them with my office hours for the next term so they can stop by and let me know how their new courses are going. I teach a small honors section of introductory psychology in the Fall semester composed entirely of first semester students. At the end of the following Spring semester, I email all of those students and ask them "what they wish they would have known before coming to college that no one told them." I pass that information on to entering students when I participate in new student orientation during the following summer. This simple exercise, begun primarily to benefit the incoming freshmen, has had a wonderful and unexpected effect of maintaining my rapport with the Fall class. Students write thoughtful analyses of what they would have liked to know when they came to college, often pointing out how the introductory psychology class helped them adjust to college. This channel of communication also encourages students to stay in touch throughout their college experience.

At the beginning of each Fall term, I send an email to all of my former students welcoming them back to school, providing my office hours, and encouraging them to let me know how their summer went and what courses they are now taking. This allows me to keep track of students as they progress through their college experience, figure out which students are no longer in school, and help students make decisions about which future psychology course would best suit their needs.

The point is that ending a class, and keeping in touch with students, requires just as much thought as beginning a class.

# End-of-Term Reflections

At the end of the term, I try to integrate as many sources of information about my class as possible. First, I ask myself about my overall impression of the term. Were there things I didn't like (e.g., the students were too quiet or too much time was spent on one topic)? How will I fix those issues next term? Were there things that went really well (e.g., the group presentations on the classic psychology article)? How can I ensure that these will go well again next term?

Second, what did my students think about the course? How were their mid-semester evaluations similar to or different from their end-of-term comments? Did I effectively address problems that students were having with the course? Was I able to expand the things that students liked about the course? What suggestions did students have to improve the course?

## Students' end-of-term evaluations

The same set of teacher behaviors that elicit favorable or unfavorable student evaluations during my course tend to result in favorable or unfavorable ratings at the end. I am usually not surprised by my formal end-of-term evaluations (summative evaluations). And I value what students have to say—after all they are the "consumers" of my course. Contrary to what you might hear from some of your colleagues, student evaluations are reliable and valid sources of information about your course. There is a considerable body of research that shows that summative student evaluations show good interrater reliability, ranging from .74 to .95 (Marsh & Roche, 1997). And high summative student evaluations are strongly associated with desirable teacher characteristics such as enthusiasm, energy, and interest in teaching the course, but not with gender, age, ethnicity, teaching experience, or research productivity (Cashin, 1995). These evaluations are *not* significantly related to potentially confounding factors such as the level or type of course being taught, the time of day it was taught, class size, or students' age, gender, year in school, grade-point average, personality traits, and prior interest in the subject matter (Cashin, 1995; Marsh & Roche, 1997). Summative evaluations *are* related to the amount of work assigned and to the leniency of the grading system, but the correlations are not in the direction that critics of student ratings might predict. Indeed, teachers who employ more stringent grading standards and assign heavier student workloads (up to a reasonable limit) tend to receive higher summative student evaluations than those who are more lenient and less demanding (Marsh & Roche, 1997, 2000). The validity of student ratings is also suggested by the fact that these ratings don't necessarily improve as teachers gain experience, but they do tend to improve after teachers engage in specific and structured efforts to improve their teaching (Marsh & Roche, 1997).

## Feedback from colleagues

Many introductory psychology faculty have the opportunity to have the department head or a senior colleague visit their classroom to provide feedback. I value this feedback as much as I do my student feedback because I know that my colleague observer will be able to comment on aspects of my teaching that my students will not. For example, was my content up to date? Did I explain a complicated concept well? Are there better examples of concepts that my colleague uses? How appropriate are my syllabus, exams, paper assignments, and other course materials? What do I do well in class? What should I work on improving?

More and more colleges and universities are actually requiring such classroom visits as part of a peer evaluation program (DeZure, 1999). But even if your department does not require peer observation of your teaching, ask a colleague—someone who can be both candid and supportive—to visit a couple of your classes each term. These visits can provide insights into your teaching and can be especially useful if you schedule them on days when you are giving a particularly difficult lecture, administering or returning a quiz, performing a dramatic demonstration, or engaging in some other aspect of teaching about which you feel less than confident and would like to improve.

To get the most from each visit, meet with your colleague before the class to describe your goals for the class to be observed, outline and explain the methods you will be using, and identify the aspects of your teaching that you are most interested in improving. After the class visit, set up a meeting to discuss your colleague's observations. In this meeting, be open and willing to accept criticism as well as praise. You might also want to ask the person to visit again later in the term to assess the results of your efforts to improve in areas of weakness. In fact, the true value of colleague visits lies in the feedback that comes during the detailed discussion that follows them. (For guidelines on conducting peer observations, see Millis, 1992).

Keep in mind, too, that though they cannot visit your classroom personally, colleagues who teach introductory psychology at other institutions can provide feedback via email or other electronic means about the organization and content of your course, the quality of your exams and quizzes, and ideas you might have about dealing with various problems and issues in your course.

# Self-Evaluation

There is no doubt that the process of collecting, reviewing, and analyzing feedback from others can be of enormous benefit in improving your teaching skills, but self-evaluation can be valuable, too. As noted earlier, reflecting on your teaching is a good way to begin the self-evaluation process, but you can also develop a teaching portfolio and, in particular, a portfolio for your introductory psychology course.

## Teaching and course portfolios

A *teaching portfolio* is a dossier containing syllabi, exams, quizzes, student evaluations, and the like from all the courses you have taught. Detailed suggestions about how to create such a portfolio are available in several sources (Centra & Gaubatz, 2000; Davis, 1993; Edgerton, Hutchings, & Quinlan, 1991; Knapper & Wright, 2001; Seldin, 1991; Shore et al., 1986). Ideally, you will begin to save such documents during the first introductory psychology course that you teach as a graduate student or instructor. Starting early allows your teaching portfolio to grow as you collect and organize packets of materials related to each course.

The *course portfolio* allows you to focus not only on what you did in your introductory course and how you evaluated your students, but also on "what, how and why students learned or did not learn what they were taught (or what the instructor intended them to learn)" (Cerbin, 2001).

As your teaching and course portfolios expand along with your teaching experience, it should include material that goes beyond copies of your syllabus, exams, paper assignments, and the like. It should also contain your written reflections about the introductory psychology course, about specific teaching experiences, and about teaching in general (Rodriguez-Farrar, 2003).

A statement of your philosophy of teaching is an important component of these reflections (Korn, 2003). In fact, most teaching portfolios begin with a teaching statement that is a reflection about how teachers see themselves as teachers, and especially of those things they value in the teaching domain. Each teaching philosophy statement is unique, of course, but they often begin by posing and answering questions such as "Why do I teach? How do I teach? Why do I teach the way I do? What are my teaching goals, methods and strategies?" (Rodriguez-Farrar, 2003). Having your teaching philosophy clearly in mind can ease the process of making decisions about course organization, planning, policies, and rules. For example, reviewing your teaching philosophy from time to time can remind you of why you decided on requiring (or not requiring) class attendance or why you use so few (or so many) definitional items on exams and therefore whether it now makes sense to change those elements of your courses. (My teaching philosophy can be accessed at this book's web site ⓤ.)

## Tips From Experienced Teachers

As you reflect on your course, on your teaching, and on your teaching plans, don't forget that experienced teachers can provide valuable advice, and don't be shy about asking them for it.

In 1998 Richard Leblanc won the Seymour Schulich Award for Teaching Excellence. He summarized good teaching in a list of top 10 requirements (Leblanc, 1998). According to Leblanc, good teaching is about passion—motivating students and helping them learn how to learn. It is about substance and keeping on top of your field. It is about "listening, questioning, being responsive, and remembering that each student and class is different" (p. 1). Good teaching is about style —being entertaining with substance and using humor. It also is about "caring, nurturing, and developing minds and talents" (p. 1). Good teaching involves a commitment of the entire organization, as well as mentoring, teamwork, and recognition among peers. Finally, he says:

> At the end of the day, good teaching is about having fun, experiencing pleasure and intrinsic rewards . . . like locking eyes with a student in the back row and seeing the synapses and neurons connecting, thoughts being formed, the person becoming better, and a smile cracking across a face as learning all of a sudden happens. (Leblanc, 1998, pp. 1, 7).

These are excellent tips for becoming a good teacher, and I would like to add a few of my own that have kept me sane throughout my teaching career.

- You do not have to conform to someone else's ideal of a "good teacher" in order to be a good teacher. Be yourself. If you have a humorous streak, don't try to suppress it in the classroom. But if you don't normally make witty comments, don't try to be "funny" in class. Students can like and respect teachers who display almost any interpersonal style as long as that style is authentic and as long as it is clear that the teacher cares about them, and about teaching the course. By the same token, students tend to dislike even the flashiest, funniest, or most scholarly style if it is seen as phony.
- Do not throw away any introductory psychology course material for at least two years after each term is over. This means archiving student emails, keeping copies of exams or exam answer sheets and even keeping student papers that were not handed back. It may only be after you throw something away that you find you need it! So create a system for storing course documents, organized by term and kept safe for at least two years. I use four cardboard boxes each marked by semester and year, and empty them only when the two-year archival period is over.
- Find time on campus and at home for relaxation (King, 2002). I like to schedule a daily walk, and by arranging to walk with a colleague on most days, I find that I actually do it. When I get back to the office, I often find that my efficiency is improved.
- Connect with your colleagues (King, 2002). Talk about issues that you are facing with your peers—preferably face to face but at least by email or phone. Especially, if you are facing a student problem or a difficult decision, talk to your colleagues about options for handling it. Like most people, I tend to develop a narrowed focus when under stress, and I find that colleagues usually come up with options and perspectives that I might have otherwise missed. I also meet with all of the introductory

psychology instructors weekly. We take that scheduled time to talk about teaching content, but also to share problems, ask for and give advice, and generally support one another. In addition, I participate in my campus's Center for Teaching Excellence. I attend book groups composed of faculty from across campus to discuss new books on college teaching. I attend and present at our annual Faculty Retreat, with a focus on promoting active learning. These experiences have enriched my own views on teaching and helped me establish and expand my base of teaching colleagues across my campus.

- Manage your time (King, 2002). Always easier said than done—but don't try to do too much in one day. However, don't procrastinate and let tasks pile up, because you can eventually feel overwhelmed. Instead, try to develop and stick to a schedule that spreads your tasks out in a way that moderates your workload. My colleague, Doug Bernstein, and I developed a calendar-based "master list" of course-related tasks that must be completed each week, beginning several weeks before the introductory course begins, and continuing throughout the semester. The master list reminds us, for example, that well before the semester begins, we have to order our computer answer sheets, check out our classrooms, and perform a variety of other tasks that make the beginning of the semester run smoothly. The master list also alerts us when it is time to request exam rooms, when we need to order our end-of-term evaluation forms, when we need to start writing our course-wide midterm and final exams, when we need to request proctors, and the like. If any items on the master list require that we contact someone on campus, we include that person's phone number and email address on the list next to that item. By consulting this master list every Monday morning, I can be assured that I will remember to do everything necessary for my course that week. You probably carry an informal master list in your head, but I encourage you to develop a written version by jotting down all of the course-related tasks you do each week throughout the semester. Keep adding to the list as you think of new things, and you will be amazed at how much time and trouble you save.
- Take your teaching seriously, but not so seriously that it impairs your performance. Keep in perspective the problems inherent in teaching introductory psychology, or anything else. By this I mean, don't focus so much on problems that you ignore all of the

positives and achievements in your teaching. Enjoy watching your students "get it" (King, 2002).

## Some Final Thoughts

Michael Loui, a colleague of mine in engineering, says that

> Effective education is moral education. In the classroom, we teachers are role models, and through our assignments and grading criteria, we state implicitly what is important, what ought to be valued. For example, if we encourage collaborative learning, then we say that cooperation and teamwork are important. If we base half of the grade on a paper on content and half on presentation, then we say that content and presentation are equally important. If we adhere to the syllabus and give exams on the dates previously announced, then we say that consistency is important. If we base part of the letter grade on classroom participation, then we say that each student's contribution to the discussion is important. (Loui, 1997)

Samuel Gorovitz from Syracuse University agrees.

> Ofttimes we tend to be so taken with the accuracy, insight, and eloquence of our lectures that it takes reading student examinations to remind us how far short we have fallen of achieving the goal, which is after all, not to perform an entertainment that gives the impression to us or to the students of being uplifting or edifying, but to bring about specific changes in the minds of the students. If we do not succeed in changing the interiors of students' heads, then our universities are simply overpriced day-care facilities for late adolescents. (quoted by Loui, 2003)

I reflect on these words of wisdom when I am feeling down about my teaching, when things have not gone well, or when I know I need to redo an entire day's content in introductory psychology. We all have days when our classroom is alive with excitement and teaching is going well, as well as days when planned demonstrations and activities don't work, when students are mystified by even the most carefully crafted lectures, and when the process of handing back exams turns ugly. That is all part of teaching. However, by engaging in reflection, using student and colleague feedback, and working to improve our introductory course, we can expect to have more "exciting" days of teaching and fewer "ugly" days. I wish you joy and excitement in your own introductory psychology course. And, as I pointed out in the first chapter, I would love to hear from you— both about how valuable you might have found this book and about what you wish I had included, but didn't. You can email me at gossluca@uiuc.edu.

## References

Angelo, T., & Cross, K. P. (1993). *Classroom assessment techniques: A handbook for college teachers* (2nd ed.). San Francisco: Jossey-Bass.

Cashin, W. (1995). *Student ratings of teaching: The research revisited. Idea Paper No. 32.* Manhattan, KS: Kansas State University, Center for Faculty Evaluation and Development.

Cashin, W. (1999). Student ratings of teaching: Uses and misuses. In P. Seldin (Ed.), *Changing practices in evaluating teaching: A practical guide to improved faculty performance and promotion/tenure decisions* (pp. 25–44). Bolton, MA: Anker.

Centra, J., & Gaubatz, N. (2000). Is there gender bias in student evaluations of teaching? *Journal of Higher Education, 70,* 17–33.

Cerbin, W. (2001). The course portfolio. *American Psychological Society Observer, 14,* 16–17, 30–31. Available at http://www.psychologicalscience.org/observer/0401/tips.html

Davis, B. G. (1993). *Tools for teaching.* San Francisco: Jossey-Bass.

DeZure, D. (1999). Evaluating teaching through peer classroom observation. In P. Seldin (Ed.), *Changing practices in evaluating teaching: A practical guide to improved faculty performance and promotion/tenure decisions* (pp. 70–96). Bolton, MA: Anker.

Edgerton, R., Hutchings, P., & Quinlan, K. (1991). *The teaching portfolio: Capturing the scholarship in teaching.* Washington, DC: American Association for Higher Education.

Eggleston, T., & Smith, G. (2002). Parting ways: Ending your course. *APS Observer, 15*(3), 15–16, 29–30.

Hendersen, R. (2002). Introductory psychology forum: Case studies for increasing student engagement. Presentation to 2nd annual Summer National Institute on the Teaching of Psychology, June 24, 2002, St. Petersburg Beach, Florida.

King, R. (2002). Managing teaching loads: And finding time for reflection and renewal. *APS Observer, 15*(1), 13–14, 35–36.

Knapper, C., & Wright, A. (2001). Using portfolios to document good teaching: Premises, purposes, practices. *New Directions for Teaching and Learning, 88,* 19–29.

Korn, J. (2003, July). Writing a philosophy of teaching. Retrieved 5 October, 2007 from http://www.teachpsych.org/resources/e-books/eit2003/eit03-07.pdf

Leblanc, R. (1998). Good teaching: The top ten requirements. *The Teaching Professor, 12*(6), 1, 7.

Loui, M. (1997). *What do we teach when we teach? Ethical values in the classroom.* Speech given at the Graduate Teacher Certificate ceremony April 28, 1997, University of Illinois, Urbana-Champaign. Retrieved 5 October, 2007 from https://netfiles.uiuc.edu/loui/www/values.html

Loui, M. (2003). *What do professors do all day and why do they do it?* Presentation April 23, 2003, University of Illinois, Urbana-Champaign.

Lowman, J. (1995). *Mastering the techniques of teaching* (2nd ed.). San Francisco: Jossey-Bass.

Maier, M., & Panitz, T. (1996). Ending on a high note: Better endings for classes and courses. *College Teaching, 44,* 145–148.

Marsh, H., & Roche, L. (1997). Making students' evaluations of teaching effectiveness effective: The critical issues of validity, bias and utility. *American Psychologist, 52,* 1187–1197.

Marsh, H., & Roche, L. (2000). Effects of grading leniency and low workload on students' evaluation of teaching: Popular myth, bias, validity or innocent bystander? *Journal of Educational Psychology, 92,* 202–228.

Millis, R. (1992). Conducting effective peer classroom observations. *To Improve the Academy, 11,* 189–201.

Rodriguez-Farrar, H. B. (2003). The teaching portfolio. The Harriet W. Sheridan Center for Teaching and Learning at Brown University. Retrieved October 5, 2007 from http://www.brown.edu/Administration/Sheridan_Center/publications/handbooks/teach_port.pdf

Seldin, P. (1991). *The teaching portfolio: A practical guide to improved performance and promotion/tenure decisions.* Bolton, MA: Anker Publishing.

Shore, B., Foster, S., Knapper, C., Nadeau, G., Neill, N., & Sim, V. (1986). *The teaching dossier: A guide to its preparation and use.* Ottawa: Canadian Association of University Teachers.

Zakrajsek, Todd (2004). Teaching a course you feel unprepared to teach. *American Psychological Society, 17*(11), 33–34, 44.

# Appendix: Professional Development Resources in the Teaching of Psychology

A wide range of useful resources is available to help high school, community college, and college and university faculty and graduate students become more effective teachers and to develop professionally as teacher-scholars. In particular, psychology has been at the forefront of all disciplines in promoting effective teaching. This appendix contains a listing and brief description of many of these resources. This listing is not intended to be exhaustive, but it is designed to offer you a solid picture of the many excellent sources to which you may turn to learn more about teaching well, to hone your teaching style, and to join with others who value teaching as much as you do. The listing below includes teaching organizations, teaching conferences, and books on teaching.

## Teaching Organizations

### Society for the Teaching of Psychology (STP; Division 2 of the American Psychological Association) (http://teachpsych.org/)

STP promotes the effective teaching of psychology at all levels of education. Its web site receives hundreds of thousands of hits each year, testifying to the usefulness of its electronic resources. In addition to these resources, many of which are available through its wildly popular Office of Teaching Resources in Psychology (OTRP; http://teachpsych.org/otrp/index.php), STP also publishes one of the premier disciplinary pedagogical journals, *Teaching of Psychology* (http://teachpsych.org/top/topindex.php), and electronic books, which are downloadable in several formats and are free of charge (http://teachpsych.org/resources/e-books/e-books.php).

## Education Directorate of the American Psychological Association (http://www.apa.org/ed/)

This arm of the APA focuses on promoting education in psychology at all levels. It offers many programs and initiatives aimed at enhancing both faculty development and student learning.

## Association for Psychological Science (http://www.psychologicalscience.org/)

APS is devoted to promoting psychology as a science, including promoting the teaching of psychological science. Part of its web site is devoted to information on teaching (see http://www.psychologicalscience.org/teaching/). APS sponsors a preconference institute on the teaching of psychology (overseen by STP) at its annual convention and includes several hours of teaching-related programming within the convention itself. APS also publishes a regular column on teaching in its monthly magazine, *The Observer*. These columns have been bound into two volumes entitled *Lessons Learned: Practical Advice on the Teaching of Psychology*, which are edited by Barry Perlman, Lee McCann, and Susan McFadden (1999–2004). Finally, APS oversees the APS Fund for the Teaching and Public Understanding of Psychological Science, which provides small grants for local, regional, national, and international teaching-related initiatives and supports other worthy causes related to "giving psychology away."

## Canadian Psychological Association Section of the Teaching of Psychology (http://www.cpa.ca/sections/teaching/)

The general aim of the Section on the Teaching of Psychology is to provide a forum for the exchange of information, ideas, and data concerning all aspects of teaching, including methods and styles of teaching, innovative pedagogical techniques, and aspects of student behavior and evaluation. To this end, each year at the Canadian Psychological Association Convention, the Section offers a teaching-related symposium, paper session or workshop, the ongoing general theme of which has been since 1989, "Improving the teaching of psychology."

## British Psychological Society Division of Teachers and Researchers (http://www.bps.org.uk/dtrp/ dtrp_home.cfm)

This division of the BPS aims to be the professional home for any psychologist whose principal activities are in research, in teaching, or in a combination of both. It was formed to address the professional issues which concern that significant proportion of the Society's membership who do not offer direct psychological services to client groups, but undertake academic duties in schools, colleges, universities, and research establishments or are undergoing training to equip themselves for careers in these settings.

## Educational Psychology, Division 15 of the American Psychological Association (http://www.apa.org/ about/division/div15.html)

Division 15 is dedicated to supporting research on teaching and other aspects of education at all levels. It publishes a quarterly journal, the *Educational Psychologist*.

## PT@CC, or Psychology Teachers at Community Colleges (http://www.apa.org/ed/pt@cc_update.html)

PT@CC is an APA-supported organization dedicated to providing support for psychology faculty who teach at two-year schools. One of PT@CC's many goals is to stimulate research in teaching and learning at the community college level.

## TOPSS, or Teachers of Psychology at Secondary Schools (http://www.apa.org/ed/topssinfo.html)

TOPPS is an APA-backed organization that provides supports for high school teachers of psychology.

### CTUP, or the Council of Teachers of Undergraduate Psychology (http://www.am.org/ctup/)

CTUP is an independent organization that promotes the teaching of psychology by sponsoring workshops, symposia, posters, and talks at regional and national psychology conferences.

### CUPP, or the Council of Undergraduate Psychology Programs (http://www.am.org/cupp/)

CUPP is an independent organization that focuses on improving teaching and learning in psychology at the program/departmental level. CUPP sponsors events at regional and national psychology conferences and its members often serve in advocacy positions within other teaching-related psychology organizations.

### Higher Education Academy Psychology Network (http://www.psychology.heacademy.ac.uk/)

This is a UK government-supported organization whose aim is to promote excellence in the learning, teaching, and assessment of psychology across the full range of curricula and activities relevant to UK higher education.

## Conferences on the Teaching of Psychology

### National Institute on the Teaching of Psychology (NITOP; http://www.nitop.org/)

NITOP is considered to be the world's premier conference on the teaching of psychology. Its annual meeting is held in early January in St. Pete Beach, Florida. NITOP's venue includes plenary sessions, concurrent sessions, workshops, poster sessions, and participant idea exchanges. Many of the top names in both psychological research and the teaching of psychology present their work at NITOP.

### American Psychological Association (APA; http://www.apa.org/)

The APA holds its annual meeting in August, but occasionally in July. STP (Division 2 of the APA) sponsors the bulk of the conference programming related specifically to the teaching of psychology.

## Association for Psychological Science (APS; http://www.psychologicalscience.org/)

APS sponsors a pre-conference workshop and a day-long Teaching Institute as part of its annual meeting, which is held each year in late May. In addition, sessions on the teaching of psychology are embedded within the regular conference programming. STP oversees the pre-conference workshop, the Teaching Institute, and all conference programming related to the teaching of psychology.

## Best Practices (BP) Conference

This conference, which is sponsored by both STP and NITOP as well as by the Center for Teaching and Excellence at Kennesaw State University is held each year in October. The conference was originally held in Atlanta but will take place in various other locations in the future. The conference focuses on a different theme each year— so all plenary sessions, workshops, concurrent sessions, and poster sessions are related to that theme. The themes in years past have included such topics as teaching introductory psychology, teaching research methods and statistics, diversity issues, and starting and finishing the psychology major.

## Regional Conferences on the Teaching of Psychology

Several independent regional and state conferences devoted to the teaching of psychology are held annually. For a listing of these conferences, their dates, and locations, go to http://teachpsych.org/conferences/conferences.php. This web site also lists more general teaching-related conferences in addition to those meetings devoted to the teaching of psychology.

## Books

The books referenced below represent a partial, but compelling, list of excellent texts on the teaching of psychology, teaching across higher education, and careers in teaching. Although most of the books are recent, those that are not represent what many consider to be classics in the area. They are well worth the time you might invest in reading them.

Bain, K. (2004). *What the best college teachers do*. Cambridge, MA: Harvard University Press.

Baiocco, S. A., & DeWaters, J. N. (1998). *Successful college teachers: Problem-solving strategies of distinguished professors*. Boston: Allyn and Bacon.

Boice, R. (2000). *Advice for new faculty members*. Boston: Allyn and Bacon.

Boyer, E. L. (1990). *Scholarship reconsidered: Priorities of the professoriate*. San Francisco: Jossey-Bass.

Brookfield, S. D. (1990). *The skillful teacher*. San Francisco: Jossey-Bass.

Brookfield, S. D. (1995). *Becoming a critically reflective teacher*. San Francisco: Jossey-Bass.

Buskist, W., & Davis, S. F. (Eds.). (2006). *Handbook of the teaching of psychology*. Malden, MA: Blackwell.

Darley, J. M., Zanna, M. P., & Roediger, H. L. (2004). *The compleat academic: A career guide* (2nd ed.). Washington, DC: American Psychological Association.

Davis, S. F., & Buskist, W. (Eds.). (2002). *The teaching of psychology: Essays in honor of Wilbert J. McKeachie and Charles L. Brewer*. Mahwah, NJ: Erlbaum.

Duffy, D. K., & Jones, J. W. *Teaching within the rhythms of the semester*. San Francisco: Jossey-Bass.

Dunn, D. S., & Chew, S. L. (Eds.). (2006). *Best practices for teaching introductory psychology*. Mahwah, NJ: Erlbaum.

Forsyth, D. R. (2003). *The professor's guide to teaching: Psychological principles and practices*. Washington, DC: American Psychological Association.

Fox, R. (2005). *Teaching & learning: Lessons from psychology*. Malden, MA: Blackwell.

Glassick, C. E., Huber, M. T., & Maeroff, G. I. (1997). *Scholarship assessed: Evaluation of the professoriate*. San Francisco: Jossey-Bass.

Goss Lucas, S., & Bernstein, D. A. (2005). *Teaching psychology: A step by step guide*. Mahwah, NJ: Erlbaum.

Huber, M. T. (2004). *Balancing acts: The scholarship of teaching and learning in academic careers*. Washington, DC: The Carnegie Foundation for the Advancement of Teaching and the American Association of Higher Education.

James, W. (1962/1899). *Talks to teachers on psychology and to students on some of life's ideals*. Mineola, NY: Dover.

Keith-Spiegel, P., Whitley, B. E., Balogh, D. W., Perkins, D. V., & Wittig, A. F. (2002). *The ethics of teaching: A casebook* (2nd ed.). Mahwah, NJ: Erlbaum.

Lowman, J. (1995). *Mastering the techniques of teaching* (2nd ed.). San Francisco: Jossey-Bass.

McKeachie, W. J., & Svinicki, M. (2006). *McKeachie's teaching tips: Strategies, research, and theory for college and university teachers.* Boston: Houghton Mifflin.

Palmer, P. J. (1998). *The courage to teach: Exploring the inner landscape of a teacher's life.* San Francisco: Jossey-Bass.

Perlman, B., McCann, L. I., & Buskist, W. (2005). *Voices of experience: Memorable talks from the National Institute on the Teaching of Psychology.* Washington, DC: American Psychological Society.

Perlman, B., McCann, L. I., & McFadden S. H. (1999). *Lessons learned: Practical advice for the teaching of psychology, Vol. 1.* Washington, DC: American Psychological Society.

Perlman, B., McCann, L. I., & McFadden S. H. (2004). *Lessons learned: Practical advice for the teaching of psychology, Vol. 2.* Washington, DC: American Psychological Society.

Puente, A. E., Matthews, J. R., & Brewer, C. L. (1992). *Teaching psychology in America: A history.* Washington, DC: American Psychological Association.

Sternberg, R. J. (Ed.). (1997). *Teaching introductory psychology: Survival tips from the experts.* Washington, DC: American Psychological Association.

# Index